Inside Asquith's Cabinet

INSIDE ASQUITH'S CABINET

From the Diaries of
Charles Hobhouse

EDITED BY EDWARD DAVID

St. Martin's Press
NEW YORK

All rights reserved. For information, write:
St. Martin's Press, Inc., 175 Fifth Avenue, New York, N.Y. 10010
Printed in Great Britain
Library of Congress Catalog Card Number 77-84941
ISBN 0-312-41868-X
First published in the United States of America in 1978

Contents

Illustrations

ACKNOWLEDGEMENTS

Grateful acknowledgement is given to the following for their kindness in allowing the reproduction of illustrations: 1, 2 Sir Gerard
Fuller, Bt.; 3, 5, 12, 13 Mary Evans Picture Library, London;
4, 8, 9, 15 Sir Charles Hobhouse, Bt.; 6 Cresset Press, London,
publishers of *Memoirs* (1945) by Viscount Samuel; 7 from *Prophets,
Priests and Kings* (1908) by A. G. Gardiner; 10, 14 Paul Popper
Ltd., London; 11 Hodge & Co. Ltd., Glasgow, publishers of *Trial
of the Seddons* (1914) ed. by F. Young.
    The photographs for plates 1, 2, 4, 8, 9 were taken by Stephanie
Hobhouse.

Editor's Note

Charles Hobhouse's diaries consist of three soft-covered exercise books which cover the years 1893–8 and 1904–15. The manuscript runs to well over 300,000 words. Any editor faces the problem of selection but here there is a vast quantity of material ranging from the utterly trivial to the highly significant. Inevitably whatever balance is struck between the gossipy anecdote and the sober account of a serious Cabinet meeting it can be criticised. What I have tried to do is to present a picture of Charles Hobhouse which conveys the breadth of his interests while concentrating attention particularly on the later years of the diaries, when as a Liberal Minister he was involved in the most intense political activity. I have been more ruthless in excluding material, mostly ephemeral social comment, from the earlier diaries. In the later years the proportion of material which I have retained is far higher and the balance of the book as a whole is weighted towards the years when Hobhouse was a member of the last Liberal Cabinet which this country has seen. In all about a third of the original has been selected. Both the professional political historian and the general reader will find the description of British political life in the setting of high society of absorbing interest.

I have corrected dates in the manuscript which were erroneous and inserted them when they have been omitted. The many abbreviations used by the diarist have been unscrambled so that on first sight the reader will find the full name or title of a person or office. As familiarity increases, so I have retained abbreviated forms e.g. Ll.G. and W.S.C. are Lloyd George and Churchill; W.R. and McK. should become obvious as Walter Runciman and Reginald McKenna. It would be pedantry too to write in full Chief of Imperial General Staff when C.I.G.S. is used in the original text. Reference to the Dramatis Personae should unravel any difficulties. In these I have included the most prominent figures of the time, as well as those less familiar to our generation, indeed relatively unknown, who figure prominently in the diaries.

I have occasionally included other material to illustrate some facet of Hobhouse's career or character. Those letters of his which have survived were often particularly interesting. In this connection I must thank the individuals and institutions which allowed me to use collections of private papers in their possession, notably the Buxton Papers (in the possession of Mrs. Elizabeth Clay), Asquith and Nathan Papers (Bodleian Library, Oxford), Runciman Papers (University of Newcastle-upon-Tyne Library), and the Bonar Law and Lloyd George Papers (Beaverbrook Library).

During my research Mr. Stanley F. Down, Mr. A. Missen and Mr. W. James Croker responded to my request for information about Sir Charles Hobhouse. I am grateful especially for a most stimulating correspondence, conversation and hospitality from Mrs. E. G. Wilson, who was Hobhouse's private secretary from 1912 until 1914.

My particular gratitude is due to the staff of the Wills Memorial Library, University of Bristol, for their patience and forbearance in the face of endless demands on their time and energy. My colleagues and pupils in the History Department of Bristol University were an unfailing source of stimulus and encouragement. I was glad to have expert advice on various technical points from Professor John Vincent and Dr. John Cannon, while Dr. George E. Carl gave much needed help in adversity. Mrs. Peggy Roberts and Miss Elizabeth Reid gave me invaluable secretarial assistance.

This book could never have appeared without the enthusiasm and encouragement of Sir Charles Hobhouse Bt., whose interest and patience during the inevitably long process of realising the diaries in print have been a great help. Above all, without the tolerant support of my wife and the exuberant interruptions of my daughter it could never have been completed.

2 December 1976   EDWARD DAVID

Introduction

Charles Edward Henry Hobhouse was born at Dormansland near Lingfield in Surrey on 30 June 1862. He embarked on a political career at the age of thirty and eventually achieved Cabinet office when he was forty-nine. That was the summit of his ambition. Until his nephew discovered these diaries in a drawer at Monkton Farleigh he remained unheralded. Even now the information we have about him is fragmentary. Some episodes in his life are vividly recorded in his diaries, occasional writings or those letters which have survived in other collections of private papers, but for the most part his career has remained unremarked, sunk in that obscurity which befalls the not quite great men in public life. Yet as a diarist he deserves to be remembered. The diaries which have survived him provide an invaluable commentary on the social and political world of late Victorian and Edwardian England.

Charles Hobhouse was born into a tradition of public and political service. The Hobhouse family can be traced in Somerset back to 1537. In the 17th century one John Hobhouse was established in business as a Master Mariner in Minehead and in 1717 one of his sons moved to Bristol and became a merchant. Several generations of the family lived in the city, establishing long associations with Clifton, Redland and Westbury-on-Trym, and playing a prominent part in the Society of Merchant Venturers at the heart of Bristol commerce. Benjamin Hobhouse (1757–1831) and his son, John Cam Hobhouse (1786–1869), first brought the family into public life. Benjamin Hobhouse became a Member of Parliament and was a member of Addington's Ministry in 1801–4 and the 'Ministry of All the Talents' in 1806–7. Nominally a Whig, by the standards of the age he was a radical. He favoured the repeal of the Test and Corporation Acts in the 1790s, voted against the suspension of Habeas Corpus in 1797, and supported Catholic Emancipation and the abolition of the Slave Trade. He became the 1st Baronet in 1812. His son, John Cam Hobhouse, notorious as a crony of Lord Byron, sat in Parliament from 1820 until 1851, and held office under Lord Grey, Lord Melbourne and Lord John Russell. In 1851 he became a peer, taking the title of Lord Broughton de Gifford. When he died in 1869 the barony became extinct, but the baronetcy passed to his nephew, Charles Parry Hobhouse, the diarist's father. Charles Parry Hobhouse was born in Calcutta in 1825, his mother being the daughter of John Palmer, a famous Calcutta merchant. At the age of nineteen he joined the Indian Civil Service in which he served for twenty-six years. He had a varied career, first as assistant and later as full magistrate and collector in various districts, as a judge, in the Financial Department, as a member first of the Bengal Legislative Council and then the Imperial Legislative Council of India, and finally as Judge of the High Court in Calcutta. In 1870 he returned to England to take up the role of a modest country landowner.

When he took over the entailed estates he found them in bad disrepair and had to struggle to set them in order. In 1873 he sold his property in Gloucestershire and bought instead the estate at Monkton Farleigh in Wiltshire. Desirable acquisition as this was, it proved a considerable financial strain at a time of steadily declining rents and general agricultural depression. His heir was not brought up amidst luxury. Indeed the family of thirteen children necessitated economy, and Charles was to retain a concern for money throughout his life. Nevertheless he enjoyed the conventional education of the upper-middle class. Preparatory school was followed by Eton and Christ Church, Oxford. He entered the Royal Military College at Sandhurst and was commissioned in the 60th Rifles in 1884. As a young Lieutenant Charles Hobhouse seemed destined for a military career, but family connections soon brought him into the political world.

One of his father's friends was George Pargiter Fuller, the squire of Neston Park just a few miles away from Monkton Farleigh. Fuller was the Liberal Member of Parliament for West Wiltshire from 1885 until 1895. His son, John Fuller, was to follow in his footsteps between 1900 and 1911. His daughter, Georgina, married Charles Hobhouse on 24 April 1890. He gained not only a wife but a foothold in the world of politics in the Fuller connection. His wife, Nina, as she was called, was to be a staunch ally throughout his political career. By all accounts she herself was an excellent speaker and a highly competent organiser. Certainly their marriage disproved any popular view of the effect of the strains of political life on marital harmony.

A few months after their marriage the young couple started on a round-the-world trip. The diary which Charles Hobhouse kept during the next ten months is the first evidence of his talent as a diarist. His account is largely a factual record of places visited, sights seen and people encountered. He had not yet acquired the happy knack of catching the tone of a conversation or making the point of a story which is so evident in his later diaries. Nonetheless the intensity of the Hobhouses' journeyings emerges strongly.

Their grand tour took them across Canada to Vancouver, across the Pacific to Japan, Hong Kong, Indonesia, Burma, India, over the Afghanistan border even, then through the Suez Canal to Palestine, Cyprus, Greece and through France home again. No time was wasted, to be sure. Everything of interest was seen, 'Kodaked' and briskly accounted for in Hobhouse's firm handwriting. When Nina was sea-sick, the intrepid Charles sternly recorded the ship's run that day; when slightly 'touched by the sun' in Canada the architectural merits of Toronto were dismissed in a single sentence; when visiting dubious Himalayan rulers, formal politeness masked a hearty dislike for such 'villains'. There is a certain humour, too, in the predilection for visiting prisons in every Far Eastern country while on a honeymoon! Whether the knowledge which he acquired of such institutions was useful later one cannot say, but certainly the whole trip provided a remarkable education for the future politician. At the India Office seventeen years later he was able to relate problems to his own experience in a way which Morley, his superior, could not. Later still we frequently find some esoteric piece of information, gleaned from this journey, dryly inserted by Hobhouse in some ill-founded Cabinet discussion.

When he returned to England Hobhouse made his first political speeches in support of the successful Liberal candidate in the North Buckinghamshire by-election in May 1891. A year later he was himself a Liberal candidate in the 1892 general election. It proved to be very much a family affair. His father-in-law won Wiltshire West, he himself won Wiltshire East, and his brother-in-law, John Fuller, tried unsuccessfully to capture Wiltshire North-West. Hobhouse's narrow victory (by 138 votes) over Walter Long, the rising hope of the Tory squirearchy, was remarkable. It also provoked an acrid exchange of letters between the two candidates in *The Times*, with Long accusing his opponent of falsely representing Conservative policy and drawing a characteristically pugnacious reply from the new M.P. Hobhouse had started his political career auspiciously but East Wiltshire was to be no safe refuge. Three years later, in 1895, he was defeated. He was out of Parliament until 1900. In 1899 he was looking for a constituency and was interviewed by the Liberal Chief Whip, Herbert Gladstone, who noted, rather discouragingly, 'Hobhouse: Hay fever so bad *always* in June that he can't fight country division. Told him good boroughs now very scarce—would do my best.' Gladstone considered Bath a possibility but in the event it was to East Bristol that Hobhouse went. In a letter to Matthew Nathan, whom they had met first as a young Captain inspecting fortifications in India in 1890 and who was to be one of their most constant friends, Nina Hobhouse in June 1899 related how they had '*both* had to go down to be looked at—it was the most painful performance I ever went through!' But they survived the ordeal and Hobhouse was returned to Parliament in this safe Liberal seat in 1900. He was to remain M.P. for the constituency until 1918.

As a backbencher Hobhouse's main interests were typical of his class and perhaps less typical of his party. His interest in the Free Trade versus Protection controversy was a *sine qua non* for a young Liberal politician, but his contributions to parliamentary discussion of the land question and the army were less conventional. He retained a longstanding and professional military knowledge which put him in a distinct minority within the Liberal Party. This enabled him to make damaging criticism of War Office administration during the disasters of the Boer War. As the Unionist Government under Balfour went into decline so Liberal impatience grew. There is a revealing comment on Hobhouse's character in a letter which he wrote to Matthew Nathan in April 1905 when he said 'It is weary waiting on the back benches—but it may be wearier still waiting on backbenches on the Govt. side.' But for another two years he made no overt progress.

Only in January 1907 did he gain office as Under-Secretary at the India Office. Thereafter he could feel more satisfied with the advances he made. Chairmanship of the Royal Commission on Decentralisation of Government in India in 1907–8 was followed by the Financial Secretaryship to the Treasury in Asquith's new Government in 1908. He remained at the Treasury throughout the years of crisis over the 'People's Budget' and the House of Lords. Then in

October 1911 he entered the Cabinet as Chancellor of the Duchy of Lancaster. He gained proper departmental responsibility for the first time in February 1914 when he became Postmaster-General, and there he remained until May 1915 when the last Liberal Government fell.

In 1903 Charles Hobhouse transferred a selection of entries from old diaries which he was destroying to the first of the three black soft-covered exercise books in which he was henceforth to keep his diary. As he wrote at the beginning of the first volume, 'I am putting down in this book those anecdotes of notable people which I have heard from time to time, generally at first hand.' The three volumes span the years 1893–8 and 1904–15. Hobhouse was very aware of his role as a participant in history and later especially he was consciously recording for posterity the deliberations of the Cabinet on current political problems. Later on he wrote up his diary regularly either last thing at night or early in the morning, but earlier entries were very intermittent. At first the diaries reflect the milieu of a young backbencher and his social round in the 1890s. Many of the anecdotes may appear familiar to readers, some indeed appear in other memoirs of the period. Not that this should be held against the diarist. After all, who is to say who first heard, or told, the latest story going the round about Gladstone, Disraeli or Lord Tennyson?

During the winter the Hobhouses lived at the Fullers' London house at 47 Rutland Gate. There they could entertain in modest style, dinner parties for up to twenty people, with a French chef brought in for the occasion if something extra special was required. In the summer there was always the annual problem of hay fever, which had to be overcome by a quick trip abroad or on one rather unfortunate occasion, a cruise in a Post Office cable ship! Despite his hay fever Hobhouse enjoyed the outdoor life and his stories of hunting, shooting and cricket are a happy contrast to his political accounts. One of his favourite modes of transport was bicycling, and the diaries abound in descriptions of long cycling tours which appear quite remarkable by the sedentary standards of the second half of the 20th century. What we should not forget, however, is the role of the bicycle in this largely pre-motorised age. It was the obvious, and often the only, way of travelling around the countryside. His other passion was hunting. He was a spectacular rider to hounds, renowned for his recklessness. Hence some of the more lugubrious diary entries describing heavy falls and broken bones. It remains a curious quirk of character that a man so concerned with diligent and sober management of men's affairs should be, in the excitement of the chase at least, so unmindful of the consequences of his rashness.

For the Hobhouses weekends in the country meant either a visit to a political host such as Lord Ripon at Studley Royal in Yorkshire, or joining a family party at Neston or Llysdinam where the Hobhouse, Fuller and Hicks-Beach cousins could sink their political differences perfectly happily. More frequently The Ridge at Corsham, the dower house of Neston Park lent to Hobhouse by his father-in-law, would be the setting for small shooting parties of four or five guns. The Ridge was not a very comfortable house for entertaining many guests. There were only five guest bedrooms and only one bathroom, which was for gentlemen only—ladies had to avail themselves of pitchers of hot water in their bedrooms. Naturally shooting weekends tended to be masculine affairs. The guns went out in the morning, and if the weather was suitable the ladies might join them for a picnic lunch and then return to tea at the house awaiting the menfolk later. Often these were also political occasions, especially later on when Hobhouse himself and several of the guests might be Cabinet Ministers. Then the early morning would be taken up with correspondence, dictated to his secretary who was brought over from Bath for the weekend for this purpose. There was also the administration of his own 1,000 acres at Monkton Farleigh, which marched with his father's estate.

It is worth emphasising the close-knit nature of this society. The Fullers and Hobhouses formed one close social and political group based in west Wiltshire, but significantly there seems to have been little or no contact beyond the most formal of exchanges with Walter Long, the neighbouring Tory squire. More important perhaps is the function of the country house circuit as a channel for political contacts and information. Thus at various times there were significant meetings at such places as Nuneham Courtney, near Oxford, where the Harcourts resided, or Canford Manor in Dorset where Lady Wimborne presided over the machinations of that most political of all families, the Guests—and sometimes of their cousin, Winston Churchill.

There is an obvious contrast between the frivolity of the 1890s and the more solemn chronicle of the years of the Liberal Government between 1908 and 1915. These years were among the most critical in British history. Hobhouse, even as a junior minister, was closely involved in the long-running political crisis over Ireland, the suffragettes, the Labour unrest and the constitutional struggle with the House of Lords. All these problems appear in the diaries in some form. To some extent the trials of the Government are filtered through the perceptions of a minister for a particular department. His departmental duties inevitably alter the perspective. Thus at the India Office Hobhouse was most concerned with the sometimes fundamental differences of opinion between Whitehall and Simla— and with overcoming a certain hostility from the prickly John Morley who had not wanted him as Under-Secretary in the first place. In these circumstances the wider implications of domestic politics receive relatively little attention.

More instructive is the period after April 1908 when Hobhouse became Financial Secretary to the Treasury. Then he came into contact with David Lloyd George for the first time. Lloyd George becomes one of the 'hero-villains' of the diaries. It is fair to say that of those who actually worked with Lloyd George as an administrator only Frances Stevenson, his secretary and mistress, has depicted him favourably later. Almost all were agreed about Lloyd George's gifts—most were driven to distraction by his methods. Hobhouse was no exception. His reactions also reveal the fears and suspicions of a moderate Liberal at the dangerous *socialistic* inclinations of the Chancellor. Lloyd George's 1909 Budget inspired Hobhouse's admiration and contempt in equal measure—admiration for its audacity and contempt for its formulation. After the exhausting passage of the Finance Bill late in 1909 Hobhouse permitted himself one moderately favourable comment and then lapsed into head-shaking once more. Indeed the picture he paints of Lloyd George shirking meetings in order to play golf is positively Calvinist in its disapproval!

The second of the 'hero-villains' is Lloyd George's henchman, Winston Churchill. But if in the case of Lloyd George the under-current of criticism is balanced by occasional tributes to the Welsh-man's ingenuity, then Churchill always remains *un bête noire* as far as Hobhouse is concerned. He believed that 'W.S.C.'s introduction to the Cabinet has been followed by the disappearance of that harmony which its members all tell me has been its marked feature ... personal discourtesy is C.'s chief weapon.' In short, Churchill to Hobhouse was a disruptive and disturbing influence.

These were not just differences in temperament or even ability, but they illustrated the fundamental gulf between the moderate and advanced sections of the Liberal Party. Hobhouse's reactions in the diaries are those of the 'old' Liberalism, overshadowed by the dynamism of the social reform led by Lloyd George and Churchill. Hobhouse had been elected to Parliament as a Gladstonian Liberal in 1892. He was still one in 1915. He may have warned occasionally of the danger posed to the Liberal Party by an independent Labour Party, but he shrank from the socialistic excesses of his young colleagues. He was a supporter of Free Trade and Irish Home Rule, and a reluctant subscriber to Welsh Church Disestablishment. He called himself a Radical, but even his radicalism was old-fashioned. He was prepared to attack the House of Lords and few things aroused his ire more than the discreditable money-grabbing which he observed in minor members of the Royal family. What provoked him most of all, however, was the suffragette agitation. He made his most notorious speech on the question of women's votes, although his diary is strangely silent on the subject. But his speech at Bristol on 16 February 1912 was always regarded by the women's movement as having provoked them to greater militancy by his claim that until there were comparable scenes to the smashing of the Hyde Park railings in 1867 there was no evidence of popular support for the women's cause. He was accused by *Votes for Women* of 'the most calculated and wicked incitement to violence that any responsible man, and more especially any Minister of the Crown has ever uttered.' It is perhaps too tempting to recall Hobhouse's own arguments on the subject, for he actually claimed that 'the absorption of women in politics would prejudice the number, character and vigour of our future race, would lead to the limitation of their capacity and inclination for maternity, and to their unwillingness and incapacity to manage their home [cheers] and home was the primary and eternal unit of social life in all countries [cheers].' One should perhaps add that the lawyer's test of 'the reasonable man' might be difficult to apply to a hay-fever sufferer whose morning post frequently included letters filled with grass-seed and pepper sent by suffragettes.

The outbreak of war in 1914 swept all familiar disputes aside. It also brought Lloyd George and Churchill further into the limelight and began the erosion of Asquith's magisterial authority. Hobhouse's attitude to Lloyd George mellowed as time passed. There is almost a certain affection in his comments—rather like a probation officer and some incorrigible delinquent—and Lloyd George is allowed some endearing qualities. Hobhouse records the acid John Burns comment that 'L.G.'s conscience is as good as new: for he has never used it' (4 March 1911), but also the delightful Lloyd George remark 'Good Heavens, if one mayn't tell lies at election times, when may one tell them'! (2 March 1911.) Hobhouse also gave Lloyd George full credit for the financial arrangements which he introduced on the outbreak of war. He quotes with approval also Lloyd George's prescience in discussing the final peace settlement at an early stage in the work—'L.G. hoped that it was not intended at the final settlement to strip Germany of her colonies, an issue everyone avoided replying to.' (25 November 1914.) This too is a fine example of Hobhouse's capacity for seizing on the historically significant remark, the political irony or personal idiosyncrasy. At many different levels the diarist has the happy knack of riveting attention on the real point of a particular anecdote. And he is also amusing, as for example in the final picture which he draws of Lloyd George, seen in July 1915 travelling to Cardiff to address strikers, dealing with hordes of press reporters and 'always protesting against the "odious" photographers, and then smoothing his hair and adjusting his collar and stopping at a convenient corner to allow them to catch him'! (25 July 1915.)

By contrast there is no way in which Hobhouse can restrain his hostility when writing about Churchill. Rumbustious, enthusiastic, belligerent, ambitious Churchill, unredeemed and irredeemable, is what Hobhouse depicts. It was a picture which he, and many of his colleagues, believed to be true. Churchill *was* the most distrusted man in British politics—largely because he did not share the presumptive party loyalty and shibboleths of his fellow politicians. Hobhouse in fact clashed with Churchill over navy policy in the summer of 1912 and more directly in the battle over the naval estimates of December 1913–January 1914. His account of the latter crisis, invaluable evidence as it is, is highly pejorative. Yet we should remember that few contemporaries would have quarrelled with his judgement of the young Winston in July 1912: 'He is really a spoilt child endowed by some chance with the brain of a genius' (17 July 1912), and many indeed would have claimed that it was over-favourable.

If Lloyd George and Churchill are the two obvious 'hero-villains' of the diaries they are by no means the only figures of interest. Hobhouse's felicitous style enabled him to sum up a colleague's character or ability with tremendous economy and yet great perception. Asquith, Birrell, Morley, Kitchener and many others are often quite suddenly revealed to the reader in an unfamiliar light. Hobhouse may reinforce prejudices or even be patently ungenerous in his judgement (as in the case of Birrell) but he was an acute observer who above all had a talent for describing the atmosphere of a crucial meeting, of encapsulating the main point at issue in a discussion and conveying in the most vivid possible way how a decision came to be made. It is, of course, this talent, rather than his achievements as a politician himself, with which we are concerned. But this raises the question of how accurate a commentator was Hobhouse and how sound was his political judgement? The two things are not the same, in fact, but inevitably they tend to become entangled.

As far as his accuracy is concerned he seems, so far as it is possible to check, remarkably free from factual errors. He recorded truthfully what he saw of events in which he participated. It is fair to say that his accounts of Cabinet meetings are consistent with the only other direct account of what passed there, namely Asquith's letters to the King reporting their discussions. More important, Hobhouse usually gives far more detail than the Prime Minister either had time to or wished to. Naturally his account lays emphasis on those matters which interested him. The diarist inevitably commits sins of omission. What is more difficult is the distinction which has to be drawn between historian's truth and politician's belief. This has been highlighted recently in the historical controversy over the fall of the Liberal Government in May 1915. The controversy also impinges directly on Hobhouse's credibility as a historical witness. An account of the May 1915 crisis written by Dr. Stephen Koss was founded largely upon a letter written by Hobhouse to Lord Buxton on 10 June 1915. Koss's article 'The Destruction of Britain's Last Liberal Government' (*Journal of Modern History*, June 1968) postulated the theory of a wider conspiracy involving

Balfour, Lloyd George and Churchill which also finds expression in Hobhouse's diary. This interpretation has now been attacked, with excessive ferocity, by Dr. Cameron Hazlehurst in his book, *Politicians at War*. He denounces the inaccuracy of Hobhouse's version, citing his particular mistake about the date of Lord Fisher's resignation in May 1915, and brushing aside the 'supremely ridiculous suspicions' which abounded at that time.

As it happens Hobhouse's diary makes it clear how he was misled about the date in question. McKenna was his informant, and McKenna talked of having seen the resignation note on the *Friday* night when it was not in fact sent until the Saturday. Hence Hobhouse's confusion in thinking it actually went in on Friday. However, as far as the general controversy about the 'plot' is concerned, we must realise that Hobhouse's account *was* largely based on hearsay at this time. There are two reasons for this—firstly that these events were taking place at the highest political level of all and a junior Cabinet colleague simply was not consulted about them, and secondly that the whole episode happened so dramatically quickly. Indeed the diary provides telling testimony to this fact. Historian's truth and politician's belief are indeed different things. Hobhouse's entries reflect the prevailing atmosphere of strain, suspicion and mistrust. What he shows beyond any doubt is the way in which the dilemmas of war—strategic, economic and above all, moral—beset the Liberal Ministers. In a fundamental sense his account is valuable to the historian *because* it may be wrong.

Inevitably the diaries reveal both the political prejudices and his own personality. He was well known as having a ferocious temper and when put on his dignity was apt to be prickly. Yet his judgements on others, though often stern to the point of ungenerosity, were no stricter than those he applied to himself. He possessed notions of self-discipline and honour which made for a sense of fairness. In the academic sense Hobhouse was not brilliant as many of his colleagues were, but he possessed a lively intelligence, omnivorous general knowledge and a certain perceptive common sense. If, in the diaries, he occasionally claimed rather more credit for some happening than may seem justified, then it can perhaps be pardoned, for he was, in the main, very conscious of his own limitations. In a personal sense he was not self-seeking. He was capable of sustained and generous friendship as is obvious in the case of Matthew Nathan. His ambitions, which he did not conceal, were those of a man seeking honourable employment rather than personal aggrandisement. When he found work his industry was remarkable. The disparaging remark that 'he loves the palm without the dust' never applied to Charles Hobhouse. He was indeed one of the unsung politicians. Many of the values and assumptions which he represented were destroyed by the very events which he helped to shape. He deserves to be remembered not for his political successes but for his perceptive eye, facile pen and integrity which have provided us not only with a record of those events but an account which captures the flavour of an age which we have lost.

Dramatis Personae

HERBERT HENRY ASQUITH (1852–1928): Liberal M.P. 1886–1918, 1920–4; Home Secretary 1892–5; Chancellor of the Exchequer 1905–8; Prime Minister 1908–16; created Earl of Oxford and Asquith 1925.

ARTHUR JAMES BALFOUR (1848–1930): Conservative M.P. 1874–1922; leader of Conservative Party in House of Commons 1891–2, 1895–1902; Prime Minister 1902–5; leader of Conservative Party 1906–11; First Lord of the Admiralty 1915–16; Foreign Secretary 1916–19; created 1st Earl of Balfour 1922.

SIR ARTHUR BIGGE (1849–1931): Private Secretary to Queen Victoria 1895–1901, to Prince of Wales (later George V) 1901–10; created Baron Stamfordham 1911.

AUGUSTINE BIRRELL (1850–1933): Liberal M.P. 1889–1900, 1906–18; President of the Board of Education 1905–7; Chief Secretary for Ireland 1907–16.

LOUIS BOTHA (1863–1919): Commander-in-Chief, Boer Forces in South African War; Premier, Transvaal 1907–10; C.-in-C., Union Forces in South West Africa 1914–15.

JOHN SWANWICK BRADBURY (1872–1950): Principal Clerk, Treasury; Member of National Health Insurance Joint Committee 1911–13; Joint Permanent Secretary, Treasury 1913–19; created Baron Bradbury of Winsford 1925.

JOHN BURNS (1858–1943): Labour and Liberal M.P. 1892–1918; 'first Labour Cabinet Minister'; President of the Local Government Board 1905–14; President of the Board of Trade 1914; resigned on outbreak of First World War.

SYDNEY CHARLES BUXTON (1853–1934): Liberal M.P. 1883–5, 1886–1914; Under-Secretary for the Colonies 1892–5; Postmaster-General 1905–10; President of the Board of Trade 1910–14; Governor-General South Africa 1914–20; created Earl Buxton 1920.

SIR HENRY CAMPBELL-BANNERMAN (1836–1908): Liberal M.P. 1868–1908; War Secretary 1886 and 1892–5; leader of Liberal Party 1899–1905; Prime Minister 1905–8.

1ST EARL CARRINGTON (1843–1928): President of the Board of Agricul-

13

ture 1905–11; Lord Privy Seal 1911–12; created 1st Marquess of Lincolnshire 1912.

SIR EDWARD HENRY CARSON (1854–1935): Unionist M.P. 1892–1918, 1918–21; leader of Ulster Unionist opposition to Liberal Government 1911–14.

JOSEPH CHAMBERLAIN (1836–1914): Liberal M.P. 1876–86; opposed Home Rule 1886; Unionist M.P. 1886–1914, leader of Liberal Unionists; Colonial Secretary 1895–1903.

WINSTON LEONARD SPENCER CHURCHILL (1874–1965): Unionist M.P. 1900–4; Liberal M.P. 1904–8, 1908–22; Under-Secretary for Colonies 1905–8; President, Board of Trade 1908–10; Home Secretary 1910–11; First Lord of the Admiralty 1911–15; Chancellor of the Duchy of Lancaster May-November 1915; Conservative Prime Minister 1940–5, 1951–5.

1ST MARQUESS OF CREWE (1858–1945): Lord President of the Council 1905–8; Lord Privy Seal 1908–11; Colonial Secretary 1908–10; Indian Secretary 1910–15; Lord President of the Council 1915–16; President, Board of Education 1916.

GEORGE NATHANIEL CURZON (1859–1925): Conservative M.P. 1886–98; Under-Secretary for India 1891–2; Under-Secretary for Foreign Affairs 1895–8; Viceroy and Governor-General of India 1899–1905; Lord Privy Seal 1915–16; Lord President of the Council 1916–19; created 1st Marquess Curzon of Kedleston 1921.

SIR CHARLES DILKE (1843–1911): Radical M.P. 1868–86, 1892–1911; Cabinet Minister 1882–5; career shattered by involvement in divorce scandal 1886.

ALFRED EMMOTT (1858–1926): Liberal M.P. 1899–1911; Under-Secretary for the Colonies 1911–14; First Commissioner of Works 1914–15; created 1st Baron 1911.

EDMOND FITZMAURICE (1846–1935): Liberal M.P. 1868–85, 1898–1905; Under-Secretary for Foreign Affairs 1882–5 and 1905–8; created 1st Lord Fitzmaurice 1906; Chancellor of the Duchy of Lancaster 1908–9; brother of the Conservative Foreign Secretary, Lord Lansdowne, he was a near neighbour of Hobhouse at Leigh House, Bradford-on-Avon.

FIELD-MARSHAL SIR JOHN DENTON PINKSTONE FRENCH (1852–1925): Chief of Imperial General Staff 1911–14; C.-in-C. Expeditionary Forces in France 1914–15; created 1st Earl of Ypres 1921.

EDWARD FLEETWOOD FULLER (1878–1914): brother-in-law of Charles Hobhouse.

JOHN MICHAEL FLEETWOOD FULLER (1864–1915): Liberal M.P. 1900–11; Junior Whip 1906–7; Vice-Chamberlain of the Household 1907–11; Governor of Victoria 1911–14; Baronet 1911; brother-in-law of Charles Hobhouse.

DAVID LLOYD GEORGE (1863–1945): Liberal M.P. 1890–1945; President, Board of Trade 1905–8; Chancellor of the Exchequer 1908–15; Minister of Munitions 1915–16; War Secretary 1916; Prime Minister 1916–22; Earl Lloyd-George of Dwyfor 1945.

HERBERT GLADSTONE (1854–1930): Liberal M.P. 1880–1910; Liberal Whip 1880–5, Chief Whip 1899–1905; Home Secretary 1905–10; Governor-General of South Africa 1910–14; son of William Ewart Gladstone; 1st and last Viscount Gladstone.

WILLIAM EWART GLADSTONE (1809–98): Conservative M.P. 1832–46; Liberal Conservative M.P. 1847–65; Liberal M.P. 1865–7, 1868–80, 1880–95; Liberal Prime Minister 1868–74, 1880–5, 1886, 1892–4.

SIR EDWARD GREY (1862–1933): Liberal M.P. 1885–1916; Under-Secretary for Foreign Affairs 1892–5; Foreign Secretary 1905–16; created Viscount Grey of Falloden 1916.

FREDERICK EDWARD GUEST (1875–1937): 3rd son of 1st Baron Wimborne; Liberal M.P. 1910–22, 1923–4, 1924–9, 1931–7; Junior Whip 1911–12; Treasurer of the Household 1912–15; Coalition Liberal Chief Whip 1917–21; Secretary for Air 1921–2.

HENRY CHARLES GUEST (1874–1957): 2nd son of 1st Baron Wimborne; Liberal M.P. 1910, 1910–18, 1922–3, 1937–45; Parliamentary Private Secretary to Charles Hobhouse.

IVOR CHURCHILL GUEST (1873–1939): Liberal M.P. 1900–10; Paymaster-General 1910–12; Lord in Waiting 1913–15; Lord Lieutenant of Ireland 1915–18; created Baron Ashby St. Ledgers 1910; succeeded as 2nd Baron Wimborne 1914; created 1st Viscount 1918.

OSCAR GUEST (1888–1958): 5th son of 1st Baron Wimborne; Liberal M.P. 1918–22, 1935–45.

LEWIS 'LULU' HARCOURT (1863–1922): son of Sir William Harcourt; Liberal M.P. 1904–16; First Commissioner of Works 1905–10; Colonial Secretary 1910–15; created 1st Viscount 1917.

SIR WILLIAM HARCOURT (1827–1904): Liberal M.P. 1868–1904; Chancellor of the Exchequer 1886, 1892–5; leader of Liberal Party in House of Commons 1894–8.

PERCY ILLINGWORTH (1869–1915): Liberal M.P. 1906–15; Whip 1910–12; Chief Whip 1912.

RUFUS ISAACS (1860–1935): Liberal M.P. 1904–13; Solicitor-General 1910; Attorney-General 1910–13 (with seat in Cabinet): Lord Chief Justice 1913; Ambassador to U.S.A. 1918–19; Viceroy of India 1921–6; 1st Marquess of Reading 1926.

LEANDER STARR JAMESON (1853–1917): doctor at Kimberley, South Africa from 1878; British South Africa Company administrator from 1891; captured by Transvaal forces at Doornkop, 2 January 1896, when leading the 'Raid' on Johannesburg; handed over to British Government for trial, convicted and sentenced to imprisonment July 1896; released 1897; Prime Minister, Cape Colony 1904–8; Baronet 1911.

HORATIO HERBERT KITCHENER, VISCOUNT KITCHENER OF KHARTOUM (1850–1916): Commander-in-Chief 1900–2; C.-in-C., India 1902–9; War Secretary 1914–16.

SIR FRANCIS KNOLLYS (1837–1924): Private Secretary to Edward VII 1870–1910; Joint Private Secretary to George V 1910–13; created 1st Viscount 1911.

HENRY DU PRÉ LABOUCHERE (1831–1912): Radical M.P. 1865–1906; member of South Africa Committee 1897; critic of imperialist policy.

ANDREW BONAR LAW (1858–1923): Unionist M.P. 1900–6, 1906–10, 1911–18, 1918–23; Leader of Unionist Party 1911–21; Colonial Secretary 1915–16; Chancellor of the Exchequer 1916–18; Leader of House of Commons 1916–19; Prime Minister 1922–3.

WALTER LONG (1854–1924): defeated by Hobhouse in East Wiltshire in 1892, returned to Parliament at a by-election in January 1893; Unionist M.P. 1893–1900, 1900–6, 1906–10, 1910 –18; junior office in Unionist Government 1895–1900; a contender for the leadership of the Conservative Party in 1911; Colonial Secretary 1916–18; First Lord of the Admiralty 1919; created 1st Viscount Long of Wraxall in 1921, he took his title from the Wiltshire village just a mile or so from Monkton Farleigh.

LORD LOREBURN (1846–1923): Liberal M.P. 1880–5, 1886–1905; Attorney-General 1894–5; Lord Chancellor 1905–12.

CHARLES FREDERICK GURNEY MASTERMAN (1873–1927): Radical Liberal M.P. 1906–11, 1911–14; Parliamentary Secretary, Local Government Board 1908–9; Under-Secretary, Home Office 1909–12; Financial Secretary to the Treasury 1912–14; Chancellor of the Duchy of Lancaster 1914–15; failed to gain re-election to Parliament in the by-election required on his taking that office; resigned from Cabinet 1915.

EDWIN SAMUEL MONTAGU (1879–1924): Liberal M.P. 1906–22; Indian

Under-Secretary 1910–14; Financial Secretary to the Treasury 1914–15 and 1915–16; Chancellor of the Duchy 1915 and 1916; Minister of Munitions 1916; Indian Secretary 1917–22.

JOHN MORLEY (1838–1923): Liberal M.P. 1883–95, 1896–1908; Chief Secretary for Ireland 1886 and 1892–5; opposed Boer War 1899–1902; Indian Secretary 1905–10; Lord President of the Council 1910–14; resigned at outbreak of First World War; created 1st Viscount 1908.

A. O. 'ALICK' MURRAY ('Murray of Elibank') (1870–1920): Liberal M.P. 1900–12; Comptroller of the Household 1905–9; Under-Secretary for India 1909–10; Chief Whip 1910–12; created 1st Baron 1912.

SIR GEORGE MURRAY (1849–1936): Permanent Secretary to the Treasury 1903–11.

SIR MATTHEW NATHAN (1862–1939): soldier; colonial governor 1899–1910; Secretary to the Post Office 1910–11; Chairman, Board of Inland Revenue 1911–14; Under-Secretary to Government in Ireland 1914–16.

SIR HENRY NORMAN (1858–1939): Liberal M.P. 1900–10, 1910–23; journalist, author, coalowner, expert on early commercial wireless; Assistant Postmaster-General 1910.

ALFRED HARMSWORTH, LORD NORTHCLIFFE (1865–1922): proprietor of the *Daily Mail, Daily Mirror, Evening News* and *The Times;* created 1st Viscount 1917.

JOSEPH ALBERT PEASE (1860–1943): Liberal M.P. 1892–1900, 1901–10, 1910–16; Junior Whip 1905–8; Parliamentary Secretary to the Treasury 1908–10; Chancellor of the Duchy 1910–11; President, Board of Education 1911–16; Postmaster-General 1916; 1st Baron Gainford 1917.

JOHN REDMOND (1856–1918): Irish Nationalist M.P. 1872–91, 1891–1918; leader of Irish Party in the House of Commons.

CECIL JOHN RHODES (1835–1902): founder of De Beers Company 1880; granted British South Africa Company Charter 1889; Prime Minister of Cape Colony 1890–6; censured by South Africa Committee 1897.

SIR W. S. ROBSON (d. 1918): Liberal M.P. 1885–6, 1895–1910; Solicitor-General 1905–8; Attorney-General 1908–10; created 1st Lord Robson 1910.

LORD ROSEBERY, 5TH EARL (1847–1929): Liberal Cabinet Minister 1885; Foreign Secretary 1886 and 1892–4; Prime Minister 1894–5.

WALTER RUNCIMAN (1870–1949): Liberal M.P. 1899–1900; 1902–18, 1924–9, 1929–37; Parliamentary Secretary, Local Government Board 1905–7; Financial Secretary to the Treasury 1907–8; President, Board of Education 1908–11; President of Board of Agriculture 1911–14; President, Board of Trade 1914–16 and 1931–7; Lord President of the Council 1938–9; created 1st Viscount 1937.

HERBERT LOUIS SAMUEL (1870–1963): Liberal M.P. 1902–18, 1929–35; Under-Secretary for Home Department 1905–9; Chancellor of the Duchy of Lancaster 1909–10; Postmaster-General 1910–14; President, Local Government Board 1914–15; again Postmaster-General and Chancellor of the Duchy of Lancaster 1915–16; Home Secretary 1916; British High Commissioner in Palestine 1920–5; Home Secretary 1931–2; leader of Liberal Party in the House of Commons 1931–5 and in the House of Lords 1944–55; 1st Viscount 1937.

JOHN EDWARD BERNARD SEELY (1868–1947): Liberal M.P. 1900–6, 1906–10, 1910–22, 1923–4; Under-Secretary, Colonies 1908–11; Under-Secretary for War 1911–12; War Secretary 1912–14; Deputy Minister of Munitions 1918; Under-Secretary for Air 1919; 1st Baron Mottistone 1933.

SIR JOHN ALLSEBROOK SIMON (1873–1954): Liberal M.P. 1906–18, 1922–31; Liberal National M.P. 1931–40; Solicitor-General 1910–13; Attorney-General and member of the Cabinet 1913–15; Home Secretary 1915–16; leader of Liberal National Party 1931–40; Foreign Secretary 1931–5; Home Secretary 1935–7; Chancellor of the Exchequer 1937–40; Lord Chancellor 1940–5; created 1st Viscount 1940.

FREDERICK EDWIN SMITH (1872–1930): Conservative M.P. 1906–19; Solicitor-General 1915; Attorney-General 1915–19; Lord Chancellor 1919–22; Indian Secretary 1924–8; created 1st Lord 1919, 1st Viscount 1921, 1st Earl of Birkenhead 1922.

HAROLD JOHN TENNANT (1865–1935): Liberal M.P. 1894–1918; Parliamentary Secretary, Board of Trade 1909–11; Financial Secretary, War Office 1911–12; Under-Secretary for War 1912–16; Asquith's brother-in-law.

ALEXANDER URE (1853–1928): Liberal M.P. 1895–1913; Solicitor-General, Scotland 1905–9; Lord Advocate 1909–13; created Lord Strathclyde 1914.

T. McKINNON WOOD (1855–1927): Liberal M.P. 1906–18; Parliamentary Secretary, Board of Education 1908; Under-Secretary, Foreign Office 1908–11; Financial Secretary to the Treasury 1911–12 and 1916; Secretary for Scotland 1912–16; Chancellor of the Duchy of Lancaster 1916.

I

In and out of the House
1893–1898

✳ Divided fatally in 1886 between W. E. Gladstone and Joseph Chamberlain over the Irish Home Rule issue, the Liberals did not return to
power until 1892. When Gladstone formed his fourth administration in
that year he was dependent upon the Irish Nationalists for his majority
over the Conservatives and Chamberlain's Liberal Unionists. 1893 saw
Gladstone's last attempt to impose Irish Home Rule on a party weary of
his insistence and a Parliament made sullen by the repetition of the old
Irish arguments. His obsession with Ireland excluded all other policies.
Yet for a young Liberal M.P. Gladstone was a noble figure, personifying
the true faith of Liberalism. Beneath his shade, dwarfed by his stature,
the various Liberal factions awaited his demise. Charles Hobhouse was
very much the young politician wanting to make his name and still
finding his way in the political world.

1893

13 February
Mr. Gladstone introduced his second Home Rule Bill today. Beginning at quarter to four he finished at six. The voice wonderful considering his age and length of speech. Eloquent & dignified, and very
moderate, balancing advantages and difficulties. The House crowded.
Four ladies sat *under* the floor of the House to listen. George Russell[1]
told me that having occasion to go and see Mr. G. an hour before
the House met, he found him reading South's sermons, largely no
doubt for the language.

16 March
I presented many petitions against the Liquor Bill, which is ultimately going to turn the Govt. out. A bad measure which will do the
party the greatest possible harm, and those who care for temperate
reform the least possible good.

19

20 March

Grey's[2] speech on Uganda prompted no doubt by Rosebery made great stir in the Cabinet. Harcourt & others thinking it 'too pronounced'. Mr. G.'s answer to Labouchere perfect, smoothing over differences in wonderful way. No one in the House to touch him.

19 April

Dined at C. S. Roundell's.[3] After dinner he introduced me to Mr. Gladstone who asked me to sit beside him. He told me, *inter alia*, that he thought Lowe's[4] speeches in 1866–7 had more influence on H. of C. than any other he could remember. Chamberlain & T. W. Russell and Redmond he thought the best speeches he had heard on the Home Rule Bill. Speeches had increased in length, and the custom of coughing them down had disappeared. He added that he had never known any Parliament so full of good recruits. (Flattery perhaps, but curious from an *old* man.)

✳ The Second Reading of the Home Rule Bill was carried on the night of 21–22 April 1893, by 347 votes to 304. The Committee Stage of the Bill began on 8 May.

21 April

Today Mr. Gladstone rose at 11.40 to finish the Home Rule debate full of vigour, and with great command and flow of language. John Morley moved the closure at 1.15, and the bill was carried by a majority of 43, or the same number that carried the Union 90 yrs ago.

26 April

Made my first speech in the House tonight on the Registration Bill, and got complimented by Mr. Gladstone, Mundella and others who were very kind.

11 May

Two remarkable speeches in House from Mr. G. and Chamberlain. Curious to note deference paid by latter to former since his pretty compliment to Austen Chamberlain.

17 May

Curious to note how every day discussion on Home Rule Bill

becomes more and more exclusively a duel between Mr. G. and J. Chamberlain, Balfour and Morley being merely auxiliaries.

24 May
Wilts Yeomanry inspected by Prince of Wales on Roundway Down. Devizes town admirably decorated by Mr. A. J. Randall, castellated gateways being erected at either end of the town. Yeomanry turned out 307 horses on parade. Lady Lucy Beach[5] who was also at Neston didn't altogether like going up with such a 'Radical lot'.

6 June
Today on a motion of privilege raised by J. Chamberlain of the *Daily News* charging the Tory party of habitually interrupting Mr. G. the latter repudiated the assertion. A pretty exchange of compliments took place between J.C., Mr. G. and Balfour, the latter referring to Mr. G. as 'the most prominent Parl. figure of all time', Mr. G. bowing deep and low. Afterwards as I came through the lobby at the back of the Chair I chanced to see Mrs. G. meet Balfour, and thank him almost theatrically, but genuinely, for his kind words of her husband. It was a touching sight.

16 June
Mr. G. has spoken 44 times this week, and looks as well and speaks as well as ever.

21 June
The first Ld. Lytton, while writing one of his works told his wife he must go off to the Albany to his chambers to finish his volume in quiet, and in a day or two wrote to her that he was spending his nights with his books and his days with Solitude. Lady Lytton who knew his ways presently posted to London, and then wrote to a friend that 'the monster was indeed passing his days with Solitude, but it was Solitude dressed in white muslin, and sitting on his knee.'

28 June
Mr. G. announced today his intention to closure Home Rule Bill in 4 compartments: great relief in back bench members' minds. The decision to do this rather than carry it over to autumn session due probably to his failing health.

30 June
Today at 10.30 p.m. Mr. G. made a really beautiful speech on the opium question. Several people told me that they had come down intending to vote against the Govt. but he had overpersuaded them.

1 July
Went to 75 Dean Street to see Sir J. Thornhill's house. Round the hall is a fine tempera painting, architecture by Thornhill, painting by Hogarth. Said to have been done by Hogarth in a fortnight when courting Miss Thornhill. Her father on seeing it completed, told Hogarth he could marry the girl, for he had the ability to keep her.

✳ As the Committee Stage battle over Home Rule continued parliamentary tempers became strained. On 25 July Gladstone accused Chamberlain of using 'language of habitual, gross, and enormous exaggeration'. Chamberlain's reply soon followed.

27 July
At 9.55 this evening Chamberlain in his speech compared Mr. G. to Herod. The Irish called out 'Judas' in reply. At 10 Mellor[6] rose to put the question. Vicary Gibbs tried to raise a point of order, Hanbury supporting him. In the confusion Mellor put the question, but the Tories not hearing him, sat still. Logan moving down the floor of the House saying 'Order, order' was accosted by Carson Q.C. with 'Get out of this you gang of gaggers.' He, Logan, crossed over to the front Opposition bench to reply to Carson, but greeted by cries of 'Order' sat down at the end of the bench to be 'in order'. Thereon Hayes Fisher and H. S. Foster seized him by the collar, and tried to throw him forward. The Irish came rushing down, and in a moment there was a mêlée with Col. Sanderson in the midst. This lasted 3 or 4 minutes, amidst 'hisses' from the Strangers gallery. Mellor sent for the Speaker, it was remarkable how when he and Mr. G. made their appearance, and Peel addressed the House, the air of naughty guiltiness came over the participants in the scene.

1 August
Dined with Courtenay Warner.[7] Mr. G. there. After dinner said he much regretted that owing to weakness of human nature it had been found necessary to resort to secret voting. Also at his first election at

Newark a stone just missed his head, and turning to G. N. Curzon added, 'What a lot of trouble it would have saved the country, if it had hit.'

✳ In 1892 Hobhouse had become assistant secretary to Sydney Buxton, the Under-Secretary of State for Colonies. It was the beginning of a long political friendship and it also brought Hobhouse into contact with the Colonial Secretary, Lord Ripon.

2 August

Dined with Ld. Ripon. George Russell told me that in 1878 Dizzy proposed to open the Berlin Congress in a French (!) speech. Odo Russell got wind of this, and went to D. saying that the Congress was in hopes of hearing a speech in English from the greatest of English parliamentary orators. D. fell into the snare, and delivered his speech in English.

15 August

Went to Studley Royal,[8] grouse shooting. Ugly house, comfortable and well situated. Lord Granby, De Grey, L. V. Harcourt, F. St. Quintin & self, shot 1,194 grouse on Dallowgill in ten drives, and 750 next day, the two best days they had yet recorded. . . .

Lord Ripon told me that his father having lost his elder daughter from brain fever, would never allow him to be educated, and he himself learnt to read and write by copying the addresses of the servants' letters. For the same reason he was never sent to school or college. . . .

Lord Ripon said that in time most Cabinet secrets leaked out, but that a resignation of Ld. Russell's when Premier had never so done. For two days there was no political leader, but no one had even guessed it. (He mentioned no year for this occurrence.)

20 August

Labouchere was once in Northampton forced into taking a part in a Non. Con. Chapel, and ascending the pulpit said 'Brethren, there are two kinds of prayers, oral and silent. Let us indulge in silent prayer.' They prayed silently until it was nearly time for his train, when he got up, and said he was called away, but that his last advice to them was to pray constantly, in silence!

✳ The Home Rule Bill passed the House of Commons on 1 September but a week later was decisively rejected by the Lords. Home Rule was dead but its ghost was to haunt the Liberal Party for another twenty years.

14 September
At Charlton Nailsea with Ld. Hobhouse.[9] Lord & Lady Farrer also and Sir Edward & Lady Fry.[10] Farrer told me that when he was Permanent Under-Secretary at the Board of Trade, Chamberlain had said to him that he (J.C.) had opened up negotiations in '84 with Parnell. These were broken off, and when in '85 Chamberlain tried to renew them, Parnell refused, saying 'I have now a better offer.'

4 October
Today I picked ripe green figs in the garden, saw dog roses in the hedge, and rhododendrons at Spye in full bloom, and yesterday ripe strawberries were picked at Devizes.

6 October
Speaking of Ld. Broughton (my great-uncle) C.P.H.[11] remembered Canning declaring 'that young man only wants courage to be an assassin'. Ld. B. and his sister Charlotte and my grandmother always wrote of Byron as Biron. Lady Dorchester has letters of Byron to Lady Palmerston which are quite unpublishable.

✳ When the parliamentary session was resumed on 2 November, much of Hobhouse's attention was devoted to the Parish Councils Bill. If his attitude to such local government reform was fairly radical, his views on the position of women in society were then, as later, forcefully expressed.

14 November
Read *Heavenly Twins*, written by a believer in 'woman's rights'. She has made her men vicious, her women hysterical & unsympathetic, and her 'twins' impossible.

17 November
House of Commons met today for Parish Councils Bill. Spoke on Bill for about 20 minutes, congratulated & twice referred to by Goschen[12] in reply.

7 December

There has been an undoubted Cabinet crisis. Fowler[13] nearly resigned on the Parish Councils having control over Charities. Harcourt in view of an unpopular Budget next April declared he didn't care whether Govt. stayed or went. He is also strong against Local Veto Bill.

9 December

G. Russell told me that in '85 Mr. G. was advised by him to ask J. Chamberlain to dinner to discuss the unauthorised programme. Mr. G. who never mixed private friendships & political alliances was aghast, & was with difficulty persuaded to do so. Naturally the effort was a failure.

26 December

Herbert Gladstone told me that it was a true story of his father going to Norwich to stay with the Colmans,[14] who asked *only a family party* to meet him, and being a little late for dinner, came in hurriedly and turned with his usual bow to Mrs. Colman, and said 'And are we all *mustered* here?' The Colmans never moved a muscle.

29 December

J. Arch[15] told me that he had made his Christmas dinner off a brace of partridge sent him by a local Norfolk squire, added that it was not by a long way the first brace he had had off him, but formerly not perhaps legally.

1894

✻ Hobhouse had been right to detect a Cabinet crisis in December, but it was the naval estimates which were its cause, rather than the Parish Councils Bill. After a prolonged period of uncertainty this issue led to Gladstone's resignation in March. After some days of manoeuvring between Sir William Harcourt and Lord Rosebery the latter emerged as Gladstone's successor as Prime Minister. He made an unhappy start to his premiership by an incautious reference to Home Rule in the House of Lords which provoked a Radical revolt led by Henry Labouchere in the House of Commons in the debate on the Queen's Speech. But for the remainder of the year the Irish incubus took second place to colonial affairs. Here Hobhouse was well informed through his connection with Buxton. Increasingly, however, the diary deals with an expanding social life rather than with day-to-day politics.

8 January

Today Harcourt accepted a proposal of the Tory Whips, in view of Horncastle election consequent on Stanhope's death, to limit 'allotments' under Parish Councils Bill to 3 acres pasture and 1 acre arable, and that on Rural Districts, Councils should be able to co-opt four members. The Liberal County members, Luttrell, Logan, Cobb, myself etc. strongly opposed to such limitation, as is Arthur Acland, and we think of leaving the Govt. to look after itself. Eventually we gave way.

9 January

House adjourned today on completion of Parish Councils Bill.

31 January

Today Chamberlain made his first appearance at a purely Tory gathering.

✳ Chamberlain had spoken at the Edgbaston Conservative Club, Birmingham, on 30 January. His speech emphasised the need for a great National Party committed to defence of the Empire and the maintenance of British naval superiority. He applauded the happy alliance of Liberal Unionism and Conservatism for these ends. Following the Liberal defeat in the 1895 general election he was to take office in Lord Salisbury's administration as Colonial Secretary.

14 February

Govt. today nearly defeated through compromising with Tories on Employers' Liability. A splendid meeting in St. James's Hall protesting against Lords' amendments to Parish Councils Bill.

Mr. Gladstone speaking of civilities shown him at Biarritz by Spaniards, said foreign compliments like an aged tree were pretty but hollow. The Englishman on the other hand said as it were, 'My friend, here is my house, large & comfortable. It has two sides, the inside for me, the outside for you.'

27 February

Some talk with the Marlborough masters. It seems quite clear to me that the present system of cultivating the memory, and neglecting the thinking & reasoning faculty is all wrong.

2 March

Mr. G. spoke today for the last time in H. of C. For the party the lop is irreparable, for he alone holds together our varying sections, and he is still far the ablest debater in the House. I am fortunate to have sat one year under him, and to have known what his mastery over the House was.

5 March

It is Harcourt's own fault he is not P.M. He is impossibly overbearing to his colleagues in private, and to his party in public. Lords Ripon and Kimberley I hear would have discovered failing health if Harcourt had been summoned.

The testimony of all parties, and especially of foreigners to Gladstone's single-mindedness and courage is very striking.

✳ The first day of the new session of Parliament saw a successful meeting of the Parliamentary Liberal Party at the Foreign Office where both Rosebery and Harcourt spoke. Their rivalry, and the disappointment of John Morley, was soothed over by suitable expressions of party unity. But that evening, in the House of Lords, Rosebery, in reply to an attack by Salisbury, made a near-fatal error of judgement in admitting the need for an *English* majority in favour of Home Rule before it could be passed by the Imperial Parliament. This needless concession to the Unionist case brought a swift response from Radical Liberals in the Commons on the following night. To the embarrassment of the Liberal leadership the debate of the Address resulted in defeat. It was a dismal start to an unhappy ministry.

12 March

Came to London for hasty meeting at F.O. Rosebery very nervous, made a good impression. Lambert and others told me their first feeling was that Harcourt should have been the man, but they were satisfied with Rosebery. Harcourt very warmly received, speaking almost in tears of Gladstone's departure, and feeling no doubt he should have been first and not second, was not happy.

13 March

Rosebery's incautious and unnecessary speech in the Lords upset the Irish, and today on Labby's amendment, we who to justify our speeches in the country voted with L. expecting to be 30 or 40, being joined unexpectedly by Irish, beat the Govt. by 2. Harcourt was delighted and said so.

16 March

Elected today an Alderman of Wiltshire C.C.

5 April

The real reason for Labouchere's opposition to Rosebery is this. In '92 Labby expected a Cabinet appointment. When this was not forthcoming he asked for the Washington Embassy. This Rosebery, on account of extreme susceptibility of Americans to L.'s past career, absolutely vetoed.

When Rosebery formed his Govt., it was proposed to put S. Buxton at the L.G.B. instead of Shaw Lefevre.

8 April

Dined tonight with Tom Ellis[16] and Prof. Munro to meet Mr. James Thornton, a possible candidate for N.W. Wilts. (He subsequently married my sister.)

9 April

Ld. Bowen died today. A great wit, on whom much was fathered. Two *mots* seem to be authentic. 'Truth will out, even in an affidavit', and the alteration in an address to the Queen at the '87 jubilee from 'Conscious as we are of our own defects' to 'Conscious as we are of each other's defects.'

13 April

Put today on the Committee of '80 Club to select testimonial for Mr. G. Only 3 members.

H. P. Parker of Gurkhas dining with me, said that last year, a tribe on the frontier giving trouble, the headmen were captured and brought in. They however refused to pay the fine inflicted, saying they knew the British Government would not let them be hurt. The politicals were nonplussed at this, but a native officer took the chiefs off to the guard tent, and round it so built a latrine, that anyone using it, must expose his backside. This being the greatest indignity a frontier man can conceive, in 4 days they capitulated, declaring that the devil himself could not equal British ingenuity.

2 May
Staying at Leigh with Ed. Fitzmaurice, he remembered Speaker Denison being once compelled to leave the Chair to escape vomiting from the bad smells prevalent in the House. He once met Parnell at Chicago, and a team of English cricketers there, being a man short, asked Parnell, a member of I Zingari to play. He though fond of the game declined on the ground that his political influence in Ireland would be gone if it was once known that he had ever played for an English team.

3 May
Much trouble in C.O. about Swaziland, natives refusing to come under Boers; & Cape Colony Africanders very combative.

7 May
Spoke today in H. of C. rising at 7 just after W. Long. I raised a new point in connection with Budget, & my figures being unimpeachable got a good deal of kudos from high & low.

10 May
Harcourt wound up debate today by saying in so many words, the Tories won't tax land, capital or beer. What is it they do want to tax? Is it food, coffee perhaps or better still corn? They were significantly silent.

13 June
Some talk with E. Grey on the Congo Treaty, for which he declares Germany will demand compensation either in Samoa or Walfish Bay. Personally I should like to acquire Morocco in exchange for Egypt and Gibraltar, thus obtaining an extensive and fertile country only 3 days steam from our own shore, and in which we should be free from any difficulties with colonists, with whom and our so-called dependencies I can see possible causes of friction in future.

✳ Here Hobhouse was the reverse of prescient. In 1904 Britain and France did reach agreement on colonial differences, but with France taking control of Morocco and Britain retaining Egypt, Gibraltar never entering into the bargaining at all.

17 June

A Japanese attaché who goes in for studying folklore, eastern and western, was discussing proverbs with a lady the other day. She asked him whether they had an equivalent for our 'Penny wise & pound foolish'. 'Yes' he replied, 'the Japanese declare that he who goes to bed at 7 p.m. to save candles, always begets twins.'

3 July

A good deal of trouble over Attercliffe[17] election. A fight between Liberalism & Labour is bound to come. Our aims are largely the same, the difference being between disciplined and undisciplined ideas.

13 August

Shot grouse at Ingleboro[18], 140 brace. Jimmy Farrer much disturbed at Budget, having taken 4 years to pay his duties, got 71 brace next day, and 51 brace day after that.

25 August

Went on to Brooks[19] at Rawtenstall, & Roundells at Dorfold. The latter near Nantwich. It belonged to Tollemaches, but was built 1611 by Roger Wilbraham. . . .

Mrs. Julia Roundell told me some old stories of Tennyson. He was at a garden party of Lady Middleton's who found him in an anteroom eating, or rather stuffing sandwiches. Lady M. who was a gushing sort of person said 'Oh Mr. T. I am so glad you like our sandwiches, they are of our own ham, cured by our own recipe', to this T. replied with his mouth full of them 'They're as tough as old boots.'

✳ The long summer recess gave the opportunity for more leisurely visiting. The autumn of 1894 saw one such tour.

20 October

Drove from The Ridge with Sir W. E. Hall & his wife, via Beckington

& Longleat and Nunney Castle to Hadspen. Left at 9.30 & arrived at 6 p.m.

Henry Hobhouse[20] told me that Jas. Bryce[21] opened the proceedings of the Royal Commission on Secondary Education of which 3 ladies were members & present, by saying 'Well, Gentlemen & Ladies, we may congratulate ourselves that we have no ornamental members among our number.'

Left Hadspen at noon, via Ilchester & Petherton, Shepton Beauchamp & Barrington to Jordans near Ilminster, 23 miles. Next day via Castle Neroche to Culmhead, we nearly lost our way in the rain, and came down by the Holman Clavell Inn (Holly Bram Inn, Devonian dialect). Stayed here Sunday, and found people still believed in a 'white' witch whom we saw, and in a 'wiseman' in Taunton.

Next day via Wellington, Wiveliscombe, Longford Budville, Sydenham Combe (quite as beautiful as anything I ever saw in Japan), Cleeve Abbey, to Dunster, about 29 miles. Lady Hood, her daughter Mrs. Mackinnon, and a family party. Stayed here 4 days, & left the Halls, taking on Hugh Luttrell & drove, via Lynton, Parracombe and Loxhore, to Barnstable 40 miles.

Left next day, via Torrington, Merton, Hatherleigh to Okehampton, all very beautiful scenery. Next day we walked on to Dartmoor. Nina sketched. Went to church in Corporation Chapel, good oak carving & pulpit, but a villainous choir singing fine old hymns to discordant new tunes.

Left on Monday via Cheriton Cross to Exeter, thence by Honiton Clyst to Ottery St. Mary 34 miles. The inn here kept by one Squires & his daughter, a very pretty & charming girl of a type more generally heard of in ballads than seen.

Visited Church to see Thrupp's monument of 1st Lady Coleridge, very beautiful; hands, drapery & feet exquisitely done. Thence by Honiton to Chard via Cricket St. Thomas. Fine house at Chard where Jeffreys held his assize, with barrel ceiling & pendants. So to Coker Court, near Sutton Bingham.

Next day walked to Brympton, & West Coker Manor built by Edward VI, added to in 1600. Drove to Trent House where Charles II hid. Next day walked to Montacute, a perfectly beautiful & delightful house. Some talk with Hall over Newfoundland question[22] which he is to conduct at Paris. I thought his case a weak one.

Left Coker next day 11 a.m., returned by train to The Ridge, having been away 18 days without having any rain!

22 December

The new parish councils have been elected, and the village people of this country have been put on trial, & after natural failures will do well.

28 December

Visited today the lunatic asylum on Kingsdown, the oldest licensed establishment in England, being originally licensed to Judge Jeffreys's sister. One of the inmates recognising Fitzmaurice and me, called out, 'You'll be glad to know my Lord that we are all Liberals here.'

I believe that Home Rule would be possible if the Irish contribution should be earmarked for certain services, the estimates to which they belonged taken *en bloc*, at a fixed period of the session, the Irish members attending for this period, but being otherwise excluded.

1895

✳ The difficulties of the Liberal Government, divided amongst its leaders and over policy, harassed even over the choice of the Speaker of the House of Commons, continued until the end of June. Resignation then was a merciful end, but for Charles Hobhouse it meant electoral defeat and the interruption of his political career.

26 January

Received letter from Harcourt asking me to 'move the address' on 23 January. Went to Monkton Farleigh to ask my father to help me with my speech which, of course, he refused to do.

4 February

Went through Queen's Speech with Harcourt, who told me that *he* had wanted to give Magistrates power in Local Option Bill of treating all licences as new ones. Dined next day with Govt., custom being to treat the 'mover' as chief guest. I sat therefore on Harcourt's right, the Speaker on his left, Mellor on my left [*sic*]. Harcourt told me that in the beginning even of this century the Govt. always wore court dress in the House, and (? like the actors) were always styled 'His Majesty's servants'.

✳ Hobhouse moved the address on 5 February, finding perhaps as others have done that the occasion offers little opportunity for eloquence. In the debate that followed, Keir Hardie, the Independent Labour Member for West Ham South, regarded then as a dangerous socialist, the *enfant terrible* of the House, made an eloquent plea for central government action to deal with the major problem of unemployment. The diary comment is perhaps less than generous—Hardie in fact had to speak in support of a more vapid general amendment expressing concern about economic conditions, his own amendment not having been called.

8 February
On Keir Hardie's amendment Harcourt made one of very best speeches, clear & vigorous. K.H. walked out & Ed. Strachey abstained from voting, so beat the Tories by 12!

26 February
S. Buxton told me they wanted him to go to Cape as High Commissioner. He thought Rhodes a sincere friend of G.B. and the Empire.

28 February
Ed. Grey and Bobby Spencer[23] told me Harcourt's conduct to his colleagues was abominable. Frank Lockwood[24] being attacked by him for not being on front bench replied 'Ah Sir William, I thought it would hardly be seemly for me as the youngest member of the Govt. to be too much in evidence at first.'

Got First Reading of Welsh Church Bill today. I think the glebe lands ought to remain with Church.

4 March
The progressives lost today 22 seats on the L.C.C. No doubt the 'Empire' licensing case did them harm, but the workingmen of London who have been rescued from long hours, and low wages, who have had their river cleansed, their parks beautified, and

multiplied, and their streets renovated have been singularly un-grateful to their best servants.

✳ The vulnerability of the Liberal Government was demonstrated by their difficulty in finding a successor for the Speakership of the House of Commons.

11 March
Speaker Peel[25] has announced his impending resignation. Courtney and C. Bannerman the favourites. Tories will not support former, we can't spare latter. Personally I think A. Morley[26] would do well, he would be no administrative or debating loss, but is clear headed & has a good presence.

8 April
Mr. Peel made his farewell address, language and sentiments worthy of the occasion, but he displayed curiously little emotion. Harcourt's Local Veto Bill will wreck the party.

9 April
Today Mr. Peel showed much agitation at the general leavetaking; he said a few kind words to me personally.

10 April
Mr. Gully chosen Speaker today by 11 votes, proposed by Whit-bread, seconded by Birrell. Mowbray proposed and Wharton seconded White Ridley.[27] Balfour displayed anger & bitterness, but commanded no cheers from his own side. Harcourt spoke with weight and dignity.

3 May
Voted against the Duke of Coburg's annuity,[28] a most improper proposal, considering his double nationality and his position in the German Army.

25 May
At Colonial Office all day. Much trouble over our annexation of Zambaan's territory. Boers very angry as it shuts them out from sea. They had to have rushed us as in the case of Swaziland.

1 June

Present Lady St. Leonard's went to call at Hythe on Mrs. Featherstonhaugh, bicycling in spats & a *very* short skirt. The sentry stopped her saying he wasn't going to allow a woman of that sort in that dress to go to the officers' quarters, at least *by day*.

✳ The Liberals' Welsh Church Disestablishment Bill had passed its Second Reading in March, but in the Committee Stage in May and June ran into difficulties in the form of the Radical demands of the Welsh M.P.'s led by the young Lloyd George, and Gladstone's threat to re-enter the fray as the champion of the Anglican Church. In mid-June another humiliating Irish episode showed how insecure was the Government's hold on the Commons.

17 June

Debate on Cromwell's statue, first on 14th then today. Irish of course opposed it, as did Balfour also. No one on our side even thought of giving Cromwell credit for procuring for the English people religious freedom & toleration. Today Govt. pressed by the Irish withdrew the vote, John Morley saying that he looked on Oliver as the greatest of Englishmen. I told Grey that it was the first act of the Govt. of which I was ashamed. Rosebery apparently was thrown over by Harcourt, for at a Cabinet they had decided to stick to the vote.

✳ On 20 June Hobhouse left England for a holiday in Norway where three days later he learnt that the Government had resigned. A defeat in committee over the question of the supply of cordite to the army gave the Liberal leaders the opportunity to resign from an impossible parliamentary situation.

   Polling in the general election which followed was spread over three weeks in July. Hobhouse claimed that the adverse results of Harcourt in Derby on 15 July and Geoffrey Fuller in West Wiltshire on 25 July contributed to his own defeat in East Wiltshire on 26 July. But the Liberal leaders were hopelessly divided and the Party's weakness was emphasised by the overall Unionist majority of 152 seats. Out of Parliament Hobhouse planned a trip to Persia, but his wife's ill health prevented this. During the autumn his diary entries virtually ceased. Only at the very end of the year did he comment again on the political scene.

31 December
Spoke at Bathford last night, and warned audience of complications
in S. Africa, resulting from racial hostility. Today comes news of the
Raid, the most foolish, criminal, and misorganised political venture
of the century.

1896

✳ The Jameson Raid was the *cause célèbre* of 1896. Many Liberals stri-
dently denounced the Unionist Government's policies which had led to
this situation. Others, more realistically, recognised the essential con-
tinuity of policy between Lord Ripon and Chamberlain at the Colonial
Office. Chamberlain's complicity in the Raid was the subject of much
speculation. But there was time too for the Liberals to relate the past
enmities of their leaders or to take stock of their 'coming men'.

1 January
Heard today of Jameson's Raid. Engineered no doubt by Rhodes,
and possibly *The Times* has assisted. The former will ruin his career,
whether or not he disavows Jameson.

3 January
Very serious feeling against us in Germany, fomented by Emperor's
telegram to Kruger.[29] The French too very hostile. All this very
justifiable. But why did Rhodes think he could filibuster the Boers
with a force which couldn't even fight a handful of police?

11 January
Jameson's forces numbered 500 with 20 officers! food and ammunition failing them 6 miles from Johannesburg. What a leader.
He is to be surrendered to British authorities. The arrest and
punishment of the Nat. Dep. Union. must follow, & that will
eventually lead to a racial war.

16 January
Failed today to get T. Ellis to organise Wilts., Dorset & Somerset as
a separate group of counties as Ed. Strachey[30] & I wished.

28 January

Ld. Suffolk is Chairman of the R.D.C. nominally a Liberal, and the autocrat of Malmesbury. He refuses to allow a steam roller in the district. The other day he fell ill, and E. Fitzmaurice was asked how he was, not because the Council was anxious about his recovery, but in hopes that he would be ill long enough to permit them to pass a resolution to buy the steam roller.

6 February

S. Buxton told me that J.C. had sent him the news about South Africa a day or two before the public knew it, & that he was greatly alarmed as to the possible consequences. S.B. thought neither Rhodes nor J.C. had any preknowledge of the raid.

8 February

Luncheon with S.B. He had just left Rhodes, & was sure that Rhodes was not privy to the plot. Rhodes was convinced he would never recover his position. J.C. much pleased with his 'dispatch' of today, *his* first, but as written just after his interview with Rhodes, I think Kruger will refuse to accept his suggestions, and then eventually war!

12 February

Salisbury said that the Govt. had invited Kruger to England before J.C. sent his dispatch to H. Robinson. But the dispatch was not finished till the evening before publication, and Kruger only heard of it through Montagu White.

Harcourt on Venezuela, said Queen Elizabeth had granted the whole of Venezuela to one of his ancestors, and he had the title deeds at Malwood.

17 February

Started for Malta, where E. Fuller ill, from Marseilles to Tunis by the *Transatlantique*, clean & comfortable, bad food. Great use of ironwork with admirable designs. The language a mixture of Arabic & Italian. Arrived in Malta in time for Carnival ball. Morland being A.D.C.

19 February

A good deal of fighting and drinking consequent on the Carnival.

Confetti may not be thrown at anyone in uniform, and men & officers may not wear anything else during this week.

Kruger, as I anticipated, has declined J.C. interference in Transvaal internal affairs, declaring his own competence to manage things.

✳ Hobhouse spent about six weeks in Malta and visited Sicily and southern Italy before returning to England via Genoa, Basle and Paris early in April.

5 May
Dined with G. W. Palmer[31] & next to G. W. E. Russell. Said that Mr. G. had a poor opinion of Asquith who could only make 'a good speech on a legal point', but regarded Grey as 'the coming man'. He added that in the Cabinet of '80 to '84, Dilke and J.C. were regarded with so much suspicion that contrary to all precedent memoranda were taken of decisions. On the question of the Franchise the Cabinet divided Lords 'against', Commons 'for' the Bill, *exactly*. In '85 when Parnell approached Mr. G. he had proposals in writing from J.C. upon Home Rule.

10 May
The Asquiths at Neston. She[32] and Agnes Grove discussed the problems of maternity in a manner which made J.F. & myself blush! Asquith confirmed to me H. H. Fowler's statement to me at Sprinkell that when Ld. Roseberry was asked to form a Cabinet he was given a paper signed by the *whole* of the late Cabinet (Mr. G., Ld. R., and Harcourt and *one* other excepted), saying they would not take office under Harcourt.

24 May
Walked in Hyde Park. Listened to a professor of palmistry, a discussion on the relative merits of monarchy & republicanism, the merits of the Salvation Army, the necessity, from a self-acknowledged convict, of a Court of Criminal Appeal, two comic artists and a revivifier of hair.

30 May
Visited the Trinity Almshouses in Mile End Road. Curious that

communities such as these should be in spite of socialism nowadays so little liked by the working classes.

1 August
Long told me this morning that Ld. Salisbury had done what he could to get Irish Land Bill wrecked in H. of L. Such are the advantages of a Unionist Govt.

11 August
Biked with J.M.F. & Nina to Wells. Touched the actual hurdling with which the prehistoric inhabitants of Glastonbury lined their walls.

15 August
C. W. Wright told me that he had been in Johannesburg at the time of Jameson Raid. Willoughby had neglected the most ordinary military precautions, & while paths ran along the hills above Dornkop he sauntered into the Boer trap.

20 August
Played cricket at Glanusk, made 26 runs out of 134. Went to Tredillion which the Thomases have just bought for £12,500!

24 August
I detest Anglo-Indians. They spend their whole lives in forcing Radical administration on the most conservative of peoples, and return home to be the most narrowminded of Tories, criticising a system of which they know nothing, while resenting any entertainment of opinion (contrary to their own) by English people on Indian affairs.

29 August
Bicycled from Abergavenny to Caerleon, & from Patchway to Westbury-on-Trym to look at the 'College', once ours. A central square tower, a fine arched roof to the vault all now left of the Bishop's Collegium.

Then on to Charlton to stay with Lord Hobhouse. Found Lady Norman & her daughter. He told me that Jessel who could not always manage his 'h's, was examining, through an interpreter, a

French witness in a patent case connected with sealing wax. After asking how the components were mixed he continued 'Do you then (h)eat them?' which the interpreter rendered 'Que faites-vous donc, en mangez-vous?'

4 September
Stayed with C. Roundell who showed me a letter from Jowett[33] in which he wrote that the High Church party cared more for miracles and sacraments than morality and truth.

15 September
Eshton Lady Wilson gave me as a specific for cuts some petals of the madonna lily soaked in brandy. Read again Barrington's *Memoirs* and *Don Quixote*.

16 September
Rode round Derwentwater yesterday, and Bassenthwaite today and on to Springkell.[34] Some good pictures, Mieres, Poelemberg, Weenix, G. Dow, Wandercapelle, Havel etc.

24 September
Went to Lysdinam.[35] Today Mr. G. addresses 6,000 people in Liverpool on the Armenian massacres. Europe, as in 1490 disunited, looks on while the Turk slaughters Christians. Such is our advance!

6 October
One result of Mr. G.'s speech is Ld. Rosebery's retirement. It's unlucky & unwise. Harcourt would have died & Morley disappeared before next election, if R. had only waited. (Much later Lord Crewe told me he had told no one of his intention, and had posted with his own hand the letters to the papers.)

2 November
Dined at Leigh with E. Fitzmaurice. He and Mr. G. being once at Wilton walking along the river, Mr. G. exclaimed, throwing up his arms, 'How delightful is the peace and rest of the country. What a comfort to be free from H. of C. and from Fawcett.' As they turned the corner there was Fawcett[36] fishing.

When Harcourt became Solicitor-General he, as James subsequently, refused to be knighted. Mr. G. tried every argument in vain and at last urged that ancient honour any distinguished man might covet and be adorned by. Harcourt replied 'Very well, Mr. G., if you will consent to receive this great honour, I too will yield', but he yielded first.

Some talk with Walter Long. Complained of the stationary and progressive sections of the Tories. Salisbury can only consult Duke of Devonshire, J.C., A. Balfour and Beach, and though he did not complain of only being *told* what was going on, he said he wished he was on back benches again.

1897

✳ This year saw the South African Committee proceedings of inquiry into the Jameson Raid. Hobhouse heard occasionally from Buxton, a member of the Committee, and himself attended some sessions. But his own main concerns were social rather than political, and the diary reflects the life of the English country house rather than Parliament.

7 January
Today Miners Federation passed resolution in favour of nationalising mines, land and manufactures. I think the first Socialist declaration of a large body of men which I have come across.

10 January
My sister May became engaged today to a Capt. MacTier without any means. My father takes the line that this is no affair of his, they are the only people interested.

27 January
John Fuller defeated at Salisbury today.[37] The corruption on *both* sides deliberate and great. Mrs. Fuller wisely remarked, that to wallow in the mire was bad enough, but to wallow unsuccessfully was worst possible.

31 January
Called on S.B. Rhodes will own to his share in the Raid, if so he must lose his Privy Councillorship, to deprive him of which will be

unpopular in South Africa, so probably he will be asked to hold his tongue. Harcourt asked S.B. not to go to the Rothschilds today lest he should meet Rhodes.

5 February
S.B. further said that Rhodes while 'owning up' would take care not to incriminate J.C. Apparently Flora Shaw[38] immediately after an interview with J.C. telegraphed to British South Africa Company that J.C., in view of Venezuela question, recommended them to do whatever they wished to do quickly. This they took as an unofficial hint—it was really misrepresentation by the lady.

8 February
Lord Dorchester told when he joined 60th Rifles about 1850, they were one of the few Regts. taught shooting. Strips of linen, hung in Windsor Park about 150 yds. from the shooters, were the targets, but as the practice was found to disturb the pheasants it was discontinued.

20 February
Listening to Rhodes giving evidence I was convinced that while he could calculate the results of his actions on his friends, he never reckoned what it might be on his enemies. A *statesman* omits neither.

I have felt very strongly for the Greek movement in Crete, and if means permitted I would go there myself.

24 February
J. A. Butler, Longman's 'reader', told me that Dizzy, to whom they had paid £10,000 for *Endymion*, hearing the book had failed to sell, came to them offering to return half the amount. They declined on the ground that a speculation must stand. Dizzy retired stipulating that no one should be told of the interview or its character. Two hours later the *St. James' Gazette* told the whole story, and Longman subsequently found that D. had gone straight to Greenwood with an account of what happened.

13 March
Baddish fall out hunting near Mapson's Farm close to the Fosse.

18 March
Stayed with Ld. Hobhouse in Bruton Street and attended as an Ex-Member sittings of Select Committee on Fair Wages, but with special facilities.

7 April
Wrote an article on Fair Wages Committee for *Daily Chronicle*.

✳ In the first part of April Hobhouse crossed to France for a short cycling holiday, visiting Dieppe, Rouen, Elbeuf, Dreux, Chartres and Orleans. But his thoughts still seem to have been centred on the Greek problem.

5 May
The Greeks fought their last fight today, and when it came to cold steel ran away as usual. I recollect that we have never had the *Persian* account of the Persian and Greek wars, nor their version of the battle of Salamis.

11 May
The Duke of Abercorn, Chairman of the British South Africa Company, under cross-examination. A very pitiable spectacle. Though it was on the strength of his appointment that the Company was given a Charter, he was so ignorant of their business that he did not know what Directors attended meetings, nor had he read the annual reports of the Company, nor had he *any* answers to questions save what Hawksley put into his mouth.

✳ Liberal irritation with the South African Committee was increased by the report which it produced in July 1897. Rhodes and the British South Africa Company were censured but the complicity of Chamberlain remained unproven and in Parliament the latter was able to claim that the personal reputation of Rhodes as a man of honour was unaffected by the findings. The suspicion remained that the British Government had connived at both the Raid and the subsequent cover-up.

24 June
Training with my Militia, the Barnet Rifles. Had a field day for which the men paraded an hour too early. We were then marched,

without any attempt to explain to us what part we were expected to play, to a sunk lane where we stayed three hours. We then marched through a small wood to within 300 yds. of the enemy & ordered to charge entrenchments. Some day we shall pay dearly for this foolish 'training'.

1 July
Great Military Review. 30,000 men. Cavalry very bad—infantry and artillery good: but display hardly likely to impress foreign military critics. Went to Henley. First time since Eton, season having been so early & hay fever over. Stayed with G. W. Palmers, the remainder of the party relations neither interesting, amusing nor pleasant.

24–30 July
Coaching party, G.P. and E. J. G. Fuller, selves, Rob. F., Madeleine Clutterbuck.[39] Charlton, Winchester (at St. Cross noticed that the 'Brethren' to prevent jealousies, keep a roster of the first turn to the first *cut* at the common joint), Romsey, Lyndhurst, Bournemouth, via Ringwood to Stoney Cross, via Downton to Salisbury and home.

28 July
Mr. R. P. Davies told me that when staying with M. Beach at the Chief Secretary's Lodge at Dublin, Gen. Ulysses Grant, *ex*-President U.S.A. and private citizen was there. Though the Ld.-Lieutenant was present he resented not being sent into dinner first, and after dinner made a *bolt* for the door. One of his staff asked semi-officially what the Lord-Lieut.'s position was, and was told that as the representative of the Sovereign, the L.L. had precedence even of the Prince of Wales. Sir Selwyn Ibbetson said that when the Prince Regent was staying with his father & was asked to take Lady Ibbetson to dinner, he pointed to the High Sheriff of the County, and said, 'as High Sheriff *he* takes Lady Ibbetson in.' After dinner Grant without waiting for the L.L. made his adieux and as they disappeared the Duchess of Marlborough ejaculated 'Shoemakers!'[40]

15 August
Staying at Rheola.[41] Jack Vaughan told me that when Sir William Harcourt came down to stand for Monmouthshire after his defeat

at Derby he was received by the local Liberal Association in a chapel, & the first hymn was 'Lead kindly light'.

8 September

Eshton.[42] Mathew Wilson, same kind considerate man as always, told me that the late Ld. Bathurst sent John Wallington as follows. 'Dear John, I return with thanks the horse you sent me. For getting on and off he is perfect, for all intermediate purposes quite useless.' He was once walking with Capt. Haworth, a King's Messenger, talking of the then Tichborne trial. Wilson asked H. who knew Tichborne what he was like. H. replied 'Well, there's a man the other side of the road who would strongly resemble him if he were alive.' While he was speaking the man crossed, & said 'Capt. Haworth, you remember me, Roger Tich.' He was invited to call at Capt. Haworth's house, but never came.

Robert Wilson now on the *Britannia* speaking of the bullying amongst the cadets there, said the frequent practice was to tie a small boy to the pump handle in the playground, and beat his hand with a knotted cord. In one instance the fingers nearly rotted off. Another *amusement* was to beat them with a 'Turk's Head', while one senior cadet made a junior stand at attention and then struck him in the face to see if he could knock him down. Stealing he declared to be very rife.

13 September

Springkell. Sir Henry Fowler, Ld. & Lady Frederick Bruce, and the Fergusons. Henry Fowler very bitter against Gladstone. Speaking of the formation of the Rosebery Cabinet, that he left London at 5 p.m. on the Friday afternoon [2 March 1894], after expressing himself ready to follow any leader 'as a hewer of wood and drawer of water', and on the Monday, R. asked him to go to the India Office. John Morley at first was R.'s most vehement supporter, the quarrel coming later. He said that towards the end Mr. G. would scarcely ever, even in Cabinet, discuss *politics*, that the '95 Cabinet ended not because C.B. resigned, for he was willing to go on, but because R. was determined to go. After a Cabinet lasting from 11 to 5 they decided by a small majority only to resign. His own wish being to hold on. That Harcourt and J. Morley's surrender to the Irish over Cromwell's statue was contrary to the decision of the Cabinet, &

without R.'s sanction. He added that in the '86 Govt. M. White
Ridley was offered 4 different offices, and that each offer having been
accepted was subsequently withdrawn. The last offer was the Under-
Secretary of Foreign Office, and when this was cancelled to make
room for Jas. Ferguson, W. Ridley gave Ld. Salisbury such a
whigging (*sic*), as no Prime Minister had had before.

* Such political gossip aside, the autumn was given over to more parochial
affairs, such as holding a Court Leet at Broughton Gifford (29 September) and securing a grant of £25 from Bradford-on-Avon R.D.C. to
build a road over Norrington Common, near Melksham (4 October).
The diary entries are tantalisingly brief.

28 October
The most beautiful autumn I ever recollect. Colours and tints in the
Avon Valley perfectly bewildering. Chosen Vice-Chairman of
Finance Committee of C.C.

2 November
Shot at Hadspen. Bailward of Horsington who married Margaret
Hobhouse is blind, but rides, walks by himself, Chairman of the
R.D.C. etc. Bicycled back to Ridge in 4½ hours.

19 November
West Wilts. Lib. Assoc. would have chosen me as their candidate
today, had I wished, which I did not.

28 December
Much industrial disturbances, engineers, Railway, and Cotton
operatives all on strike, which will probably not be successful.
Against the former Wilkie warned Barnes the Gen. Sec. in my hearing.

1898

* The diary for this year is fragmentary, but Hobhouse's description of
his visit to Rome typifies his eye for detail and his mixture of perceptive
comment with outlandish allusion.

March

Visited Rome this spring with Nina and Arthur Bond. Bewilderment that so much, and disappointment that so little is left, are the predominant feelings. No one can come to Rome and see the harm that clerical vanity, ambition, or ignorance have done here without realising the injury done to science by the Church the world over.

The Farnese Gardens reminded me of Omar Khayyam. 'I sometimes think that never blows so red, The rose, as where some buried Caesar bled. And every hyacinth the garden rears, Springs in its lap from some once lovely head.'[43]

While looking at Raphael's *Two Venetians* in the Doria Gallery, a priest came & stood looking at the picture who might have sat as a model for one of the two painted.

Noticed that the bust of Cavour is the image of one Mr. Hart of Bradford-on-Avon. Is it wits or opportunities which separate the probable fame of each?

The shady ilex, the broad box hedges make one understand how Italians could be stabbed in their own gardens, their conversations overheard, and how Benedict & Beatrice could be cajoled in turn 'Mark where the fowl sits, stalk on, stalk on.'

From Rome to Venice. Equally wet. I can never forget the first impression of St. Mark.

5 May

Herbert Spencer[44] & Huxley[45] were in Rome together. Spencer told Huxley he had just been to see Raphael's *Assumption*, and disliked it so much that he sat down there and then and wrote 3 pages of notes in criticism. Huxley replied 'Had you been present at the original scene, you would probably have done just the same.'

28 May

Went to Mr. Gladstone's funeral. The music and choir in the Abbey very beautiful. Harcourt & Rosebery *next* to each other. The grey simplicity of it all in striking contrast to the noise, the glare, the crowd, almost holiday-making, who were present at Dizzy's funeral at Hughenden, where I went also from Oxford.

5 June

Heard an admirable story of Lord Tennyson. A lady was introduced to him and 'gushed' as usual. He merely grunted out 'Madam, your stays creak disgustingly.' She turned indignantly away, but at the end of the entertainment Tennyson advanced to her. She expecting the *amende honorable* stepped forward. All he said was 'Beg your pardon, ma'am. It was not your stays, but my braces.'

7 June
Field day at Aldershot very badly managed, troops taught to retire across the open in close order, obstructing their friends and exposed to their foes' fire. Company Officers without maps, uninformed of direction of attack or object of operations. Such training is a dangerous farce.

8 July
Today died my dear dog Nellie. Fourteen years my friend in every part of the world. Her jealous love of myself was her only fault in my eyes. I hope I may never forget her, and perhaps we may meet again.

1 December
Fleetwood Wilson[46] told me that in 1893, C.B. was in attendance at Balmoral, and the Queen who had been very rude over the Home Rule Bill, said at dinner one day, 'Mr. Campbell-Bannerman, I don't like the way Mr. Farquharson of Invercauld treats his tenants. I speak as a neighbour and not as the Queen. He is not a resident here now and his agent rackrents the tenants and will make no improvements.' When she had done, C.B. bent forward and said 'Well ma'am, you've admirably described a state of affairs whose existence in Ireland has made me a Home Ruler.'

II

Indian Journey
1904–1908

✳ In the 1900 'Khaki' election the Liberal Party fared almost as badly as in 1895. Hobhouse's return to Parliament as M.P. for East Bristol was only an isolated success. Divided now in their attitudes towards the Boer War, the Liberals were manifestly impossible as a realistic government for most electors. Those divisions into 'Liberal Imperialist' and 'Little Englander' factions were to persist. But after Arthur Balfour became Prime Minister in July 1902 the Unionist majority was increasingly threatened. Their 1902 Education Act reunited the Liberal Party with the forces of Nonconformity, protesting against State-financed denominational teaching. In 1903 Chamberlain's championship of Imperial Preference split the Unionist Party completely. That summer saw the formation of two rival bodies within the Unionist Party—the Tariff Reform League and the Free Food League. In the autumn Chamberlain resigned from the Cabinet and launched an aggressive nationwide campaign for Tariff Reform and Imperial Preference. Henceforth the Government was in difficulties. If anything, the fiscal controversy concealed its real vulnerability. Criticised by Labour for the 1901 Taff Vale judgement, by the Nonconformists for the Education Act, by its own younger backbenchers like Winston Churchill for its proposed Army Reforms, by the press for its mishandling of the South African War, and divided over Tariff Reform the Balfour Government went into decline. By December 1905 even Balfour's calculated ambiguities could not sustain it any longer and he resigned. The Liberals took office and in the following month won an overwhelming electoral victory. Four hundred Liberals were elected to Westminster and with the support of 83 Irish Nationalists and 30 Labour M.P.s the new Government had an incredible working majority of 356.

1904

✳ At the turn of the year Balfour was trying to avert an open rift, treading

49

gingerly between the Chamberlainite and Free Trade factions in his party. The Debate on the Address in February revealed the Government's embarrassment. Balfour and Chamberlain were both absent, the former with influenza and the latter recuperating in Egypt from the effects of his speaking tour. Morley's Liberal amendment upholding Free Trade provoked a wondrous array of contradictory arguments from Unionist Ministers. After veering from one course of action to another over the six days of debate, eventually twenty-six Unionist Free Traders voted against their own Government. The Government's morale never recovered from this division.

17 February

I met today Percy Wyndham, George Wyndham's[1] father, who told me that Arthur Balfour had been much worse than was ever admitted. He was not even allowed to see Gerald B[alfour] but lay like a log, knowing and caring for nothing. He could not be consulted, and the authoritative declarations of policy made in the Fiscal debate did not emanate from him, were not seen by him, or even known by him. He was not told till today of the important division having taken place, or its result.

✳ But after this political excitement Hobhouse's diary recorded little for many months. When he did so, it was a typically apolitical comment.

17 June

I was stopping tonight at Oban *en route* for Gairloch. At the next table to mine in the hotel were a father, mother and 3 daughters. They began to talk, and finally it was decided that 'Columba was a relative of Columbus who discovered Iona and Staffa, that he lived about the time of Sir Thomas Moore who discovered Canada, but died on his way home through the Suez Canal'! Such is knowledge in the XX century.

2 October

Sir W. Harcourt died suddenly yesterday. To his friends who knew him and to the public who did not know him at all he will be a loss. To those who like myself only knew him politically his departure will be a relief. His bad temper and want of political courage made him an impossible leader and unbearable colleague. We invariably congratulated ourselves when Harcourt was out of the House. He was latterly completely under the control of his son Lulu, who has little ability and a great love of intrigue.

5 November
John Bailey[2] said that it was within his knowledge that Haldane had at the request of mutual friends spoken seriously to Asquith as to his tendency to take too much champagne, the reproof being taken in very good part, & *acted* on ?

6 November
Bailey also said that the terms of the letters addressed by Queen Victoria to Dizzy were not only intimate, but almost unwarrantably affectionate. He in turn wrote daily to the Queen describing parties, ladies, dresses etc. He bewailed Bismarck's habits of smoking, but since nothing could be got from him till the end of his 3rd cigar, Dizzy suffered the smoke & beer of German habits.

15 November
Staying with the Sydney Buxtons last week. Lord Stanley of Alderley, in other ways a curious creature, married a wife of no known nationality or language, probably a Spanish gipsy. The only language she spoke was French & that very badly. She said of a butler discharged for stealing cigars that he was dismissed 'parce qu'il avait une infidelité avec le fumier'.[3]

1905

✳ During this year the diary again reveals how far removed from the centre of the political stage Hobhouse was. The relatively infrequent occasions on which he played what he thought was a significant part are carefully recorded. But only at the end of the year does he provide much insight into what political events were taking place with his account of the formation of the Liberal Government.

31 March
I dined last night with Ld. Rosebery, and sat next to him. He said little that was ·interesting, wouldn't talk politics, but one trait I

learnt. He reads an enormous number of daily papers *himself*, & leaves or trusts nothing for his secretary to transact.

14 April

Someone told me yesterday that when Mrs. Chamberlain first married & came to England with J.C. that Mrs. Asquith went to call on her and made a great fuss over her during the visit. On leaving Mrs. Asquith said 'Good-bye, dear Mrs. Chamberlain, or may I call you Jessie?' 'Certainly,' said Mrs. J.' if you wish to do so, but I was christened Mary'! The conjecture is that Mrs. A. was thinking of Jesse Collings.[4]

2 July

Came to Portugal to be free from hay fever. Oporto, Lisbon and Cintra. At Hotel Costa met Sir Maurice & Lady de Bunsen, British Minister.[5] The only Catholic country I know where the priests are not in evidence and the churches really clean. A quiet, orderly, taciturn people, it is difficult to know why there is so little prosperity, but poverty, begging, and its relief by almsgiving seem universal. Belem is the only building architecturally interesting.

Someone told me yesterday that going to see Huxley, he, as a youth & inquisitive, asked Huxley if he prepared his speeches carefully, to which Huxley replied, 'Yes, especially those passages in which I let my emotions overpower me.'

12 August

I had a bad fall from my horse on July 15: got concussion of the brain, dislocated my shoulder, & sprained my ankle. Nina was with me & got me back from Kingsdown to The Ridge very quickly.

Mathew Wilson told me that some years ago when driving through Wales he chanced when stopping at Crickhowell to get an attack of toothache. He asked the landlord if there was a dentist in the place. 'Yes,' said the other, 'a relation of my own,' & then added, 'not exactly a relation, but my wife had a child by him before I married her.'

✳ Although the Unionist Government was foundering, the Liberals seemed incapable of maintaining a united front. Rosebery as ever was an unpredictable destructive force, taking issue with Campbell-Bannerman over Home Rule. The speech Rosebery made at Bodmin on 25 November provoked a major row, all the more serious because Balfour was on the brink of resignation. During November the struggle for supremacy in the Unionist Party had become open warfare, with Chamberlain securing the support of the National Union of Conservative Associations for 'whole-hog' tariff reform against Balfour's own advice. As a last tactic the Unionist Prime Minister resigned on 4 December, perhaps believing, certainly hoping, that the Liberal divisions would prevent them from forming a Government.

27 November [?29 November]

On Saturday last Ld. Rosebery very unnecessarily attacked C.B. (by implication) for reviving the Home Rule cry, and declared that he could never serve under such a banner. On the Monday [27 November] I went to London for a 'Thames Conservancy' meeting, and [found] the political world in a ferment: Liberals of all shades of opinion very angry with Ld. Rosebery: Tories correspondingly jubilant. Lawson Walton[6] very indignant at R.'s want of tact. Even Ld. Burghclere[7] was apologetic for R. At Brooks's I met S. Buxton & hearing he was dining that night with Asquith urged him to see A. at once and get him to telegraph to Ed. Grey who was speaking at Newcastle the same night. After some reluctance S.B. consented to seek A. and next day appeared an excellent speech from E.G. saying there was no cause for difference: *and* a letter from S.B. saying Asquith was very *angry* with R. & E.G. had spoken after telegraphic communication with A. Satisfactory interference of mine!

8 December

I went up on Thursday [7 December] to the meeting of the Royal Commission,[8] dined and went to the play with Sydney Buxton. He told me that most important people were against forming a Liberal Ministry but C.B. had determined on trying, as the alternative was Rosebery being sent for, trying, failing, and the return of Balfour and the discredit of potential Liberal Ministers. In the formation of the Cabinet there was no difficulty arising from differences of political views, but questions of personal preference were considerable. Morley (who has no knowledge and has shown no aptitude for finance) wished for the Exchequer, but after considerable discussion has given way to Asquith. He goes to the Indian Office. The King wanted Grey to have the F.O. and to lead the Lords, but Grey refuses to take a peerage on any consideration. Tweedmouth who otherwise would have to lead H. of L. is personally unpopular and ineffective. C.B. who would make a better leader there than anyone is unwilling to go. Neither Rosebery nor Dilke has been approached.

9 December
Today Friday [8 December] Sydney told me he had been offered and accepted the Postmaster-Generalship with the Cabinet. He was disappointed at not getting the Board of Trade or Local Government Board, but as regards the latter a letter he wrote 2 months ago to C.B. pointing out his possible difficulties (if there) with his constituents,[9] settled the question no doubt. Sydney is an ineffective speaker in H. of C. and I fear not too popular.

10 December
I heard from Alick Murray of Elibank regretting he could not come here (to Corsham) today. From his ambiguity of expression I gather he has had the offer of a 'Court' appointment which I heard mooted some time ago. He has good manners, a nice fellow, but too addicted to writing letters & making speeches, and is obstinate without firmness, and I doubt his judgment.

19 December
Edmond Fitzmaurice has accepted the Under-Secretaryship at the F.O. It was first offered to Burghclere who accepted. But in his letter to C.B. he said that it was taking a step downwards and that he ought to be decorated for this, meaning this as a joke. C.B. took it seriously, perhaps glad to do so, and regarded it as a practical refusal.

E.F. also told me that I had been considered for the Financial Sec. at the War Office and the Under-Sec. at the Local Government Board. For the former I had to give way to a Scotchman, and in the second to a business!-man, who knows nothing of Local Government, but who happened to be a Leaguer.[10]

1906

✳ The diary for this year is in the form of a continuous narrative. The

Liberal general election triumph is not even mentioned. There is a sense of 'marking time' as far as Hobhouse was concerned.

Not a year of satisfaction in any way. On 3rd March I was offered by the Prime Minister a Church Estates (and Ecclesiastical) Commissionership. I accepted after some internal debate and consultation with S.B. and A. Birrell. The work if properly done requires constant attendance, and is at present entirely in the hands of Sir Alfred Porter, an able man, but too long an autocrat.

On the end of March I was appointed Chairman of the Select Committee on Post Office wages & services. A difficult, laborious and thankless task. I have found the Members, with the exception of Claude Hay,[11] very pleasant to work with, but it has involved about 6 months' work of 12 hours each day.

On June 22nd, I went as Chairman of the Church Liberal Members to a meeting at Lady Wimborne's. Bishop of Ripon, Weldon, Drs. Meyer & Guiness Rogers, and 10 or 12 others.[12] Ripon very eloquent on the Church attitude. Meyer saying that the giving of denominational teaching in single school areas was a stumbling block to the Nonconformist conscience, impossible. Ripon answered that the refusal to allow teachers liberty to give this touched C. of E. conscience to an extent that would produce passive resistance far in excess of the Free Churches. Meyer evidently surprised, asked Ripon to repeat & explain, which was done with evident effect on Meyer. I asked Meyer whether he would undertake to form a Committee of Free Churchmen to moderate Free Church opinion, just as we were trying to do with the Established Church. Weldon objected, but the others all accepted the proposal, and Meyer & G. Rogers consented so to act.

On Sunday [date unknown] Birrell came to see me, telling me that the Cabinet were alarmed at his concessions to the R.C.s & C. of E. and that he had reached his tether of yielding in the *Commons*. But C.B. was not allowed away from his wife, and Asquith so sulky at Sir C. Tennant's will that he would take no part in anything.[13]

Mrs. John Bailey told me that her brother Alfred Lyttleton[14] declared that it was a mistake to suppose Balfour was the only obstacle to a compromise. The whole of the Tory leaders were unanimous in their opposition. If so nearly the whole of their followers are against them.

1907

✴ In January Hobhouse was appointed Under-Secretary at the India Office. His misgivings about working under John Morley were shared by the latter. Morley had wanted T. R. Buchanan as his Under-Secretary and in fact threatened resignation when he did not get his way. But Campbell-Bannerman refused to budge. Morley, as usual, remained in office. He still hankered after Buchanan and eventually got his man when Asquith reconstructed the Government in April 1908. His relations with Hobhouse seem to have been harmonious enough, but this might explain Morley's offer of the Bombay Governorship to his junior minister within a few months, although Hobhouse interpreted this as a sign of favour at the time. In any case, in October he was appointed Chairman of the Royal Commission on Decentralisation of Government in India.

The first diary entry of the year was a review of his first few months in office.

18 May
On Jan 28 I got a letter from the Prime Minister offering me the Under-Secretaryship of India, which I accepted. I went to London and saw Geo. Whiteley.[15] He begged me to be careful in my dealings with J. Morley whom I should find vain, capricious, and peevish. Sydney Buxton and Walter Runciman, both intimate personal friends of J.M. repeated the caution and opinion, adding that while J.M. could be more delightful than anyone he could also be more disagreeable. An opinion I have found absolutely accurate.

I attended my *second* Ministerial dinner, sitting in strict order of precedence between H. Samuel and Dr. Macnamara. C.B. opened the proceedings by reading the King's Speech, telling us he had had special injunctions that there should be no escape of 'this gas'. I got many friendly words on my appearance as a Minister, and John Burns, Asquith, and S.B. all told me that each was the special cause of my promotion and each gave me to understand that my Chief would not remain long in his place! I found J.M. very frigid at first. He begged me to learn the work of the whole office, and during the debate on the King's Speech, when there was talk on an Indian amendment he told me to be ready to take the answering of it. The principal questions in the Office are Russian agreement to cover Thibet, Afghanistan, and Persia. The Russian F.O. are very desirous of coming to an understanding, and Isvolsky[16] will do or make any sacrifice to that end, but he has to deal with *his* War Office and the Grand Dukes. Our F.O. have made the serious blunder of not suggesting our lines of influence should commence, like the Russian, at Zulfikar, and there'll be a row in the country when the truth comes out.

The other questions are that of Indian Railways, their finance and extension; of the abolition of Indian opium growing, and the revenue which will thereby be lost; of Kitchener's Army Re-organisation Scheme, and of the Baghdad Railway, not so immediately pressing, but in which Russia, France and England are working together. The entente, so far as it affects Indian affairs is very real, and very important. But in relation to Afghanistan it will be invaluable, and *therefore* at present the Russian *War Office* is very hostile. . . .

Hamlet Lodge, Cowes, for Easter recess, our party Lady Dorchester, Lady Roden,[17] Ld. Munster, Ld. & Lady Arran, and Godfrey Baring.[18] Pleasant but not instructive. Lord A. a Radical Unionist. Visited the Parkhurst Prison, and the New Naval College at Osborne. . . .

I had a long conversation with Lady D. She has given Ld. Rosebery to read, and, if he desires, to prepare for publication the 525 unpublished letters she has, written by Lord Byron to her father. Some she told me were of the grossest character. John Cam Hobhouse and Douglas Kinnaird[19] being as bad as Ld. Byron. She asked me to collaborate with her in bringing out her father's Life, which exists in 5 long & diffuse volumes. Her idea is to reduce it to 2, and make one volume from social notes & from his records of journeys with Byron, and the second from his political notes which are very copious & rather interesting.

We have long been considering a dispatch which will sanction a great change in the form of the Government of India. The change is due to the direct suggestion and insistence of Lord Minto.[20] He is, I imagine, a stupid and mentally timid man. The disturbance which exists in India has alarmed him, and in ignorance of the native character, he thinks concession will lead to calm. J.M., much I believe against his will, consents to the proposed changes, thinking that he as a Liberal cannot refuse changes which Minto a Conservative, advocates. The Governor-General's council, except Baker[21], are against him, but the Secretary of State's Council is for change, though not universally. Lee Warner[22] particularly strong against. We had settled our dispatch when news of sedition came, which has postponed the *publication* of intended changes, but all Secretary of State's Council agreed that disturbances ought not to prevent, though they should postpone alterations.

9 June

John Morley is more friendly on the whole, and I have effected some things, e.g. the division of the Indian Army into a Northern and Southern Force, and prevented centralisation at Simla. I have also advocated and obtained inquiry into the method of financing and controlling Indian Railways.

We have dined with the Shuttleworths[23], Harcourts, Denmans[24], Lady Dorchester, T. Ashtons[25], Tufnells[26], etc. and Douglass Hogg, Radnors[27], C.B.

I went with other Ministers to the Guildhall when the City conferred its freedom on the Colonial Premiers. The Hall itself was used for lunching in, an adjoining Chamber being fitted up with pews like a church, and a red carpet up the 'aisle' along which all guests walked with an usher to announce them. The sight of Jameson, Moor[28], and Botha meeting in congress on good personal terms with each other, to consult with Laurier[29], a quasi-Frenchman, and the British Govt., must have caused heart burnings in Berlin, just as they caused pride and satisfaction here. Such a sight may have been possible in Ancient Rome, it certainly has never been known since, for we and they alone seem to hold the secret of administrative absorption.

I was asked by Haldane to assist him with the Territorial Forces Bill, and thus had much work added to the Indian Office business besides the Post Office Report. However it was good practice and when Morley having made his own magnificent speech on the Indian Budget went away for three hours, and left me in charge of the House and with the duty of replying I did so, with trepidation indeed, but much less so than if I hadn't the previous three days' practice. My work this week has been, all Monday & Tuesday from

10 a.m. to 11 p.m. at the War Office. Wednesday 10 a.m. to 3 p.m. India Office getting up an answer to Dilke on Indian Military expenditure. 3 p.m. to 11 p.m. H. of C. on the bench with War Office Bill. Thursday 10 a.m. to 11 p.m. at India Office and H. of C. with Indian affairs, no dinner till 10.45 p.m. Friday, Saturday & *Sunday* at India Office 10 hours a day on Post Office Report.

17 July

On my return from Portugal, where I had been for a fortnight's holiday chiefly at Thomar and Busaco, Morley to my great surprise and in very complimentary terms offered me the Governorship of Bombay, from which Ld. Lamington was retiring. I asked for time to consider, and having consulted S. Buxton, one or two private members and Asquith as to my future chances of advancement in the House, I declined J.M.'s offer.

26 July and later

I got out the Report of the Select Committee on the Post Office today. It has been the most laborious work on which I have been ever engaged. Claude Hay, contrary to all traditions of public and private honour, has shown this Report previous to publication to the press etc. Throughout the Committee he has only been kept in order by Wardle's[30] honesty, and Ward's[31] absence from our deliberation. I wrote and re-wrote myself the whole actual wording of the Report 4 times. There has been much abuse from the employees of the Post Office, and some praise from the Treasury (Sir G. Murray). Wardle was brought to account before the Labour Members' Committee by the Postmen's Federation, but has I understand proved his case, so far as the former are concerned.

4 October

Today I received from J. Morley the offer of the Chairmanship of Committee on Indian Decentralisation of Government. It means 5 months' hard work in India, as many more on our return to England, and the disarrangement of all our autumn plans. I accepted, chiefly because I had refused Bombay, and partly because it affords an opening if done successfully, of further political advancement. The complexity and size of the problems involved do not lead one to expect success, while I shall be lucky to avoid failure.

20 October [Letter to Walter Runciman from The Ridge, Corsham][32]

My dear Walter

Your very kind letter of the 16th has just reached me. It was most welcome, not only as the message of a friend, but because it gave me a stimulus when such was badly needed. I confess myself very apprehensive as to the result of my mission. We are to take 4 or 5 months in traversing a continent almost—in probing the Governments therein—which are almost as numerous as those of all Europe—and in constructing a system which shall be an improvement on present systems. Put the problem to yourself in that light, and you wonder at my apprehensions of error and incompleteness. On the other hand it is the second mark of confidence I have received from J.M. in the last 3 months, and to me no one could be more considerate.

I am asking one or two friends to dine with me at *Brooks's* on Thursday next 24th. Could you join us at 8.15 p.m. there, it would give me much pleasure if you would.

Yours as always
C. Hobhouse

26 October

I have had various conferences with Sirs Walter Laurence, W. Lee Warner, H. Barnes etc.[33] on the way to get at the truth of Govt. in India. One of the most difficult points will be the relations with the Native States. Morley has himself been most helpful, but he knows nothing of internal administration. No one could have been kinder or more considerate than J.M. has been to me since the first two months of our co-operation. He is amenable to praise, particularly of his literary work, but is suspicious of flattery, very greatly impressed with the responsibility of his duties, and alive to the dignity of Secretary of State, and an absolute master in his own office and in India.

✳ The Commission on Decentralisation was partly a response to the political unrest of 1905–6 centred largely on Bengal and partly a challenge to the bureaucratic centralisation of the Imperial Government at Simla. There was implicit conflict between the established order of the Imperial Government and the Indian Civil Service and the Radical Government at Westminster. The Commission's terms of reference were to inquire into the financial and administrative relations between the Supreme Government and the various provincial Governments and between the latter and those authorities subordinate to them, and 'to report whether, by measures of decentralisation or otherwise, those relations can be simplified and improved, and the system of Government better adapted both to meet the requirements and promote the welfare of the different provinces, and (without impairing its strength and unity) to bring the executive power in closer touch with local conditions.'[34]

Hobhouse was in fact a substitute for the original choice of Chairman, Sir Henry Primrose, whose health had forced him to resign. His colleagues were Sir F. S. P. Lely, a retired Bombay Civil Servant; Sir Steyning Edgerley, a member of the Bombay Government; Romesh C. Dutt, a retired Indian civilian and leader of Congress; W. S. Meyer, secretary to the Government of India Finance Department; and W. L. Hichens, a former official in South Africa.

[Undated]
Left Marseilles Oct. 31, and reached Bombay, cyclone in Arabian Sea, Nov. 15. Stayed with Sir G. Clarke[35] at Government House. He is delighted with his grandeur but very able and hard-working. The formality observed by subordinate Europeans in Indian Civil Service to their superiors, out of hours, is absurd, and the habit of discussing their work also out of hours paralyses their powers of recruitment and observation.

Went to Government House, Madras (22 Nov.) and found the same ceremony, only more so. Sir Arthur Lawley[36], his wife and staff, all hailed from South Africa, and received a Radical Under-Secretary with as much stiffness as hospitality allowed. He appears hard-working, slow, and reactionary, his two members of Council, Forbes and Stokes both out of date, all are out of touch with each other. We examined 40 witnesses here and at Madras in 8 working days.

At Rajahmundry the Municipality entertained us at a garden party with conjuring, sword play, fireworks etc. Nina was too unwell to see this. The noticeable thing about Rajahmundry entertainment was the performances by the daughters and betrothed wives of Brahmans, in public, of physical drill and songs, such an exhibition would not only have been impossible, but unthinkable 10 or 20 years ago.

Reached Rangoon about Dec. 10, stayed with Sir C. Fox[37], greatly grown since last visit in 1890. Dined with Sir H. White[38], Lieutenant-Governor, an able man, but desirous of doing *everything* himself. Authorised his chief secretaries to speak the views of Government, and then wrote two voluminous memos to set them out afresh. His house and park quite charming. The officials are overworked young, and government is greatly overcentralised. It ought as far as possible to be separated from Burma: distance, language, race, system of government all demand separation in domestic affairs.

1908

After visiting Madras and Burma, we reached Calcutta on Dec. 24, in time to see the race for the Viceroy's Cup, the great social event of the Calcutta season. I was not prepossessed by Society here. They demand, often by letter and even in person, hospitality from the Lieutenant-Governor of Bengal, or from the Viceroy, and though this is dispensed at the rate of two or three dances a week besides formal dinners, they grumble at everything.

As to their patriotism, it was exhibited by a refusal of the Volunteer Artillery to go on the 1st January parade because the Royal Field Artillery and not they were to fire the King's salute, while the Volunteer Cavalry also refused to parade because they were in the 2nd Brigade and the Native Cavalry were in the 1st. We stayed first with Sir Andrew Fraser[39], Lieutenant-Governor of Bengal, and then with Lord Minto, the Viceroy. The first of these is not a strong administrator, but knows and is liked by the natives, more so than any other Governor whom I met. Lord Minto is also not a strong man, but has good judgement, which he allows other people to overrule: he thinks and works slowly. His Council is a weak one, collectively and individually, except Mr. Barker and Lord Kitchener. Of the latter I saw a good deal. He is not cultivated but is artistic, and shows it by collecting Oriental china and by the habit of house-decorating. He is a delightful personality, not too scrupulous as to how he gets his way, but sensible and moderate. A man of strong will, but no overpowering genius.

From Calcutta we went to Dacca to stay with Sir L. Hare[40], not a strong but an amiable man with the best A.D.C., Capt. Denning, I have so far met. Sir Lancelot Hare thought agitation was dying down, and would only be revived by a proposal to reunify Bengal. The attack on Mr. Allen[41] was managed by a gang of students, but without direct and organised conspiracy. He was not hopeful about the future peace of India. Thence we went to Nepal, 80 miles from the frontier station at Raxaul, which we did in 24 hours partly by palkee, partly by riding. We stayed with Manners Smith[42], an energetic tactful officer, not brilliant but a good frontier political. The Maharaja Sumshen Singh is a capable and wise administrator, who has apparently reconciled the leading contending factions, and holds the Army. All the principal posts in the country are given to one or other relations. He understands perfectly and speaks English fairly. His palace has an excellent supply of electric light and water. We saw the Maharani and the women's quarters. She was pretty, not very dark, and the interior of the palace was beautifully clean. I reviewed his Army, 13,000 strong, they were well drilled, and clothed, but badly equipped. He deserves a free hand to buy arms, and from fear of subsequent Chinese pressure would probably be a most useful friend in case of any serious trouble in India.

From Nepal to Calcutta to stay with the Mintos. The Government of India under pressure from Lord Kitchener perhaps, and Richards, Findlay and Miller[43] now refused to give evidence before us. A threat to resign and thus indict them before the bar of public opinion at home, brought them to their senses, and having gained the substance I was willing to concede the shadow. Incidentally I am not impressed with the ability of the Indian Civil Service. All able writers, they are too fond of writing and too many of them lose their sense of proportion, and mistake length of argument for soundness of view. Who writes most, lasts longest. There are plenty of good slaves and office men, but most of the men are in their places 5 years too late. A too prolonged *first* stay in the country, and too much quill driving in a horrible climate saps their energies comparatively early, and after 50 though they may retain and even acquire knowledge, they lose originality and their experience is tarnished by timidity.

At Calcutta I met many natives, Hindus and Mahommedans, most of them well-educated pleasant men, very much in earnest at getting some share in the government of the country, but none I think likely to hold their own if India was left unsupported by the British Army. Probably honest, from their standpoint, zealous for law and order, an enervating climate and almost hereditary habit of submission would render them quite incapable of standing for a moment against the northern tribes. On the other hand while we rule India, on quasi-Western methods, we must employ the educated native, or his talent for journalism and petty intrigue will render 'responsible' Government almost impossible.

From Calcutta to Nagpur. Mr. Craddock, Chief Commissioner, an able man surrounded by incapable assistants, mostly connected by blood or marriage to each other. Not much 'unrest' at present. The fort at Nagpur intended to be a 'refuge' in case of trouble holds about 50 British Infantry, and just outside it 50 Native Infantry. It is a bare rock without trees or shade, or buildings to shelter, from climate, those who would have to collect there. The growing number of non-official Europeans, planters, mine managers, mill managers, engineers, railway men etc. would be cause of anxiety and responsibility in case of mutiny, against which the Government of India have apparently made *no* provision. The soldiers might be able to stand a siege here and there, though this I doubt looking to the ridiculous *size* of the Lucknow and Cawnpore forts, but the civilians and non-officials would be a burden thrown upon our resources, which humanity and necessity would compel us to accept, without adequate power to bear it.

✳ From Nagpur in the Central Provinces, the Commission moved on to Benares, and into the United Provinces of Agra and Oudh, to Lucknow.

From Benares to Lucknow, the Lieutenant-Governor Sir John Hewett, said to be the ablest man in India, certainly the most autocratic. Here again there seemed to be no first-rate young men. We motored out to Bari Banki, to see a famine relief work, and a Swadeshi spinning and technical school. The relief work employed about 3,000 men, women and children, in digging earth out of the fields, carrying it 20 to 50 yds. to a road already amply wide, and making it unnecessarily spacious. So far as 'value received' went, the work was quite useless, but it acted as a test of hunger, and prevented imposture. The signs of famine are a peculiar yellow tinge under the eyes of the cheekbones, and in the children a falling away of flesh over the buttocks, and *then* the general leanness.

The technical school employed about 50 persons in spinning cotton and silk on hand looms invented by the Salvation Army, and simplified in the school, so that the cheapest only cost Rs 15. The peculiar and satisfactory feature about this work is that people who would be ashamed to work in a shop or factory will do so at home and then earn a sufficient livelihood. . . .

From Agra to Jaipur and then Ajmer. The interest of the place centred on the Mayo College, built for the education of the sons of ruling chiefs or noble houses. The building itself is fine, well situated, but the surrounding grounds ought to be larger. Each state has its own separate boarding house, and the pupils are looked after by native tutors, but the teaching is done by Englishmen. The affairs of the College are managed by a Committee of Ruling Chiefs who take the greatest interest in it, and attend meetings regularly. There are about 130 students of ages varying from 24 to 9 years. The progress is fair on the whole, and a post-graduate class in estate, and State, management has been of great service. This and the Daly College at Indore solve the question of education for boys, but do not get over the difficulty of providing a well-educated boy with a well-educated wife, an essential companion if the boy is not gradually to slip back into an Oriental ruler pure and simple. . . .

From Ajmer to Udaipur. Mr. Claude Hill the Resident. The Maharana an intelligent man of the bluest Rajput blood, old-fashioned. We had a very frank talk together, he told me he thought discontent in Bengal was serious, but subsiding, hinted that the Sikhs were intriguing, but said he had nothing to complain of.

Mr. Hill and I rode out one morning to call on a border baron who was ill. We rode up to the castle gate, guarded by armed retainers, inside a great courtyard with horses stabled all round, mostly bitted and saddled, on one side stood a battlemented dwelling house, and labourers and tenants were going to and fro with produce and food. Wouwerman could have found a very congenial subject.

From Udaipur to Kotah. Resident Major Peacock. The Maharao is quite the best Chief I have seen, simple in tastes, unostentatious, thrifty without being a miser.[44] I took a great fancy to him. He is himself a rich man, and very desirous of visiting England, but will not do this until the *State* has repaid its debt to the Government of

India incurred for famine three years previously. He has got his city cleaner than any town I have seen in either British or native India. We visited the old Castle, in the city, with some very curious wall paintings and oil paintings. The keep is, as usual in India, built on and round a mound in the centre of the Castle. Like most of the modern Indian Chiefs he is monogamous and childless.

From Kotah we *drove* to Bundi about 40 miles through a level plain in which many of the villages were in ruins or half-deserted, a result of the famine of 1900 and the fever of the following year. Bundi stands in a pass of the hills with the streets climbing up the hillside and only just wide enough to let an elephant pass along them. We were received with great state by the Resident, Major Berkeley, guns firing and an escort of cavalry meeting us. We camped outside the city and next morning the raja Rao came to call, a man of good and old family, but a drinker who had had more than one warning. We returned the visit at once, riding through the city on elephants. As the place is one of the very few unreformed states, the colours and uniforms were picturesque and varied, lancers, footmen with pikes, heralds, all blazing with varying hues, while the gentry and nobility came in spotless white and turbans. After the reception we went up into the Castle where was the remains of some fine ivory work inlaid into the doors. In the afternoon a leopard was turned out of a cage, and ridden down and speared by two or three of the court, about 50 or 60 being mounted.

From Bundi, drove back same afternoon, dined with and at Kotah, and went on same night to Indore to stay with Col. Daly, Agent to the Governor-General. Holkar[45] was at the Mayo College, and a good deal of anxiety was felt as to his future, signs being not wanting to show that he would be troublesome. Fortunately his wife had lately had an heir, but the fact that a schoolboy should have a wife and family points to the difference between our ideas and theirs, but remember not a difference between our flesh and blood and theirs.

The only pleasant thing about Indore was the public garden, and next day we motored 70 miles through Mhow to Mandou . . . and trained to Bombay having seen six of the Rajputana States and travelled 1,300 miles therein in fourteen days!

Reached Bombay March 5, stayed with George Clarke at Government House. Lady and Miss Clarke had joined him since our previous visit. The former was very ill, the latter had taken up an attitude of intimacy and friendship with natives which right in itself, was far too precipitate and previous to effect its object, viz. to bridge over the gulf between European and native. We stayed 8 days, heard 30 or 40 witnesses, amongst them Messrs. Tilak[46] and Goghale[47]. The former seemed a vicious but forceless character, the latter a man of good character, full of good and honest intention, but subject to imagination and impulse to such an extent that he became little more than a dreamer. By intention, however, a patriot and no friend of England.

The officials, except Mr. Jenkins, were commonplace tools. Indeed the Indian Civil Service have woefully disappointed me. Apt to be timid, not by any means resourceful, not too hard-working, as I count *hard* work, physical courage and energy are their chief virtues. Very greedy of patronage and power, they try to lord it over soldiers, engineers, railwaymen and merchants as if India, its trade, its inhabitants and its Government had been created solely for their aggrandisement. It is an oligarchy in danger of running mad, and hydrophobia is worse and more speedy in India than elsewhere.

By sea to Karachi, where we stayed with the Commissioner, Mr. Younghusband, hard-working and conscientious. Scinde is semi-independent of Bombay and ought always to remain so. Customs, climate, language and trade set it apart, and as yet there is little 'trouble'. Karachi itself is a sand-swept desert, artificial town and artificial harbour, due entirely to the commercial enterprise of the British merchant, and depending entirely upon the Punjab grain trade.

From thence to Quetta two days of sand and discomfort. At Sibi we branched up the Bolan pass, steep mud-coloured mountains, without plant or scrub, the strata sharply uptilted at 35 or 40 degrees, and the railway creeping up flat valleys with bottlenecks in which however were a considerable number of flocks of goats and sheep. Quetta which is about 5,000 feet above sea-level stands in the corner of the second large plain, stony and arid, but partially watered by *kranzes*, or underground channels with surface openings every 100 yards or so. Where the water touches soil, crops of grain and fruit grow freely. The 'Defences' which extend 8 or 10 miles out are a costly pitfall carefully designed to be graves for artillery and infantry of the defence. They can be turned from the S.W. and enfiladed from the N.E., both of which are 'undefended' positions while the forts on the extreme west could be taken in reverse and rendered untenable by half a company of infantry.

At Chamman 70 miles out, on the Afghan border, is stored the 'Kandahar Railway'.[48] Chamman itself is a mud fort standing in the plain, where gradually an entrepôt of trade is arising, convenient as a camping ground. This we visited and I galloped half a mile into Afghanistan. The Kojak tunnel is a good piece of engineering about 3 miles long and luckily is about a quarter mile north of a great fault in the strata which is constantly being affected by the earthquakes.[49] Quetta will most probably be off the line of invasion, though it does lie along the route of one of Alexander's incursions. The rainfall of central India is gradually shrinking, and lack of water and difficulty of moving a huge modern army will induce future armies to move southwards by Nushki. . . .

From Quetta to Peshawar, vile, hot and dusty journey. Stayed with Sir H. Deane, Chief Commissioner, an able determined man, but not so good an administrator as Sir H. MacMahon at Quetta. Peshawar cantonment is an ideal garden city, houses have good gardens, streets have flower borders along their whole length, and water is plentiful. The city is walled and stands in a large, rich and fruitful plain, being itself surrounded by walled gardens. The population is vile if faces are any index of character. The climate is relaxing.

I drove out one day to Ali Musjid and on to Landi Kotal. . . . From Landi Kotal—which is a large mud fort standing in a little plain about 1 mile long and 1½ miles wide, and round on little eminences are detached posts—I walked under escort to Mt. Pisgah on the actual border, about a mile and a half. Afghanistan lay below us with narrow fertile valleys and the Kabul river. I saw Torsuffah which Lord Kitchener wanted to make a large cantonment, a senseless plan—ungetatable and arid beyond description; and I could make out the localities of Shillman Loi and Shillman Gakka, the latter being the terminus of 'mile 300' railway. If K.'s railway was constructed as he wishes the rails would be brought to a point at which they stop above a scarp of 1,200 feet down which it would be almost impossible either from the cost or from engineering difficulties to carry this railway. Shillman Gakka might be the terminus, but the route over the hill would be the way. On my return under escort to Landi Kotal I noticed a particularly villainous face. Its owner during the previous winter had quarrelled with his brother and one afternoon had shot him and his two elder boys, had then taken the two remaining children of about 8 and 10 and pounded in their heads with a stone; and finally to prevent any chance of a blood feud being perpetuated had gone to the brother's hut, thrown the widow, who was pregnant, on the ground and jumped on her till she died. As far as I could gather, public opinion was on the side of so smart a man!

✷ As well as the constant fear of the Russian 'menace', and the intermittent tribal rebellions, Hobhouse noted the persistent apprehension of political insurrection amongst the Indian Government.

Sir Harold Deane told me that during the late troubles he had *no* means whatever of finding out what was going on. The utmost he could glean from the Mahommedans was that Hindu emissaries were trying to embroil them with the Government, and that if anything serious and definite was planned he should have a month's notice beforehand. The Hindus of course said nothing, even his best friends. He was very pessimistic, saying that he hoped things might last 10 years. My colleague Meyer gave a little longer time, about 20 to 25 years for the extinction of the British Raj.

✷ After further exploration of the North West Frontier forts in the Swat valley, the whole of which required overhauling, according to Hobhouse, the travel-worn Commissioners made their way to Simla, the effective headquarters of the Imperial Government, situated high in the Punjab hills.

This latter [Simla] a disagreeable place, difficult to get at, and its only recommendation is the coolness.

We examined the Members of the Council and their Secretaries to the Government here for five days. Mr. Baker, Financial Member and Mr. Meston, Financial Secretary, were both able men, especially the latter. Sir Harvey Adamson, Home Member, was a man of good sense, but Sir Herbert Risley, the Home Department Secretary, though brilliant was of soft fibre. Mr. Miller, Revenue and Agriculture Member, was weak and worked out, too fond of writing minutes critical of his *subordinates*, as well as of their proposals, a fatal fault. Neither Mr. Jacob, the Engineering Secretary, nor Mr. Carlyle, the Revenue Secretary, were of much account.

I stayed at Simla from April 1st to the 9th with General and Mrs. Mahon, he being Inspector-General of Ordnance Factories, and a clever man: young and one to be pushed forward.

❋ Hobhouse left Bombay for England on 11 April. The Commission had travelled more than 12,000 miles in India and heard over 300 witnesses. Nine volumes of evidence accompanied the Report when it was published eventually in February 1909. In urging the advance towards a greater degree of local self-government, the Report marked a further step in that direction. In conjunction with the administrative reforms introduced by Morley in the 1909 Indian Councils Act, the Decentralisation Commission went far to break down the established thinking of the Indian Government and Civil Service. Its most fundamental proposal was that local government should be vested in village *panchayats* or councils with powers to administer local affairs within the village as well as summary jurisdiction in petty legal cases (a proposal from which Hobhouse himself dissented). In general there was to be a devolution of authority from the remote Imperial Government to the Provincial Governments, where the Councils were to be enlarged to include Indian members, and the granting of greater responsibilities to the local District Officers. The end-result was, perhaps, what the conservative spirits of Indian administration had feared. There had certainly been difficulties and obstruction placed in the Commission's way, but Hobhouse could rightly consider his own contribution as a thorough piece of work, well done. His reward came in a telegram which he received on 15 April at Aden *en route* home. It came from Asquith, the new Prime Minister, inviting him to be Financial Secretary to the Treasury in the new administration which he was forming, following the death of Campbell-Bannerman.

1 Charles Hobhouse in 1915 by G. Swaish. This was painted a year
after his appointment as Postmaster-General

2 Nina Hobhouse *c.* 1915 by Norna Labouchère

III

Lloyd George the Irresponsible
1908–1911

✳ In April 1908 Asquith's appointment of Lloyd George as Chancellor of the Exchequer and Winston Churchill as President of the Board of Trade significantly altered the balance of the Liberal Government. Their dynamic enthusiasm impelled the Government into what Churchill had called the 'untrodden field' of social reform. The old Liberalism of Free Trade, Retrenchment, Temperance Reform and Welsh Church Disestablishment was to be transformed by their reforming zeal. With Asquith's benign support they passed legislation for Old Age Pensions in 1908, the Wages Boards and Labour Exchanges Acts 1909, and the National Insurance Act 1911. These achievements were the result of individual ministerial initiatives rather than any overwhelming commitment by the Liberal Party as a whole. Indeed, in 1908 Liberal morale was low. Despite the massive House of Commons majority since 1906, Liberal legislation had been hamstrung by the entrenched Conservative majority in the House of Lords. For three years Liberal Bills which had been passed by the Commons had been rejected or drastically amended by the hostile Lords. Legislative casualties included an Education Bill, Licensing Bill, Plural Voting Bill, and the Scottish Land Values and Small Landholders Bills. By the end of 1908 Liberal frustration was mounting. The Liberal leadership seized on the 1909 Finance Bill as the instrument to negate the Lords' veto and to push ahead with social reform. Lloyd George's 'People's Budget' provided the means both of raising Party morale and outwitting the Lords. When the 'unthinkable' happened and the Lords rejected this 'money bill', there followed a bitter constitutional crisis, two general elections in 1910, and the triumph of the Lower House with the Parliament Act in 1911.

Throughout this period Hobhouse represented that moderate Liberal opinion which was at best rather uncomprehending and at worst suspicious of the motives of the two radical demagogues, Lloyd George and Churchill. As Financial Secretary to the Treasury he came into contact for the first time with Lloyd George's working habits. Hob-house played the part of the industrious subordinate, but his exasperation with his superior's methods and his doubts about the direction in which the Liberal Government seemed to be moving were evident. Prepared to attack the 'old enemy' of the House of Lords and hereditary privilege, he was not prepared to countenance what he regarded as profligate government expenditure. He personified, in fact, the prevailing tensions within the Liberal Party.

1908

10 July

On returning to England at the end of April, I learnt, by degrees, about the formation of the Cabinet. Asquith had offered John Morley the Exchequer, but in such a manner that he couldn't accept.[1] Then Haldane was half-offered it, and I was to be Under-Secretary at the War Office with the lead in the Commons. Haldane wished to leave the War Office but finally Lloyd George was given the Exchequer. He asked for Macnamara as his Financial Secretary but George Murray begged for me, though we had no acquaintance, and Asquith said 'yes' at once.

I have learnt by experience much more of my colleagues than I could ever have done at the India Office. Practically nothing occurs in Cabinet without the Treasury knowing, and by degrees I am obtaining some control over Murray.

Lloyd George will look at no papers, and do no office work. He even refused to go to the Bank to negotiate a loan, but went off golfing, leaving Murray and myself to deal with the matter.

Murray is hard-working, cynical and devil-may-care, very fond of a gossip, and generally spends an hour before lunch in talk of every kind.

Birrell with whom I have much to do is the most cynical man in public business it is possible to conceive. He cares nothing about the rights or wrongs of a public matter—his sole concern is whether the Irish party will accept it or not. The cattle-driving; the Congested Districts Board which pays labourers wages for repairing their own fences; the management of the Irish Land Act of 1904, all alike testify to his incompetence as an administrator, though as a friend or companion he is quite charming.

27 July

Winston Churchill's introduction to the Cabinet has been followed by the disappearance of that harmony which its members all tell me has been its marked feature. He and Lloyd George have embarked on a crusade against expenditure and are fighting Asquith, Grey and Haldane. I cannot help suspecting that Winston Churchill is deliberately urging Lloyd George to ride for a fall. Lloyd George and Churchill have a good case, but personal discourtesy will not help them, and that is C.'s chief weapon.

The King presented us yesterday with a bill for £1,300 for jewellery given away during his Scandinavian trip. I have sent it back to D. Probyn[2] saying I will not defend it in House of Commons. The things were in nearly every instance given as personal presents, and bore the E. and A. cypher.[3]

5 August

Lloyd George has an extraordinary power of picking up the essential details of a question by conversation. He *refuses* to read any office files or papers, but likes people to come and *talk*. He also possesses a great gift of imposing on people the idea that he sees and agrees with their side of a question to the exclusion of all other aspects.

But his absolute contempt for details and ignorance of common facts of life make him a bad official, and about the end of June Asquith instructed me to come and see him weekly on the financial position, and let him know how things stood.

5 September

W. S. Robson the Attorney-General went into Brooks's the other day and meeting Ed. Gully they began talking about Speaker Lowther and Robson said he was far the best Speaker of modern times. Gully could only acquiesce, when Robson suddenly woke up to his mistake and bolted into the smoking room where he found Sidney Peel, son of Lord Peel to whom he recounted his story: S. Peel without a smile said 'If you only go downstairs you'll probably find Arthur Brand to whom you can repeat your views a third time'![4]

17 November

I have seen much of John Morley this last month. He is much perplexed and alarmed over India. He said Ld. Minto and Sir A. Fraser both wrote cheerfully—trouble disappearing etc.—the morning of the attack on Fraser.[5] The Viceroy's Council are weak, but K. is quite ready for a military [? rising] if that should occur. Curzon had warned him to look out for civil disaffection. Haldane yesterday said to me that the Germans had meant a *quarrel* with France, till they found that we would actively support France, and secondly that their own people were against them. He had calculated that he could mobilise two divisions in 10 days *and* put them on board ship: and let the Germans know this.

The Cabinet yesterday really discussed Birrell's Land Finance Bill. A Committee which I attended consisting of Churchill, George, A. B. [Birrell], Crewe and Runciman had met previously (though Ll.G. had shirked the first meeting to play golf!) and yielded to A.B. In Cabinet however he could find no support for his 12% bonus: he will probably take some opportunity in House of Commons to give the Irish *all* they want. He is the most cynical and reckless administrator, all he dares for is a quiet official life, and will throw away money or principles like water to get peace.

I have separately tried to get Harcourt and McKenna to get up some interest in our reckless expenditure, and hope I may have alarmed the latter, for he came to me to explain the economy of his new contracts. Ll.G. is now on a new tack, he encourages ministers to spend, so that he may have justification for the extra millions he proposes to ask for next year.

8 December

If the Cabinet give Ll.G. his way, he will find the money for next year which will probably be £12 millions in excess of this year's requirements by lowering the range of the income tax so as to fully tax people with incomes of £500, by a surtax on incomes over £5,000; by a 2/- capital tax on non agricultural land: and by high licences and increase on tea. Such proposals, if propounded to the country, ought to insure the rejection of the budget by the Lords, enforce a dissolution, and ensure our irretrievable defeat.

1909

✳ As the year began the Cabinet was split over the naval estimates, a recurring source of friction within Liberal ranks every year until the outbreak of war. McKenna originally asked for six dreadnoughts to be built in the 1909-10 programme to match German naval expansion. Lloyd George and Churchill, the 'economists', launched a strenuous attack but were outmanoeuvred on this occasion, the compromise solution achieved providing for building four ships immediately and four 'later'. The additional ships were in fact authorised in July. More significant, in order to convince the Liberal left wing of the need for this expenditure, a case had to be made emphasising the seriousness of the naval situation. In turn the Unionist press were able to exploit this alleged weakness, charging the Liberal Government with neglect of defence expenditure.

Lloyd George's Budget was 'the main business of the year'. By including social reform proposals within a 'money bill' the Chancellor sought to regain the legislative initiative lost through the Lords' opposition. Lloyd George introduced the Finance Bill on 29 April. He had to meet the cost of the increased naval expenditure as well as Old Age Pensions. An estimated deficit of £16 millions had to be met by increased taxation. Thus income tax and death duties were raised; more significantly 'supertax' was introduced on incomes over £5,000. Licence duties on tobacco and alcohol were increased to bring in an additional £3½ millions. This imposition consolidated Nonconformist temperance support but Lloyd George's most provocative measures were aimed at his old antagonists, the landlords. Both in Cabinet and outside his land taxes caused the greatest controversy. Yet his proposals for a tax on unearned increment in land values, a capital tax on the value of undeveloped land and minerals, and for a reversion duty on any benefit accruing to a lessor at the end of a lease brought in only £500,000 revenue. It was the political implication which raised controversy. His land taxes enabled him to embark on Land Valuation proposals under cover of the Finance Bill. Essentially the Budget was an attack on privilege. Indeed the new petrol tax and motor vehicle tax underlined this sectional attack. This 'People's Budget' gave the Liberal Party a new battle standard. But technically, as Hobhouse pointed out, it was a complicated and confused Bill. Its progress was arduous and prolonged. It eventually passed the Commons on 4 November. On 30 November the Lords rejected it. The 'impossibility' that a 'money bill' would be rejected had happened. The Lords for their part pointed to Lloyd George's provocation—not least his notorious Limehouse speech in

July—but their action brought the two Houses of Parliament into direct collision. On 2 December Asquith moved a Commons Resolution condemning the peers' action and the following day Parliament was prorogued. The scene was set for a general election in January 1910.

7 March

I got 4 days' holiday at Xmas and 4 days more just before the House met on Feb. 16. The interval between the two sessions having spent in preparing the Report of the Decentralisation Commission, which I presented on Feb. 28. The draft report written largely by Mr. Meyer was much altered by myself and Mr. Hechens, and though there was some compromise to get a unanimous report, the sentiments of the Members were wonderfully similar.

The Cabinet met very late. Lloyd George instead of working at the details of his budget having gone off to Cannes to play golf. When he returned instead of sitting down to the Budget he began to 'collect ideas' by talking to journalists and by confiding to the Editor of the *Daily Chronicle*[6] his views of what the Budget should be. Together with Churchill he formed a cabal which was to pledge the Cabinet in advance and if they didn't agree, to offer resignation and a newspaper war on those who remained. McKenna was to be the first victim and Haldane the second. The P.M. was not strong, he discussed McKenna's programme with him—accepted it *en bloc*, and then threw him over, but as the Admiralty stood together the Cabinet 3 days ago accepted 4 dreadnoughts at once and 4 later if wanted. Haldane got his estimates by agreeing to help Lloyd George through the House with his Land Valuation Clauses. The whole Cabinet atmosphere has been upset by Churchill, before whose advent there was no electricity. Meanwhile Chancellor of Exchequer insisted on drafting 3 different methods of Land Valuation, each more unworkable than the other but did produce what we call the Frankfurt tax, being a duty on transfers of land, with a super tax on increments. This can be worked simply. Conferences of the Cabinet Finance Committee consisting of Crewe—Lord Chancellor—McKenna, Haldane, Buxton and Chancellor of the Exchequer sit nearly every day, for several hours with them are Robson, Ure and myself. The Chancellor of the Exchequer won't read and can only pick up ideas by talking.

12 April

The last month has been a stormy one in the Cabinet. The dreadnought one was composed only after Ll.G. and W. Churchill had used every artifice and talked to their proposal in vain, by the P.M. and Grey taking McKenna's views, who had said he would not stand substantial reduction. He asked for 6 immediate dreadnoughts; they offered 4 immediate and four postponed, which latter he *could* not build: so much for the wisdom of compromise. Then in order to pacify a supposed left-wing cave, the P.M. and McKenna overstated their case. The bulk of the Cabinet cannot be got to understand that the left wing is as impotent and numerically weak as it is vociferous. During this month a tardy consideration of the Budget has been in progress. George has demanded the preparation by Depts. and Draftsmen of successive schemes of Licences, land taxation, and death duties each more impossible than the other, and every week the Cabinet has thrown out scheme after scheme, very often to have the same scheme brought up in different language a week later. Neither he nor the Cabinet have had time to consider details of clauses, and it was only owing to my searching scrutiny of some of his land tax proposals, and to my communications with the P.M., Haldane and Harcourt thereafter, that the Govt. failed to adopt *sub silentio* an absolutely unworkable scheme.

The Heads of Dept. are in a state of revolt and insubordination which is quite indescribable—my own position *vis-à-vis* with the Chancellor of the Exchequer is very uncomfortable. He will neither give nor receive advice, and regards Murray and myself as mere marplots.

Nina heard yesterday, *au contraire*, that by the Dept. I was regarded as the best Financial Secretary that they had had for more than a generation: but this is only by contrast.

16 April

After 4 days' holiday I got a bad chill, laid up for 4 days, only at the end to get a telegram from Morley to say Buchanan was ill, and would I take India Bill through H. of C. Committee. I telegraphed assent.[7]

28 May

Yesterday Sir Steyning Edgerley came to me with the suggestion that Sir Jacob Sassoon would buy the *Duchess of Milan* Holbein for the country if he was assured of a peerage later. As however Asquith had an offer from Sir G. Donaldson to do the same thing for a baronetcy the proposal was waived aside.[8]

We issued the Finance Bill yesterday much improved by the 3 weeks' debating on the resolutions, and though crude enough yet wonderfully improved in arrangement as well as provisions. The skirmishes between Harcourt and Ll.G. in Cabinet have been severe and sustained, but Asquith has taken little part against George of whom he is afraid.

4 June
Lord Carrington wrote to me today that the Duke of Bedford had refused the Govt. offer of £400,000 for 12,000 acres of the Thorney estate in Lincolnshire. Considering that 10 years since, he wrote a book to prove it brought him in nothing at all, it is clear that his arithmetic now or then was sadly at fault.

17 June
Saw John Morley yesterday. Lloyd George had proposed to Cabinet to guillotine the Finance Bill. J.M. said at once that if they did so, he would part company at once. Harcourt took the same line: and eventually only Winston Churchill supported Ll.G. They then discussed India, and agreed that I ought to be relieved of the double duty. Subsequently J.M. and Asquith agreed on Emmott, who however refused to budge, except to a better place. I hear from Runciman that Ll.G. had proposed a successor to Emmott whom he thought would be more pliable as to closure: but when this person whose name I don't know was approached he gave Ll.G. some plain speaking about corrupt bargaining. Asquith I am told by Walter Runciman agreed to Ll.G.'s arrangement. It is difficult to say whether he is helping Ll.G. ride for a fall, or whether he is afraid of his influence with the press and of his popularity. Asquith sent for me that afternoon and said he had recommended me for a Privy Councillorship, and this was approved. Both he and J.M. said very kind things about industry and ability: the former deserved and the latter not.

20 June
Sir Ernest Cassel has been pressing George Murray to go to Con-

stantinople as head of his new Bank. George Murray who was also much importuned by E. Grey consulted the P.M. Asquith is much afraid of being left alone *vis-à-vis* with Ll.G. and said he couldn't spare him. Thereupon Cassel went to Babington Smith,[9] and the latter agreed to go for a salary of £10,000 p.a. Buxton is much disconcerted at his departure, and consulted me as to a successor. I have recommended to him Hirtzel of the India Office, as a man of great discretion and courage.

1 July

There has been some trouble about filling up the vacancies caused by Fitzmaurice's and Buchanan's retirement. H. Samuel went to the Duchy—and Ll.G. recommended Masterman for the Home Office—as Masterman gave much trouble during the first two years of the Govt.[10] and has attended few divisions since, the Whips were furious, as were others in the Cabinet. Asquith has however been drinking during the last week or two, pretty hard and is losing all pluck where Ll.G. is concerned, and gave in. Having got so much Ll.G. then asked that Herbert Lewis[11] should be sent to the Education Office, and Charles Trevelyan changed to the Local Government Board. Runciman refused at first but the P.M. begged it as a personal favour, saying that he had refused to bring in R. Lehman[12] at Winston Churchill's request and refused to appoint a new Welsh Whip, and Ll.G. would make life unbearable. Runciman said he must consult C. Trevelyan and so the matter stands.[13]

3 August

Went to see J. Morley at the India Office. He and Asquith much exercised over the next Viceroy. If the legislative reforms are taken well next January they will appoint a civilian, i.e. a non-soldier but if the extremists continue active or threatening, they will appoint Kitchener, as a sign that all blood letting is not to be all on one side. Meanwhile K. is to go to China and Japan, thence to Australia, and to then take up the C.-in-C. in the Mediterranean.

As regards S. Africa the P.M. wants someone who is strong enough to help the Union Govt. stand up to Lord Milner, should he become Colonial Secretary in the next Govt. It is possible that S. Buxton might do. Winston Churchill wanted to go, but the P.M. wouldn't look at him; Pentland wouldn't do either, for 'he had the brain of a rabbit, and the temper of a pig.'[14] If Sydney this would leave the Post Office vacant, which might come to me. The Cabinet had been unanimous against a Consolidated Fund Bill in lieu of an Appropriation Bill, and for the first time Asquith had asserted himself against Ll.G. and given him a 'good trouncing'. I was much 'cheered' on introducing the Appropriation Bill this evening.

4 August

Lloyd George brought his 'Development Bill' before the Cabinet. McKenna, Harcourt and Runciman attacked its principles and details, and Asquith refused to allow it to be accepted hastily, so the Cabinet consideration was deferred a week; very disappointing to Ll.G. and Churchill, the latter of whom had anticipated a fresh debauch of oratory.

28 September

I am informed by the Press Association that I am now promoted to their 'half column' list, by which they convey a considerable compliment.

Jack Tennant told me that about a month ago, Asquith sent for him, and told him that a Mexican company were bringing out a large flotation, and that he (A.) had mentioned to the promoters that Tennant would be a likely person to take a large 'line', and that he expected Tennant to do so. Imagine Mr. Gladstone as First Lord mixed up with company promotion!

31 October, Nuneham[15]

I had some talk with Lloyd George today. He said the Bishop of Llandaff had come to him from the Archbishop of Canterbury. The latter had been talking over affairs with Lord Lansdowne. Lord L. said that he had done his best, but that the 'backwoods' men had been too many for him, and he should have to give way. I asked Ll.G. what he really wanted, the Budget to pass, or be rejected, and suggested that the author of a successful financial scheme such as his was far more likely to go down to posterity than one who was Chancellor of the Exchequer merely, as others had been before him. He agreed but added that he might be remembered even better as one who had upset the hereditary House of Lords. I think he will now do all he can to make it impossible.

I am told of a private meeting of A. J. Balfour and Lord Lansdowne with the Brewers' Committee who threatened in perfectly plain terms to stop party funds unless the Lords threw out the Bill. On the other hand on Thursday after I had refused to accept an amendment by which mortgage charges should not count against the Supertax, A. J. Balfour said to me as we were going into the lobby, 'Why on earth could not you have accepted our amendment?' If the Bill was to be rejected in any case I don't see why he should have troubled as to its contents.

3 November

I made last night my first set speech on 'behalf of the Govt.', spoke for 30 min. to wind up the debate, held the audience and am told the effort was a distinct step forward.

The debate was dull, and at one time only one Tory was present in the House, and on 5 occasions when a member addressing the House sat down, no Tory rose to speak.

22 November

We had the usual 'Colston' meeting tonight. Winston Churchill the principal speaker and brought his wife. He had plenty of good stuff very theatrically delivered, and very full notes which he carefully *read* from. He certainly held his audience fairly well, but it was the attention of amusement and interest rather of conviction and conversion.

20 November

Yesterday a proposal came from the Colonial Office that as the Duke of Connaught, the Duchess, and Princess Patricia[16] are going to East Africa they should be allowed a remission of customs dues on entering the colony—and further that as they were going to quarter themselves on the Governors of E. Africa and Uganda, these officials should be given £500 each to meet the cost of entertaining Royalty. I proposed, as the Duke draws £25,000 p.a. *and* half-pay of a Field Marshal—to refuse, but Asquith's comment was 'Very shabby, but under present circumstances, we had better pay.' Asquith then went on to talk about the Lords. Three courses were open to him. To pass a Bill continuing the Tea Tax and Income Tax at present rates, and to this the Lords would agree: or he could collect taxes under fresh resolutions of Commons—either of these courses would acknowledge the legitimacy of Lord's interference with finance: while the second would probably bring the Executive and the Courts into collision. He proposed therefore to refuse to collect any taxes after the prorogation. Both Chalmers and Guillemard[17] assured him that such a proceeding would only cause an ultimate loss of half to three-quarters of a million sterling—I said I thought much more—2 or 3 millions—and to this he agreed. I then asked him what he proposed to say about a Second Chamber. He said he favoured a *Second* Chamber—(though Vaughan Nash, his Private Secretary has just previously told me he thought the P.M.— like Birrell—was a single Chamber man)—but that he would in order to save a second dissolution later on, on that point, make it quite clear to the King that if the country gave him a majority this time, he must have power to create peers in the event of the Lords refusing his proposals for their reform. His proposals he said would be those of the Cabinet Committee of 1906 which Campbell-Bannerman didn't accept, viz. that the Lords would be allowed to reject a Bill *once*: but that if submitted to them again, they would have to attend a joint session of both Houses, in such proportions as to give the Govt. of the day a majority in the joint Assembly. This doesn't quite suit my own views, which would be for an elected body, but it would be better than the existing state.

21 November

I have refused today to sanction an increase to the Lord Chancellor's Private Secretaries. He has permitted them to be scandalously rude and obstructive to Liberal M.P.s: and he must now reap his harvest. I have got Ll.G. to support me so far. The difference to doing business with him and with the P.M. is most marked. Lloyd George can never concentrate his attention on anything for more than 5 min. together, he is wonderfully quick at picking up an argument as he goes, and his conduct of the Finance Bill has been a parliamentary feat unexampled, but he is idleness and ignorance personified. He had a diplomatic cold to avoid going to Windsor yesterday, and the Governor of the Bank of England coming by appointment today to discuss a Loan requisite to finance the country after the Lords rejection, he was found to have slipped off to golf.

6 December

Rosebery came to see Lady Dorchester the day after his speech in the Lords. I dined with her that night. Lord R. was depressed, said he had been 'persecuted' into speaking, particularly by 'the women'; he knew that he had lost his popularity with both sides—but he had acted as his conscience dictated.[18]

I went down to Wilsford near Amesbury, after speaking at Salisbury, to stay with Sir E. Tennant,[19] and spent a delightfully restful Sunday. He told me, as a large shareholder in *The Times*, that Moberley Bell, its manager had proposed to attack the Lords for proposing to reject the Budget, but that the Directors, under pressure from Buckle, had gone the other way. He confirmed to me the fact that Walter had parted with *all* his interests in the publication of *The Times* on condition that his 'printing' bill, which was overdue and unpaid, should be met without question. This amounted to over £300,000. George Murray said he and A. J. Balfour had lately been in a country house together, and that the latter had said, truly, that he had never known anyone so absorbed in his own comforts as Asquith was habitually.

1910

✻ In January the election was fought on the old Free Trade v. Tariff Reform battleground and on the Government's record of actual and attempted legislation. Implicit in the campaign was the constitutional question of 'Peers versus the People'. The result was no great endorsement for the Liberal Government. With 275 seats against the Unionists' 273, the Liberals were dependent for a working majority on the 82 Irish Nationalists and 40 Labour M.P.s. Nor did the result strengthen the Liberal case for using the Royal prerogative to create sufficient Liberal peers to secure the passage of a Liberal Parliament Bill limiting the veto powers of the House of Lords. In December 1909 King Edward VII had demurred at this proposal, indicating that he would only give the pledge required on these lines after the result of a second general election. 1910, therefore, was dominated by two questions—what policy should the Liberals adopt to deal with the Lords, and when the second election would take place.

30 January

We finished the election in E. Bristol on January 17th, the poll being Hobhouse 6,804, Batten 4,033, Sheppard 2,255. The surprises of the fight were three. First that my majority was so big, next that Labour, in the person of Mr. Sheppard polled so little; and thirdly that Mr. Batten the Tariff Reform candidate came second on the list. His meetings had been interrupted and his speeches inaudible, in spite of my constant protests to my own friends.

After the election I spoke in N.W. Wilts., Notts., Derbyshire, E. Wilts and W. Wilts. Our losses I think were due partly to 'out-voters', partly to beer and fear, and partly to the inability of many of our candidates to state their case, i.e. for Free Trade, in a way to be understood by the people.

After doing arrears at the Treasury, Nina and I came out to Cannes to stay with Lord Rendel[20] at Chateau de Thorenc and found the only other guest was H. H. Asquith.

2 February

Asquith told me a delightful story of Lord Shuttleworth. He in 1894 was Secretary to the Admiralty and was riding with Lord Spencer the 1st Lord in the Row, when Asquith walking with Ld. Rosebery passed them. Ld. R. wishing to signal Spencer, whistled softly at him. Ld. Spencer didn't hear—or see, but Shuttleworth heard though didn't recognise, and turning to Ld. Spencer said 'Who are those two impertinent boys whistling at us?'

Ld. Rendel, well known as an intimate friend of Mr. Gladstone told us last night that there were sharp divisions in the Gladstone family over Welsh Disestablishment, Lady Fred. Cavendish and Mrs. Drew and Stephen Gladstone being much opposed to it. Rendel could never get Mr. G. to pronounce quite definitely—until the formation of the 1892 Govt. when he was staying with Ld. R. in Carlton House Terrace. He said that Morley, Harcourt and Rosebery were coming to see him (though the latter never came), and that Rendel's views would need consideration. Presently he came back saying 'Why, I thought that M. and H. were your friends?' stopped and continued 'What do you really want for Wales?' R. replied 'A Land Commission, Disestablishment, and a Welsh University.' Mr. G., who when he wished, by Asquith's and Lord Rendel's agreement, could be very brief and businesslike, answered after a pause,

'Well you can have your Bill and a University, but not the Commission'—and so at length yielded. The Commission came afterwards.

Asquith is very pleasant, full of chaff and conversation, eats too little but drinks too much. Loves motoring, and takes a short walk in the afternoon. He is much given to laughing at Mr. G.'s 'small nationalities' views.

He showed me today a telegram from E. Grey saying he, Haldane and Winston Churchill had had a full and satisfactory talk, and adding a request that H.H.A., R. B. Haldane, Crewe, Morley and Ll.G. should dine with him at the earliest moment.

4 February

Lord Rendel told me he owed his first introduction to Mr. G. to the fact that he was the correspondent of Sir Harry Parkes and Sir R. Hart at the time of the Jules Ferry Tonkinese war. The French wanted to make peace, as did the Chinese, but each wanted to 'save their face'. Rendel tried to persuade Ferry to invent a victory, but instead the French had a reverse and Jules Ferry was dismissed.

Asquith told me today that the Admiralty had just found out that the Austrians were building, in defiance of their official statements to the contrary, and in anticipation of *their* parliament's sanction, two dreadnoughts—Italy must follow suit and our naval estimates must go up. Ll.G. must change to another Dept.

7 February

Rendel had a capital story of Harcourt being introduced to the Marquise d'Hautpont who was head of the French family of Harcourts and très grande dame. She was very civil but rallied him on his Liberal principles and went on to ask him how it was political differences in England permitted of personal friendships—while in France political reverses or successes meant bitterness and chicanery past belief. Harcourt replied that she had forgotten that the English cut off the head of their king just 150 years earlier than the French guillotined theirs.

Asquith had a good story of Bethel, Ld. Westbury, meeting Sir R. Earle, just retired from Chief Justiceship, and asking him why he didn't come and sit in the Privy Council. 'Well,' said Earle, 'I would were I not blind, old, and deaf.' 'That', said Bethel 'need be no hindrance. I am old, . . . is deaf, and Colville is stupid—yet we make a very tolerable tribunal.'

10 February

Lord Rendel told me that besides the public, and real reason, of failing health, Mr. G.'s retirement in 1894 was due largely to the increased naval expenditure demanded by Lord Spencer. Ld. S. came indeed to one of Mr. G.'s last Cabinets pledged to the Admiralty to get his money or resign. He got his money, but Mr. G. resigned. Ld. Rosebery was not recommended by Mr. G. who had indeed told Rendel that Rosebery had been a great disappointment in Cabinet, vacillating and resourceless. Rendel went on to discuss Admiralty policy in building and arming ships. Premising that he is an interested party, his argument came to this. The armour plating 'ring', which charges the Admiralty £100 to £120 a ton for steel plates which cost £40 to £60, was *forced* on Elswick by the Admiralty. Elswick discovered *Krupp's* secret for plating and instead of paying £60,000, as first demanded, entered the 'ring' without payment. All profits on all contracts have to be divided amongst *all* members of the ring, who are scattered over the whole world. The Admiralty are trying to avoid a similar ring in shipbuilding, and *have* dry-nursed Vickers and *are* dry-nursing the Coventry Co. But as a matter of fact Vickers-Maxim of Furness and Beardmore of the Clyde, are running in double harness and Vickers and Elswick are half and half owners of Whitehead's works at Finme etc. and pool contracts from Brazil and the Argentine, and there are all kinds of subterranean arrangements between these big firms, who though big are yet unable, like *Insurance* Companies, to take the whole of the risks of contracts running into millions.

Rendel argued therefore that the Admiralty, while thinking that they were extending the sources of supply, were in fact only increasing their own expenses, in as much as contracts and orders placed with nominally separate and competing firms were in reality being pooled by these firms, and the prices paid, and profits resulting had to find dividends upon the capital of all the firms involved.

His suggestion was that *one* constructing firm, capable of supplying *all* naval requirements was the cheapest policy therefore as the profits of only one business would have to be provided. He admitted that Elswick had not behaved well or wisely to the Admiralty.

3 H. H. Asquith, captioned 'Brains', by Spy in *Vanity Fair*.
Hobhouse: 'Extraordinary quickness in seizing the right
point'

4 In October 1907
Hobhouse was appointed
Chairman of the Royal
Commission on
Decentralisation of
Government in India.
He is seen here with his
private secretary, Charles
Waley Cohen, during
his long tour

5 A. J. Balfour in 1895 as
leader of the Conservative
Party

20 February

Returned from Cannes to find a letter from Asquith saying that he regretted he could not offer me a seat in the Cabinet 'as there was an overpowering necessity for my remaining in effective control of the Treasury'. I went to see him and told him I could not remain any longer working with Ll.G. He said he recognised the difficulty, and experienced it himself, but appealed to me on personal and political grounds not to resign, adding that I had clearly the first claim on the Cabinet, and that the Treasury had said they would put up the shutters if I was transferred. I replied that these opinions were flattering, but that I wanted a transfer, finally after half an hour or so I said I would take time to consider my position. In the middle of the week George Murray wrote begging me to stay on. On Friday [18 February] I wrote to H.H.A. saying I would stay on, but that I noted his promise of the first seat in the Cabinet.

✳ During the spring, the Cabinet was split between those wishing to tackle the Lords' veto powers by some immediate measure and those (such as Hobhouse) who desired a wider reform of the composition of the Second Chamber. The Government also faced difficulties with the Irish over the 1909 Budget which had been reintroduced in the Commons. In 1909 the Irish had opposed the Budget because of the duty on Irish whiskey. Now they threatened to withdraw support from the Budget unless the Government produced a Veto Bill to deal with the Lords. In the long term the Irish wanted a Home Rule Bill safe from the perpetual animosity of the Lords. Immediately, they were testing the Government's nerve, trying to extract concession on the whiskey duty. This the Cabinet eventually refused to consider. Instead on 14 April Asquith firmly stated the intention of proceeding with a Parliament Bill to restrict the Lords' veto, and committed the Government to a policy of securing guarantees to pass that Bill. In effect the King was to be asked to pledge that in the event of a second Liberal election victory, he would create sufficient peers to neutralise the Conservative majority in the Lords. The first part of this strategy was successful, the Budget passing the Commons with Irish support on 27 April, was accepted by the Lords on the next day, and received the Royal Assent on 29 April, exactly one year after its first introduction.

10 March

There have been many difficulties in the Cabinet. Grey declared he was going unless the Navy was increased, and the Govt. made an elective chamber their first plank. He got his way on the first but had to give way on the second. Harcourt, Loreburn, and Morley very nearly left over the Reform of the H. of L. which they desired to leave untouched.[21] Asquith promised me an untrammelled hand in the administration of the Treasury, which made Ll.G. very angry, and no one seemed to have liked J. Pease's translation.

Ll.G. has been having a series of interviews with J. E. Redmond and P. O'Brien, and later with Tim Healy and W. O'Brien at Sir Hudson Kearley's house.[22] I gather that Healy was more buyable or complacent than Redmond.

6 April

This series of conferences has been continued. Last night they terminated for the time being in a quarrel of a personal nature when Ll.G. told Redmond in round terms that he might go to the deuce. Amongst other meetings has been that at luncheon in Thurloe Square, Alick Murray's house, between Murray and Rufus Isaacs and the Prince of Wales with Sir A. Bigge.[23] The Prince of Wales being very anxious for an accommodation between the two Houses.

We have had great trouble over Ll.G.'s ignorance of financial necessities. Yesterday the Cabinet discussed dates of business, and every day was allotted and Asquith told H. of C. what was arranged. I came into House ten minutes too late, and found this done and George had not known that 'Supply' was exhausted on the 14th and consequently a vote must be taken before that day. Not knowing this he couldn't tell the Cabinet. In order therefore to protect Asquith from the charge of making arrangements he couldn't keep, or being ignorant of financial necessities, I arranged, against the wishes of the Treasury who wished to intercept Revenue or to use the Paymaster-General's balances—to finance the Irish Education vote from the Civil Contingencies Fund—and the Post Office requirements from the Treasury Chest Fund. Having so *decided* I told the Chancellor of the Exchequer whose only comment was that all these names were Greek to him, and I must do as I thought best.

16 April

The meeting of the Cabinet on Friday [8 April] was very stormy. Ll.G. began by talking about 'little concessions he proposed to make to the Irish' and recited various odds and ends of things. After some discussion the P.M. said suddenly 'Well but what about whiskey?' 'Oh,' said G. as if it was an affair of no consequence, 'I propose to let them off the whiskey tax.' There was a general outburst of refusal, headed by a homily from the Lord Chancellor and eventually G. said it was impossible for him to stay, his word was pledged; W. Churchill said the same and they took an almost formal leave of the Cabinet.

On Tuesday [12 April] the Cabinet met again, and Asquith said *at once* 'We must decide definitely what to say.' To everyone's surprise Ll.G. said, 'Well I have been into the question of the whiskey tax with my advisers, and I think it quite impossible from the fiscal point of view to abandon the tax, and I shall tell the Irish so quite plainly.' Then with hardly another word Asquith said 'Then it's quite clear to everyone that the Budget goes forward without any change whatever,' and they went on to discuss the terms of his pronouncement. Both my informants W.R. and L. Harcourt were agreed that Asquith for the first time this session had taken a strong line and stuck to it.

The true cause of Ll.G.'s volte-face seems to be that Alick Murray had told him that he would find no support amongst the advanced section of Liberals, and that if he left the Cabinet his party would be entirely covered by his hat.

I saw the P.M. this morning, he confirmed to me that there was no bargain with Redmond, who in his interview with H.H.A. had admitted that he had been completely outmanoeuvred, as he had been made to declare that all he cared about was Home Rule whereas his real object was remission of whiskey tax—I asked him whether we should take a month or 6 weeks' Supply and he suggested 6 weeks. He then told me that the Duke of Connaught was going to Canada, partly because the King wished to make amends to the Duke—and partly because the Canadians wished it. He said the King was pressing for Ld. Kitchener going to India, but Morley disliked it—and that he would be inclined to consider my name.

29 April
Dined last night with Ll.G. to celebrate the passing of the Budget of 1909–10. The party were 11 in number. Asquith, W. Churchill, Robson, Masterman, Elibank, Sir R. Chalmers, Bradbury, W. H.

Clark, Fred Guest, Ll. George and myself. We had a pleasant evening. The P.M. wearied almost to breaking strain; Ll.G. and Winston
very certain of immediate and certain success if we are driven to an
election; very wild about finance, sinking fund should be suspended,
and £300 millions borrowed for Navy and social programme.
Winston's motto being 'economy unless you can use your money for
a splash'. Masterman charging Robson and myself with a 'Hob-
housian' policy of 'piano piano'.

30 April
I came on Winston Churchill and Ll.G. colloquing a day or two
ago. Winston arguing for the retention of the whiskey tax, and
backing his views by damning the temperance people and saying
that the whiskey tax represented 'piety indispensable' party. The
noticeable feature was Winston suggested, Ll.G. accepted or re-
futed suggestions, and Winston caved in, with a biting phrase or
two, *but* caved in.

✳ The sudden death of Edward VII on 6 May temporarily stopped the
'guarantees' policy in its tracks and precluded a summer general
election.

15 May
Nina, John Fuller and his wife, had started with me for a motor
tour round the S. and W. coast of Ireland, crossing at Fishguard.
On arriving at Swansea Nina and I heard of the King's death at
midnight on the 6th, we stayed therefore 2 nights with Sir John
Llewelyn[24] at Penllegaer, and returned via Bigsweir to Neston. I
went by train on Tuesday 10th for the meeting of H. of C. There I
saw Ll.G. who said he had just come from King George. The latter
said that his father did not grasp the danger he was in till the afternoon of Friday and about 4.30 said 'I think I am really very ill' and
then suddenly put out his hand and became and remained comatose.
He only rallied for a few moments when Mrs. Keppel[25] told him a
mare of his had won a race at Kempton, and he sent an unintelligible
message to his trainer, Marsh, but he didn't recognise Mrs. K. Jack
Pease told me that the P.M. had confided to him a warning given by
Sir T. Barlow that the King might die quite suddenly any minute. I

heard from Geo. Murray that Queen Alexandra has already begun to say that the King's death was largely due to the anxieties caused by the politics of his Ministers. He said he thought that King George meant well, but was weak and talkative adding that at a dinner at which he, G.H.M., was present the Prince of Wales leant forward and in a loud voice said 'I can't think Sir George how you can go on serving that d–d fellow Ll.G.' The princess has apparently shrewdness and common sense, which with a profound dislike of her mother-in-law may induce her to keep on friendly terms with the Liberals, and also make her husband do the same. My brother-in-law John Fuller made a very imprudent speech on the 4th inst. in which he said the King would have to bow to the will of the people, hardly a proper expression for a Court official. This some busybody, almost certainly Walter Long, sent a report of to Marlborough House. Then King George sent a message to J.M.F. that he needn't mind, and that he should in no way take any notice of the incident.

18 May
I attended yesterday in Westminster Hall, the service there held for the late King. The ceremonial entry was managed without any hitch of any kind, though there was a fierce dispute over the right of the Grenadiers to attend the bier at Buckingham Palace and to carry it at Westminster, the Life Guards claiming this as their privilege. Queen Alexandra had for once discarded powder and paint. She, the Duke of Connaught and the Grand Duke Michael were the people most outwardly affected.

9 June
There has been a sharp contest between Lords Farquhar and Beauchamp over their respective duties and powers.[26] It began when the King of Portugal came to Windsor in the autumn of 1909, and the then Queen proposed that Winston Churchill should *not* be asked, as the other Ministers were—to Windsor. Lord Farquhar agreed to omit him, but Beauchamp insisted that he and the Lord Steward's Dept. regulated these things, and sent him an invitation. The dispute culminated over the King's funeral when Beauchamp was elbowed aside by the Earl Marshal and by the 1st Commissioner of Works.
On Saturday last the King paid a visit to J. Chamberlain which

lasted 1½ hours. As Chamberlain is inarticulate, Mr. Wilson his secretary, and Austen Chamberlain the son were translators and spokesmen. But on the previous day, Mr. Garvin, Editor of the *Observer* and author of its 'Compromise' policy and articles, spent a couple of hours with the 2 Chamberlains in Princes Gate as I was informed on the authority of Mr. Garvin's intimate friend R.C. Hawkin. There is little doubt that the King went to be informed as to the nature and extent of the compromise into which the Tariff Reform section of the Tory party are willing to enter. Following on this the Cabinet decided on Monday that Asquith should open negotiations with Balfour and Redmond, as to a truce first, and a subsequent compromise as to the Second Chamber. Redmond is ready, almost willing, but is very frightened as to his party and as to his position in Ireland.

10 June

I have proposed to the Treasury that they should devolve much greater powers than heretofore on the Postmaster-General. Immense power and much time is wasted over the recruitment of an extra postman, or the employment of a charwoman, under existing rules. I am proposing to sweep away all such petty control, which only results in small economies and in the neglect of observing real extravagancies.

It appears that the *present* King has pressed very hard for Lord Kitchener as next Viceroy of India, but John Morley has stood out against such a proposal. Then George Murray was sounded, but refused, and now the person most likely to be sent is Charles Hardinge of the Foreign Office.[27]

✳ In the summer another embarrassment facing the Government, and a particular concern of Hobhouse, was the growing pressure for legislation to give women the vote. Since 1903 the Pankhursts and the Women's Social and Political Union had maintained a militant campaign for votes for women. Heckling politicians, marches, demonstrations, assaults on Cabinet Ministers, imprisonment and forced feeding all fuelled the flames of agitation. Yet by 1910 little headway had been made and the opponents of women's suffrage remained unconvinced. So in 1910 militant action was suspended and the struggle moved into the parliamentary arena. In the spring the all-party Conciliation Committee had formulated a Bill to extend the franchise to women occupiers only. This narrow measure, which would enfranchise about one million women, was designed to win Conservative support. Its limited nature had the effect of dividing the pro-suffrage forces, some fearing the Tory bias of the group enfranchised by the Bill, and others on principle seeking a wider basis for women's suffrage. Hobhouse himself had no doubts—he was an out-and-out opponent of women's suffrage. The Liberal Cabinet included Grey, Lloyd George, Haldane and Churchill as supporters, and Asquith, Harcourt and Burns as intransigent opponents. But on 23 June the Cabinet agreed that this private member's bill should be allowed a Second Reading debate. This took place on 11–12 July.

18 June

Talking yesterday to Lady Dorchester, she told me that her father before *finally* deciding to burn the Byron Memoirs, gave them to Mr. Parke afterwards Ld. Wensleydale to read and pass opinion on. The verdict, written in a letter which I saw, was that 'they could only have been written from a brothel.'

Dined with Haldane in Queen Anne's Gate. Edmund Gosse,[28] Burghcleres, Mr. J. R. Green and a German diplomat. Many ridiculous stories about Ld. Portsmouth[29] late Under Sec. at W.O. He asked the German to stay at Guisachan, sent him out stalking, and at dinner, 6 or 7 others being also present, had half a bottle of champagne put in front of himself, and offered the others a whisky and soda. Burghclere narrated that when he was dining with P. cigarettes were offered to the guests, but cigars to the host. Birrell who was of the party insisted on a cigar, and on one of the same sort as P. was smoking. Eventually *two* were brought down, 'one, as P. said, for Birrell, and the rest could toss for the other.'

Went early next day to Downing St. found Ll.G. tête-à-tête with the editors of *Daily Chronicle*, *News*, and *Statesman*,[30] telling them their proper attitude on 'Woman's Suffrage' which he said truly enough if raised now, would completely dish H. of L. question.

I find the antisuffrage party very slack and frightened and inert, disposed to let the 2nd reading go unopposed. So I went to Ivor Guest (A. St. Ledgers) and sent him off to try and get hold of Cromer and Austen Chamberlain and with Loulou Harcourt to meet in my room to concert opposition to the Bill.

28 June

I found that opposition to the Women's Suffrage Bill was quite un-organised in H. of C. so today I got Lord Cromer, Austen Chamber-lain, and L. Harcourt to meet in my room. Cromer[31] whom I met for the first time was very garrulous and unpractical, talked about a 'meeting in the autumn' while the Bill was hanging over his head in the summer. Physically he seemed well, and was very vivacious, but no driving power was apparent behind the flow of words. A.C. was practical and straightforward and agreed to organise the Tories; Loulou to induce the P.M. to speak, while I undertook to stir up our rank and file. The Anti-Suffrage Women's Assoc. certainly justified their refusal to accept the responsibility of the vote by exhibiting a state of do-nothingness and incapacity which was typical of women's capacity to do serious work.

30 June

The King I find left a fortune of £200,000 to the Queen for her life. She is now trying to evade payment of supertax, and income tax, and death duties. As A. J. Balfour said at a meeting of the Civil List Committee, 'It would be interesting to know what are the revenues of the Court of Denmark.'

We were beaten over the Women's Suffrage question by a majority larger than I had expected.[32] Ld. Curzon, who started the next morning collecting funds for an anti-suffrage campaign told me he collected £10,000 the first morning.

What will eventually ruin the reputation of this Govt. is its absolute contempt for economical administration. Its Govt. is good and pure, but most of the Cabinet, save McKenna & Runciman, seem to think you can, and ought to, buy political gratitude by largesse to this and that class of people.

The Session finished today characteristically. I refused the Colonial Office £10,000 for Cyprus. The matter was referred to a Cabinet Committee of W. Churchill, McKenna, Ld. Crewe, Ll.G. and Asquith. On the facts the Committee agreed with me, but Ll.G. *spontaneously* said that as Winston Churchill's word was involved he could not but give way. Finance he took no account of.

17 September

After the Session was over I went into Camp at Tedworth with my

Regt. the 6th Battalion Gloster Regt. of which I had been in Command for 8 years, this being my last year. We had 900 men in camp and only one misdemeanour during that time. The fault of the Territorial System at present is that the Brigade Commanders are inefficient, being old and discarded officers. As a consequence the Territorial Officers despise their leaders, and the force suffers.

At the end of the set field day, Sir Chas. Douglas gave an excellent résumé of the proceedings, criticising in detail, the movements. The necessity for following the details, which must after all determine the result, is too often overlooked, perhaps from incapacity to see their interdependence.

After this we paid visits to Lady Dorchester at Cowes, Ld. Devonport near Denbigh, W. Younger at Auchen and to Ardgour which had been taken by my brother-in-law, Robert Fuller, for stalking.

While I was there I went with Stafford Howard, an able and amiable man to visit the new Govt. 'forest' at Inverleiven on Loch Awe. 1,200 acres were bought for £26,000 from Malcolm of Poltalloch, and, so far, divided into 12 areas of 150 acres each to be planted yearly, owing to the ravages of blackcock, and rabbits during the recent very hard winter, most of the 1st year's planting must be done over again. Mr. Boyd the forester said he found great difficulty in keeping men through the year, in spite of comfortable quarters and constant employment.

18 September

Saw Hugh Luttrell. Conversation turned on Florence and Temple Leader who long lived there. Leader had told Luttrell that he, Brougham (the Ld. Chancellor) and two others were upset out of a carriage, and for a joke, and without Brougham's knowledge, wrote to a notorious busybody one Col. MacGregor, an exaggerated account of the accident, hinting that B. was *in extremis*. Col. Mac-Gregor ran across Col. Wellesley of the Household who carried the news to Windsor, and so to *The Times*. He added that Lord B. read the 'leaders' next day, friendly or not with roars of laughter.[33]

25 September

We went from Edinglassie on the Don where we stayed with H. J. Tennant to Abergeldie Castle, lent by the King to Lord Carrington.

Mrs. Tennant was a Miss Abrahams an Irish woman, and a factory Inspectress of great beauty and cleverness. She makes an admirable wife, but an abominable housekeeper.[34] From Edinglassie I walked over the hills to Crathie, crossing the watershed of the Don and Dee, about 17 miles. At Abergeldie we found the Carringtons, and their daughter and son-in-law Mr. & Mrs. Nunburnholme. He, I found, was the managing partner of Wilson the Hull shipping line—and an excellent though silent man.[35]

The garden though small was delightful, and the Carringtons charming. It is refreshing to see a man of wealth and social standing so earnest and sincere in his political aims.

We had a 'command' to dine at Balmoral on Sunday the 25th and found ourselves the only outside guests. The party was small. De Soveral, Ld. Rosebery and Neil Primrose,[36] R. B. Haldane, Sir George Reid the Australian, Lord Revelstoke, and ourselves, with the Household. Nina being the only lady, except Lady Mary Trefusis in waiting, sat next the King. I between Lady Mary Trefusis and Sir H. Legge. When the ladies had gone, Sir G. Reid began to chat to Haldane about the Budget and then turned his attention to Rosebery who didn't at all like it. He bears out in every relation of life his Eton tutor's early description of him 'He loves the palm without the dust.' The wit was poor, but not unnatural, and the King laughed continually and loudly. I had some talk with the Queen after dinner, in which he also joined. She speaks with a noticeable German utterance but not unpleasantly so, and was anxious to be at ease, which she soon showed she was. Clearly they liked leading the simple and healthy life of a country gentleman.

✳ Between June and November there were discussions between the Liberal and Unionist leaders in an attempt to resolve the constitutional impasse. Initially this constitutional conference was concerned with relations between the two Houses of Parliament over financial legislation, possible methods of resolving disagreements between them, and reform of the House of Lords. Later Lloyd George extended the scope of the discussions with an extraordinary memorandum which proposed a Coalition Government with an agreed programme including social reforms, compulsory military service, land reform, Imperial Preference and a federal solution to the Home Rule problem. The exciting prospect of a 'Ministry of All the Talents' appealed not only to Lloyd George but also to Churchill, F. E. Smith and Austen Chamberlain—significantly, the very figures who were to be leading Coalitionists in 1922. Back-benchers of both main parties and the uninvited Irish and Labour parties regarded these proceedings with unconcealed suspicion. The extent of Lloyd George's proposals were not revealed at the time to the party as a whole, but he was the object of Liberal suspicion, expressed not least by Hobhouse, for years to come. Ultimately the conference proper broke down over Home Rule, the stumbling block to any agreement on the items on the original agenda, on 10 November. Fortified by favourable by-election trends, the Liberal Government decided on an early election. After a critical forty-eight hours George V was persuaded to give a reluctant pledge to create peers if necessary to pass the Parliament Bill. The December election which followed produced an almost identical result. The Liberals and Unionists both had 272 seats; the 84 Irish and 42 Labour M.P.s again held the balance.

30 October
I found amongst my papers today the following charges for the 5 days' entertainment of royalties during the Court mourning.

Food at Buckingham Palace	£3034.0.0
Food & hire of plate Windsor Castle	691.0.0
Wine and beer do.	919.0.0
Fuel and Light do.	70.0.0

I saw Alick Murray last night at Cox's Hotel, Jermyn St. He said he had been sent for to Buckingham Palace, where Knollys had asked him to say 'what sort of fellow C.E.H. was', as the King wanted to know. Alick gave a satisfactory certificate of character and Knollys said that the King had been told by the Tories that H. was a very bad-tempered man, and as he would see probably a good deal of me in the immediate future, he wished to be reassured.

Apparently in September John Morley sent in his usual letter of resignation which Asquith this time didn't decline to receive, and J.M. not getting a request to stay on followed it up early in October with a renewal of resignation to date from Lord Hardinge's start for India. It was at first suggested that Crewe should go to the India Office, Buxton to the Colonies, Harcourt to Board of Trade and I to the Works: then it changed to Harcourt going to the Colonies and Crewe to India. I have had no intimation from Asquith.

Lloyd George has I hear behaved very handsomely over my work with him, said agreeable things as to industry and capacity. If I move Mackinnon Wood is to be my successor, as George does not like Seely.

George has lately come from Somerset where he says Ed. Strachey's oratory is as flat as his cider. E.S. is to be made a peer at Xmas, and Francis Acland is to have his place and seat, which I doubt if he will hold.[37]

Lloyd George was arguing at the Board of Trade with some officials as to the promotion of a junior in the Dept. Under some pressure they confessed their objection to be that he was 'not a gentleman'. 'But', said George, 'I'm not a gentleman. Mr. Kearley here (his Under-Secretary) is not a gentleman. I am a Welsh country solicitor, and Mr. Kearley is a grocer.' Kearley who, though a grocer, was also a millionaire and is now a peer, didn't like it.[38]

I saw Sir R. Finlay's list of fees for appearing as Canadian Counsel at the Hague (Newfoundland) arbitration. He didn't want to go, and charged accordingly £11,692 for 11 weeks' work!

4 November
J. Morley finding that no one appeared to be going to beg him to remain in the Cabinet went to Asquith yesterday, and requested to be allowed to stay, hinting not obscurely that he might turn very nasty if his wishes were not met. Thereupon the previous arrangements were cancelled, and I lost the Cabinet!

Meanwhile some very curious movements were taking place. A. J. Balfour has been daily at 11 Downing St. for the past fortnight, the topics of conversation being the demerits of his late colleagues and those of Ll.G. So far has the *rapprochement* gone that it was *seriously* discussed between them whether they couldn't arrange for the existing Govt. to be defeated over the Finance Bill, Balfour was then to become P.M. with Ll.G. as his second in command, but not at the Exchequer. Asquith to go to the Lords, perhaps as Lord Chancellor if he was agreeable. Winston Churchill and Lyttleton were to be provided for. Burns and McKenna were to be shunted without mercy. A Govt. so constituted was to carry on over the Coronation and if possible over the autumn while its creators were passing their policy.

The scheme sounds fantastic and improbable, but it has been

seriously considered and debated, and the P.M. at least has not been ignorant of it.[39]

9 November
The Tory conferenciers met at Lansdowne House, and though they all 4 recommended acceptance to their colleagues, the latter largely through Ld. Halsbury's violence rejected agreements.[40]

20 December
I was elected Member for the fourth time for East Bristol on Dec. 3 1910 by an increased majority amounting to practically 3,000. The struggle turned practically on Free Trade and Protection. My opponent speaking strongly against the House of Lords. I visited 8 other constituencies subsequently and until the termination of the campaign which left the Govt. with a majority of 126. Alick Murray had hoped to win from 15 to 25 seats, and actually 100 votes would have won us 9 seats.[41]

Balfour's pronouncement for a referendum on Tariff Reform no doubt won the Tories some seats and saved them others, but it will cost Acland Hood his position as Chief Whip & possibly Balfour his position, though probably his parliamentary value is still unexhausted.

The King has insisted on the prosecution of a paper which has revived the gossip about his marriage to Miss Culine Seymour, at Malta with whom as a matter of fact he never happened to be there.[42]

1911

※ Hobhouse's diary is curiously detached from the main events of 1911. The Parliament Bill passed its Third Reading in the House of Commons in May. Under the threat of a large creation of Liberal peers the Lords divided into two groups, the 'Hedgers' led by Lansdowne and Curzon and the diehard 'Ditchers' led by Lord Halsbury and Willoughby de Broke. After a dramatic debate on 9 and 10 August sufficient peers voted for the Bill to head off the 'Last Ditch' opposition. The Parliament Act ensured that no 'money bill' could be rejected by the Lords, their veto power was a delaying power only, and the duration of Parliament was reduced from seven to five years. At the same time as this final act of the constitutional drama was taking place the country faced a double crisis. At the end of June there was a diplomatic crisis over the sending of the German gunboat *Panther* to Agadir to bring pressure to bear on France to gain territorial compensation for Germany in the Congo. Here Sir Edward Grey and Lloyd George combined to make a strong protest against the German action. Lloyd George's 'Mansion House' speech on 21 July marked his emergence in the 'patriotic' role to the dismay of some former Little Englander allies. While the diplomatic situation remained unsettled the Government faced the threat of a national rail strike in August. This presaged the pattern of industrial militancy which bedevilled the Liberal Government in the years before the First World War.

For Hobhouse, however, this year at last saw his Cabinet ambitions fulfilled. At the end of October, offered the Chancellorship of the Duchy of Lancaster and a seat in the Cabinet, he 'accepted the first because of the second'.

2 March

We went to Antibes to stay with M. Larens and then to Cannes to stay with Rendels at Chateau de Thorenc. Beautiful weather.

I saw Asquith just before I started for France. He was looking much healthier. There was clearly a *rapprochement* between Lloyd George and Balfour based on the elimination of McKenna, and a Navy Loan, the transportation of Asquith to the Lords, the postponement of Home Rule, and the acceptance of Colonial Preference. How, knowing all, the Prime Minister can consort with Lloyd George it is difficult to understand.

Henry Norman, who was at Antibes, told me that two years ago he motored across France with Lloyd George who for two days did nothing but criticise his colleagues, large and small. Grey and myself were excepted from blame!

While at Thorenc, Lloyd George came across to see me, and became very talkative about the Conference. He praised Cawdor[43] highly as always seeing and taking the right point, saying little, and anxious to settle. He said that—and here was characteristically contradictory—one day Cawdor came in very silent and sulky and changed in manner, and he Lloyd George guessed it was all up.

A few minutes later he said that the Conferenciers had parted hopeful of agreement, and that only the Lansdowne House meeting prevented it, from which A.J.B. came direct to him, looking white as a sheet, and like a beaten dog. From what I heard Milner, Curzon and the younger men raised no objection to Welsh Disestablishment and little to Home Rule, which Londonderry, Halsbury & Co. wouldn't hear of, and partly desiring to get rid of Lansdowne, and partly wishing to keep Tariff Reform to the fore they carried the meeting against A.J.B. and Balfour.

We went over to Antibes and dined with him. He spoke openly of meeting Balfour, but as if it had all been about Conference. He let fall 2 illuminating remarks. Speaking of recent political libel cases, he exclaimed 'Good Heavens, if one mayn't tell lies at election times, when may one tell them'. Later on he complained of perpetual politics, and of the constant abuse showered on him, and even of hissing when he went to visit the King at Braemar. He declared the weekly dinners of Grey, Haldane, W. Churchill and himself with Crewe, & sometimes the P.M. had alone kept the Cabinet together.

4 March
Talking of Ll. G. yesterday John Burns, who hates him cordially, said that he had a conscience as good as new, for he had never used it.

8 March
Sir Francis Younghusband told me that when Sir Henry Mac-Mahon[44] came to see King Edward to give him an account of the Ameer's doings in India, MacMahon gave him a full account of all that happened to which the King listened intently. When the story was finished, the King said 'It's all very interesting Sir Henry, but you should never wear a coloured tie with a frockcoat!'

The present King has been responsible entirely for his visit to India where he has been pressing us to give a crore of rupees to distribute as largesse.

10 March
A packet of coins arrived today in the Treasury, 200 gold nobles of Edward I. They were found in Norfolk near East Bergholt by two labourers, in a pottery vessel. I could just hold them on the length of my hand, they were very resilient, and apparently had never been in circulation.

11 March

Richmond Ritchie, the Permanent Under-Secretary at the India
Office, told me that during St. John Brodrick's tenure of the
Secretaryship at the India Office, Arthur Balfour used to come
regularly to the Office and overhaul all the important correspondence.
At the time of the Thibet imbroglio Balfour called a Committee of
Lord Lansdowne, Brodrick, Ritchie (as head of the Political
Department of the India Office), Godley, then Under-Secretary,
and one or two others. Balfour opened the proceedings by saying
that when a difficulty of the Thibet sort arose, as a rule he preferred
to take the advice of the man on the spot, but when as in this case
he profoundly distrusted the man on the spot (Curzon), he naturally
turned to the political chief at home. In this case however he felt
no reliance possible on the opinion of the political chief at home,
and he therefore called a Council of War! And yet Brodrick stayed
at the India Office.[45]

✳ In May Hobhouse visited Ireland on a tour of inspection of harbours
and public works. Accompanied by his wife, he visited Wexford,
Waterford, Killaloe, Athlone and finally Dublin.

17 May

The impression left by things seen and heard was that the Catholic
Clergy and ultra laymen were not desirous of realising Home Rule:
they liked it for political reasons, but under a Home Rule Assembly
expected a transference of power over things educational which
would reduce their power and influence. On the other hand a per-
ceptible percentage of gentry and landowners had lost fear of Home
Rule, if they could be assured of fair dealing thereafter and especially if the power of raising money by taxation was strictly
limited. Even in the four or five years since I was there a great
change had come over the appearance of the land, better cottages,
cultivation and clothing, and though every boy and girl looked forward to emigration, yet still decrease of population was slower.

15 July

I had two long talks with the Prime Minister yesterday and today.
He said in definite language that early in the autumn he intended to
move Samuel to the Board of Agriculture, and that I would be

offered the Post Office. I replied that I should prefer the Board of Agriculture. He then asked me as to the qualities of various people in the Civil Service: Chalmers, Guillemard, Nathan. I advised Babington Smith for Treasury, but he was clearly disinclined for a fight with Lloyd George, and said he would offer Smith the Inland Revenue. This was done by telegraph, but Cassel would not release B. Smith. I then suggested Nathan for the Inland Revenue and this was concurred in, and accepted. A further proposal was made that B. Smith should return to Post Office but this I can hardly think he will accept.

20 July

I gathered that there had never been any difficulty with the King as to creation of peers: he was ready to redeem his promise at any time, but A. O. Murray told me that when he was in Scotland with the King, Knollys was sent to A. J. Balfour with a message, but A.J.B. refused to accept it from anyone but Asquith.[46]

18 July

We had a very pleasant dinner at the Prime Minister's to say fare-well to George Murray. St. Aldwyn and A. Chamberlain were asked but could not come. Harcourt, Haldane, Runciman, Sir John Kempe, R. Chalmers, A. Thring,[47] Col. Williams M.P., M. Nathan, Sir Geo. Murray, Lloyd George, Sir Thos. Heath,[48] Francis Hopwood,[49] McKenna and myself. Asquith made the most perfect short speech, regret, chaff, praise perfectly blended. Murray was much moved. He will be a great loss, not of intellect, but of character and common sense. His failure, and a serious one, was his refusal to work with Ll. G. It was not right, and his influence might have seriously modified, and improved legislation.

9 October

In the last few days of the session I got through Committee a Bill for an extension of the Old Age Pensions Act, and one providing a new system of pensioning Colonial Governors, and a third Bill dealing with Merchandise Marks. I then went to Cowes to stay with Chattie Dorchester, but was recalled to Bristol where I managed to bring the coalminers, who had given notice of an immediate cessation of work, to agreeing to Board of Trade arbitration. Their wages are lower than those of any other miners in the U.K., the companies are barely paying their way, while Lady Smyth is taking £4,000 p.a. in royalties. Such inequity cannot last.

We visited the Youngers at Auchen, Rob Fullers at Ardgour where I got two good stags, Jack Tennant at Edinglassie, R. D. Holt[50] at Abernethy Forest, another two stags, and Sir J. Ferguson at Springkell.

I found Lloyd George very much *au mieux* with E. Gray. The Germans had tried to force on Ll.G. the role of a second Delcassé,[51] but Grey so strongly supported Ll.G. and was so firm and peremptory that the Germans retreated precipitately.

IV

Chancellor of the Duchy

1911–1912

✳ The office of Chancellor of the Duchy of Lancaster then, as now, was hardly onerous. This was the traditional method of appointing a minister and bringing him into the Cabinet without departmental responsibilities. The Chancellor's actual duties, to oversee the Duchy estates, were virtually nominal. One authority considers 'a Chancellor of the Duchy of Lancaster has about two hours a week of office work.' Hobhouse seems to have made the most of the slight administrative opportunities it afforded. More important was his membership of the Cabinet and his presence at discussions of the problems of the day. Henceforward the diaries are very largely based upon such discussions.

At home the troubles of the Government were centred on Ireland, industrial unrest and the suffragette agitation, but it was foreign policy and defence matters which took up much of the Cabinet's time. The Agadir crisis was resolved by a Franco-German agreement in November 1911, but it had considerable repercussions. At the height of Anglo-German tension Asquith had held a special meeting of the Committee of Imperial Defence on 23 August to discuss British strategy in the event of war. This meeting disclosed wide differences between naval and military plans. The Army assumption that the Navy would transport an expeditionary force to the Continent on the commencement of hostilities revealed the Anglo-French military conversations which had been instigated in 1906. Asquith himself looked on these proceedings with some caution, but when the news leaked to other members of the Cabinet they were furious. Morley, Crewe and Harcourt, although members of the C.I.D., had not been invited to the crucial meeting. An indignant Morley demanded why Cabinet approval had never been asked for discussions between British and French military staffs about possible military operations against Germany in the first of two stormy Cabinets on 1 November.

A second consequence of the C.I.D. meeting was the replacement of McKenna at the Admiralty by Churchill. This brought one of the 'economists' into the 'militarist' camp: it also embittered personal relations between the two men. During 1912 Churchill's enthusiasm for his new job was to become entangled with the question of Anglo-French naval dispositions, to the dismay of his Cabinet colleagues.

At the same time as the French *Entente* came under close scrutiny in the Cabinet, the House of Commons grew critical of Grey's policy towards Russia in Persia. Attempts by Morgan Shuster, the American financial adviser to the Persian Government, to strengthen the country's financial situation in the face of Russian and British influence brought drastic reaction from Russia. Grey persuaded Russia to temper some of her demands but he himself came under heavy fire from the Radical wing of the Liberal Party for apparently supporting the Russian bully. He faced uncomfortable debates on foreign policy in the House of Commons in November and December.

In a further development of the Balkan imbroglio, Italy took advantage of the crisis over Agadir to seize Tripoli from Turkey, thereby precipitating the Turco-Italian War. This revealed Turkey's military weakness and encouraged the Balkan League states to strike at her in October 1912.

30 October

On returning from political tour in west of England on 21st I found letter from Asquith offering me Duchy of Lancaster and a seat in the Cabinet. I accepted the first because of the second. The press have been very favourable, and my friends kind—I attended my first Cabinet on the 25th. It is the duty of the junior member to answer the door, and distribute any messages or papers poked in. Grey spoke at some length on Morocco, where French & Germans have come to a complete understanding & may sign any day; on Tripoli where Italy will not listen to overtures, and Aehrenthal[1] is trying to arrange concerted European action; and of Persia, where the mutual friendship, pigheadedness and pro-Persianism of Shuster the American Treasurer and the British Stokes[2] are producing a crisis. We also discussed Primrose's Home Rule report, to the financial part of which George, primed by Chalmers, took natural exception, and a Committee presided over by Asquith was appointed to examine it. Another Committee to report on Plural Voting was also appointed. Loulou Harcourt took copious notes of the proceedings.[3]

11 November

At Cabinet Wednesday [8 November] Crewe announced in a speech of 1 hour and 20 mins. that the King had to proclaim the change of the Capital of India from Calcutta to Delhi. The blow was to be sweetened by the creation of a new Governorship of Bengal, and redistribution of other sub-provinces. He expatiated on the difficulties of the Local & State Govt. side by side in Calcutta with Central & Imperial Govt., the superiority of climate, and the unanimity of Viceroy's and Secretary of State's Councils. The Lieut. Governors had not been consulted, and the strategic weakness of Delhi had hardly received consideration I discovered by questions. It seems to me that the King is responsible for the move. Asquith admitted as much to me in conversation after Wednesday's Cabinet and added that the King had asked what was the use of going to Delhi unless he could distribute largesse (which we would not allow) or make some important announcement. This argument I thought the P.M. could easily have met.

The Cabinet was very uneasy about it, the only person in the secret having been Asquith, and we adjourned till Thursday Nov. 9th, but though Beauchamp, Morley, Loreburn, and self were obviously hostile, and the others except Churchill and Burns, frankly doubtful—still the imminent departure of the King and Crewe prevented further objection or refusal. I trust we may not suffer—as I think we ought.

16 November

Morley and the Lord Chancellor reopened the discussion yesterday of the correspondence which had been passing between the French and English General Staffs, whose actions, nominally secret, yet known to be in concert, he declared to have been undertaken without the knowledge of the Cabinet. Haldane in defence said that these relations had begun with the knowledge of C.B. then Prime Minister, and Ed. Grey in January 1906. He read a memo by Sir W. Nicholson,[4] detailing all the communications. These showed that we contemplated landing 6 Divisions of Infantry with the necessary Corps Troops, somewhere in France, at (and on this French military opinion was most urgent) the very outset of hostilities. The place of operations was revised continually up to the present date. Grey and the present P.M. (Asquith) clearly knew that communications had been passing but Grey didn't seem to know all Haldane's moves, though he regarded them as committing us to co-operation with France, if her action had been non-provocative and reasonable. He read a memo which the French Ambassador had written to him showing the impressions he had conveyed to the French Govt. of British sympathies and probable action—and stating to them definitely that if France was unreasonable the British Govt. could not assist her. Asquith on the other hand said that *he* still felt himself quite free, under any circumstances, free to refuse co-operation.

The feeling of the Cabinet was clearly that the military reciprocities had committed us partially, and that Haldane had been rather 'slim' and eventually formally resolved 'that neither the General Staff of the Army nor the Navy was to enter into communication with the General Staff of any other Power in respect of concerted plans for co-operation without the previous direction of the Cabinet.'[5] The Prime Minister was asked to keep a copy of this: and Haldane was to circularise his General Staff accordingly.

I dined with A. O. Murray at the Garrick. He gave an account of recent Cabinet changes. Haldane wanted the Navy, and the P.M. wanted McKenna away from it, but it was agreed that Macnamara was not strong to face H. of C. by himself, and that a Secretary of State must be there. Then the P.M. thought of Churchill (I suspect Alick did this) whereupon McK., who had simultaneously been offered Home Office, wanted to resign. Spender[6] and Murray persuaded him not to do so, and after a second journey to Archerfield[7] the change was made. But *I* noticed how hostile was McK.'s attitude to Haldane in the Cabinet, and how unfriendly to the P.M. yesterday.

9 December

Cabinets on Wednesday and Thursday [6 & 7 December]. Grey made a long statement on Persia. It is clear both by the F.O. telegrams, Sir G. Barclay's dispatches and Sir Geo. Buchanan's[8] that the Russian Prime Minister made promises of moderation which he could not act up to—and that the anti-English party have placed him in a position very little creditable to Russian bona fides. The Russian P.M. told Buchanan definitely that Russia would withdraw her troops if Persia met the two demands and apologised; M. Neratoff said the apology had come too late—the troops had disembarked and fresh demands were formulated as a pretext for a move on Teheran.

On Thursday we discussed the opening of communications with the Irish. H. Samuel had prepared an able financial statement which we agreed should be shown to Redmond and Dillon.[9] Birrell also wanted them to see the draft Bill—to this Samuel, Runciman and I objected and eventually got our way.

24 December

Birrell gave us yesterday to understand that Dillon and Redmond had received his communications favourably. He had said nothing to them about finance, only that 'Hamlet would appear in the next scene.' Redmond had expected a greater number in *both* houses, and was anxious especially for a larger and nominated Second Chamber.

Grey's Morocco and German speeches have made a good impression on the Continent generally. Aehrenthal told Sir F. Cartwright[10] that Grey had put the English case ably, and in a conciliatory spirit. He blamed Germany for want of precision in her policy and said that it was bad policy to be unclear in *important* political issues.

Lord Acton[11] writes from Darmstadt that German feeling is very mixed. The German General Commanding the XVIIIth Army Corps sitting next an English lady at Phillippsluhe said to her 'We now know who our enemies are, and we shall never forget it.' But Princess Charles Frederic of Hesse told Sir H. Jermyngham that 'The Emperor desired a Union between the Teutonic races.'

Russian action in Persia is very troublesome. M. Neratoff the Acting Minister, at Petersburg, for Foreign Affairs is either very weak or very anti-English, probably the former. He made difficulties, and allowed himself to be overruled in the Council of Ministers, luckily M. Sazonov[12] has returned to work and pushed the difficulties on one side. But the harm done by Mr. Neratoff's ultimatums, the shortness of time allowed for their acceptance, the disembarkation of troops, the increase of demands has created a situation from which Russia cannot retreat, and which public opinion in Persia cannot accept.

Shuster's dismissal will be disastrous for Persia, he is able, of integrity—but politically so innocent of politics that he cannot see he has to reckon with the power and proximity of Russia, and her established interest in N. Persia. But the strength of his position is the support he can reckon on from the Medgliss,[13] which no successor, nominated by England and Russia can hope to get. M. Kokovstoff the President of the Council is conciliatory, and inclined to make allowance for the chaos in Persia, but shields himself behind the real or supposed temper of the Tsar at Persian delay. Sir George Barclay has under Grey's orders done everything to check the Russian move into Persia, to moderate Russia's demands, and to minimise the indemnity, and also to obtain from Russia a promise that her troops should be withdrawn *everywhere* as soon as the three demands have been complied with: 1. The dismissal of Shuster; 2. An undertaking by Persia not to appoint foreigners without consultation with the Russian and English legations; 3. An indemnity for military expenditure.

Goschen[14] writes from Berlin that the anti-British campaign has done its work and that the Social Democrats will gain but few seats, and these chiefly from the Liberal groups.

1912

✳ The year opened and closed with Ulster. While the third Home Rule Bill, introduced on 11 April, was passing slowly through Parliament, the Unionist leadership fanned the flames of Ulster resentment to try to kill Home Rule. Ulster, claimed Carson and Bonar Law, was not to be coerced into Home Rule, and without Ulster, Irish demands would not be satisfied. It was a year of violence, with Unionist threats of civil war over Ulster matched by suffragette window-smashing forays in London's West End. In part, the latter were probably provoked by a speech by Hobhouse in Bristol on 16 February, when he claimed that there was no mass support for the suffrage agitation. Whatever the cause, the suffragettes embarked on a wave of violence which had as its consequence the defeat of the second Conciliation Bill in the House of Commons at the end of March. But there was also further industrial trouble, with miners' and dockers' strikes in quick succession, and in the summer there was a characteristic Cabinet row over Churchill's proposals for the disposition of the Navy. Then, in the autumn, events in the Balkans required the Cabinet's attention.

4 February

Last week it was agreed that, in response to a message sent by the German Emperor through Herr Ballin of the Hamburg Amerika Line and Sir E. Cassel asking Ed. Grey to come to Berlin to discuss armaments, Haldane should take an unofficial journey to Berlin to 'create an atmosphere'. We all agreed except John Morley who asked for 'precedents', and was rather violent. Grey said that Metternich[15] had made no proposals as to 'expansion'—indeed Hollweg's view was that Germany wanted men, not colonies.

11 February

On Tuesday after the 'Thanksgiving' to which Nina also went, another Cabinet, chiefly on Home Rule. We finally settled on Haldane's mission, in spite of a dubious telegram to Cassel via Ballin in which the Emperor and Hollweg seemed to insist on an English attitude 'free from all entanglements' or else conversations were useless. After that, Home Rule. Ll.G. proposed that every county should be given the option of 'contracting out'—really to apply to Ulster, but nominally for every part. He was backed by Asquith, Churchill, Haldane and myself. Birrell vowed he would not touch any Bill different to that of '86 and '93. He had made no inquiry into the real condition or intentions of Ulster, and roundly declared such to be useless. He and Aberdeen seem to me to be the 2 worst administrators that any country could be cursed with.

I heard that Herbert Gladstone is coming home to be told whether there is a malignant growth somewhere or not. Very sad.

Carrington characteristically whispered to me that he had just 'handed in his cap and jacket'. Quite the last of the old school, not at all clever—but shrewd—a sincere reformer, combining aristocracy with liberalism. I shall miss him a good deal.

20 February

After a long discussion Grey and Haldane were deputed to meet Count Metternich and discuss the possibility of confining Germany's naval increases to personnel required to bring their third squadron up to efficiency. If McKenna's account to me is accurate, this is a singular deputation. McK. said that in Sept. at a special and packed meeting of the Defence Committee, Grey, Haldane, Churchill and Lloyd George decided on military proceedings against Germany.

The Prime Minister acquiesced. He, as First Lord of the Admiralty, refused to guarantee the transport of the troops, and appealed to the Cabinet. Haldane and Churchill declared the rest of the Cabinet didn't count. However when the Cabinet were consulted they were (except the 5 above named) unanimously against it. The conversations with the French Staff ceased, and preparations abandoned. As we now know the French Premier, Caillaux, was treating secretly with Germany.

McKenna and I finished today the draft of the Welsh Bill— on I hope Liberal lines. What Ll.G. will persuade the Cabinet to do I don't know.

9 March

Nina and I went to Chateau de Thorenc to stay with Ld. Rendel for a fortnight returning on March 8th. She was very unbalanced mentally. We had a complete rest; the only people we saw being the Burghcleres, Gerald Craig Sellar, and Lady Winchelsea. Ld. R. was as businesslike as ever. His principal reminiscence was Ld. Rosebery's failure as a Cabinet Minister. He said Mr. G. seldom spoke of Rosebery during his '92 Govt. without complaining of his inefficiency as a minister and uselessness in Council.

✳ In January the Miners' Federation of Great Britain had voted by ballot to call a national strike in favour of national minimum wage rates of 5/- a shift for men and 2/- for boys. Negotiations between owners and men resulted in stalemate, which the intervention of four members of the Cabinet, Asquith, Grey, Lloyd George and Buxton, as mediators did not resolve. The strike began on 29 February. Having been dragged into the dispute, the Government sought a way out, but refused either to subsidise the owners to maintain the minimum demanded or to specify the 5/- and 2/- as a national minimum in legislation. The Government eventually got out of the dilemma by passing the Coal Mines (Minimum Wage) Act which in effect established the principle of a national minimum wage by Act of Parliament, but did not specify the amount it was to be. That was left to the negotiating machinery set up by the Act on a district basis. The Bill was passed very rapidly, gaining a second reading on 21 March and receiving the Royal Assent on 29 March.

27 March

We have had a series of most serious Cabinets. Usually 4 or 5 members speak. Grey, Ll. George, Asquith usually first or last, Churchill, Morley or Loreburn, or the particular Minister whose business is under discussion. But in all these discussions everyone spoke in turn, for 2 or 3 minutes and everyone was listened to. Lloyd George was in favour of giving in to the miners' demands absolutely. Hartshorn[16] had interviewed more than once, and he had induced the editors of the *Chronicle* and the *Daily News* to take the same line. Buxton was in agreement, but as usual, with reservations. Grey at the last Cabinet [26 March] had come round to that view, but admitting that the Cabinet could not go behind the P.M.'s declarations, actually proposed that the difference between the men's demands and the cost to the employers should for a year be paid out of the Exchequer, and that during the year there should be inquiry as to nationalisation etc., he was convinced that unless we met the men there would be 'civil war', this opinion he constantly expressed. Haldane was at first vehemently against going beyond the minimum wage bill, then swung round to compliance, and finally came back to the Bill, without alteration. Loreburn was of much the same disposition.

McKenna, Runciman, Morley, Crewe, and myself were steadily and always for a Bill, *the* Bill, and if there had been any decision to go beyond it, we should have resigned.

At our last meeting the P.M. mostly adroitly said that he feared Grey's proposal was the only possible legislative alternative to the Bill, but before he had even seriously considered it the following objections had occurred to him—and then recited them and stopped. That clinched the waverers. Ll. George and I went away together he declaring that a colossal blunder had been committed. I told him that if he had yielded to Hartshorn his influence in S. Wales, and the Liberal party died together.

✳ The attempt to improve Anglo-German relations through Haldane's 'mission' in February had foundered on the British refusal to commit herself to neutrality if Germany went to war with another country, in return for which the Germans were to have withdrawn their *Novelle*, the projected naval building programme. Faced with a Germany which was building up her material and personnel so as to enable her to keep four-fifths of the German fleet in permanent commission, Churchill had presented his naval estimates in March with the warning that they would have to be increased from their £44 millions in the next year to maintain British superiority. When the German programme was passed by the Reichstag, Churchill promptly presented a £1 million supplementary estimate and announced that the British building programme would be accelerated. He also came to the conclusion that the new naval situation could only be remedied in the Mediterranean by coming to an arrangement with the French. The alternatives were either to reduce the margin of safety in the North Sea, which was strategically unacceptable; to abandon the Mediterranean completely which would be politically harmful; or to build a new fleet for the Mediterranean which would cost up to £20 millions and not be ready before 1916. The French, for their part, had earlier instigated joint naval talks and were now glad to undertake the 'policing' of the Mediterranean provided Britain looked after the northern coast of France. This proposal led to a series of contentious Cabinets.

10 May

It is noticeable how constantly our Ambassadors report that the Foreign Minister of their State desires to know what Ed. Grey would think of such and such a proposal.

At the Cabinet before the Welsh Church Bill was introduced I tried to get a sum put aside as compensation to the Church for the loss of tithe. Practically we shall give in the end her everything but that, and my belief is that with a moderate cash endowment in place of the £116,000 tithe we should get our Bill quite easily. Without such compensation we shall lose our credit, and may lose our Bill.

Yesterday Churchill proposed that the P.M., he himself, Kitchener, Prince Louis of Battenberg,[17] and representatives of the Naval and Military War Staff with Sir John Anderson of the Colonial Office should meet at Malta, hold a 'defence Committee' and settle whether the withdrawal from the Mediterranean was necessary; and to this policy he proposed as an alternative the building of 10 dreadnoughts! Happily we were all against him, being led thereto by John Morley who is a mine of Constitutional practice, and with a mind inclined thereto, and he keeps us off many rocks.

I spoke on Tuesday in H. of C. on Disestablishment, for 50 minutes—with, I was told by a good many members on both sides, general approval of matter and style. It was certainly the best speech I have made in the House.

Nina was yesterday elected at the head of the list on the Council of the Women's Liberal Association.

29 May

I went during Whitsuntide to visit the Duchy property in Needwood Forest, where recently I bought 1,000 additional acres.[18] Tutbury Castle, where Mary Queen of Scots was confined, and a fine church with a good deal of Saxon architecture on the west door and a portion of the S. wall was the most interesting *place*, but the Forest which we are extensively replanting is a fine wild country.

Thence I went to Castleton in Derbyshire, where are crumbling remains of Will Peveril's Castle, which I ordered should be strengthened, and a cavern in the mouth of which is practised rope making. There are 7 original rope walks, to each of which is attached by hereditary right, a particular family, but only 3 are still used.

12 June

At Cabinet yesterday Ll.G. tried very hard to induce us to agree to introduce legislation which would enforce the payment of a scale of wages on all employers in the trade within a given area, if associations of masters and men had agreed to the scale, and no matter how many masters or men stood outside the agreeing associations. Haldane, Buxton were with him, and Runciman partly. I raised the note of dissent, then Wood, and at the end of the discussion the P.M. sang a still stronger tune, and eventually we postponed further action till Thursday.

Ll.G. is always anxious to play up to organisations of labour, who are always abusive of him, though it is impossible to say whether his motive is fear, or the hope of disabling and replacing the leaders by himself.

21 June

In a telegram received today from Petersburg Mr. O'Beirne[19] describes the Russian Foreign Minister M. Sazonov saying to him that he could not get the French to understand that Russia's naval 'project' was directed solely against Germany. If the French don't understand it, Germany does, and it is this which causes, *inter alia*, the increase in the German shipbuilding programme.

A very long Cabinet on Wednesday [19 June], occupied with discussing Churchill's proposal to clear the Mediterranean of all battleships, and to defend Malta and Alexandria with a squadron of cruisers, and a flotilla of submarines which was 'to operate against the Dardanelles and to coerce the Turk diplomatically'. Lord Kitchener's part in this proposal is found in a proposal to increase the Egyptian garrison, and fortify Alexandria harbour.

Meanwhile without consulting the Cabinet, Churchill has moved the 8 battleships from Malta. What is not explained in this precious scheme is how we are to protect the Russian grain-trade at the outbreak of war, or in what way we are so inferior to the Austro-Italian fleet as to cause us to withdraw from the Mediterranean. There was much adverse and admirable criticism from McKenna, and as a whole we were against Churchill, but postponed decision till McK. had time to prepare a riposte.

28 June

We resumed talk about the Mediterranean yesterday. McKenna was away in attendance on the King, but he left an admirable memo. I tried to get Churchill to tell us when the German fleet would be at its full strength, and after some equivocation, there is no other word, he said 1915. We then pressed him as to the forces of France and Russia of which he had taken no account, and he had to concede their strength. Haldane who sits and purrs like a great cat, supported him, but Asquith as usual, began to lean away from Churchill to the more numerous side.

Eventually we dispersed leaving Churchill to report to us how we should stand without France, and with France as an ally. The suggested definite naval agreement with France seems to be abandoned by everyone. Grey was much impressed by my reminder that half of the corn eaten here reaches us via the Mediterranean, viz. a quarter from Russia and Rumania, and a quarter from India.

6 July

On Friday [5 July] we beat Churchill & Haldane. On the previous day the Defence Committee had sat from 11 a.m. to 5 p.m. Grey gave them an admirable picture of the diplomatic result of the withdrawal of the fleet from the Mediterranean. During the proceedings Churchill repeated before the naval & military officers his threat of leaving the Govt. and stumping the country if he could not get his way. But here as at the Cabinet this ultimatum fell quite flat, except that one or two muttered, as all felt, that they wished to goodness he would go. A War Office memo on the consequential increase of the garrison in Egypt was very effective. Finally the P.M. wobbling as he always does over to the majority declared that abandonment was impossible, and would be fatal. The next day in Cabinet he said a few words to this effect and none of us thought it necessary to dwell on our victory.

I heard at first hand the following. Churchill inspecting the fleet at Weymouth visited the *Lion*, Admiral Bayly's[20] ship. Having seen the ship, he went about amongst the junior officers and *inter alia* asked several what they thought of their Captain. This came to Captain Bayly's ears. He got Churchill out to the bridge of the ship, told him that though he was First Lord, yet he Bayly was on the ship supreme and that on any repetition of such inquisitorial methods, he would turn him off the ship. Winston took his drubbing very well, as far as temper went.

10 July

At today's Cabinet Churchill raised the Mediterranean question again and by assigning to Malta a fleet of battle cruisers incapable of meeting in action, owing to lack of sufficient armour (they having only 8″), Austro-Italian battleships, tried to show that untenable. He now proposed 4 battle cruisers and 4 armoured cruisers as the Mediterranean Fleet till June 1915, and asked us to build 3 dreadnoughts at once to come in for 1916. Up till this discussion we had always held that a 60% superiority over the next strongest fleet was sufficient. He asked us to have something like 40% over the next two strongest fleets combined. Haldane supported him strongly, Asquith hesitatingly—the rest of us opposed, Lloyd George, McKenna, Samuel and I vocally.

Our formula agreed to on Friday was 'that these must always be ready and available in home waters a reasonable preponderance of naval strength; that a fleet should be maintained in the Mediterranean always, based on Mediterranean ports equal to the fleet of the next strongest power, not counting France.'[21]

13 July

The suffragettes today tried to set fire to Nuneham, Loulou Harcourt's house. They tried about a fortnight ago to do the same thing to my house at Corsham, in both cases canvas soaked in oil was the agent, but while they burnt down my back door, at Nuneham they were caught before they had done any mischief.[22]

17 July

At Cabinets on Monday and Tuesday [15 & 16 July] we renewed discussion on the Mediterranean. Churchill was most abusive and insulting to McKenna He is really a spoilt child endowed by some chance with the brain of a genius. In the end on Tuesday he read us certain opinions of *some* of his naval experts, one by the First Sea Lord saying he would face the supposed Austrian fleet of 3 dreadnoughts and 3 Radetzkys of 1915 with confidence if he had 4 dreadnought cruisers and 4 armoured cruisers. Finally the Cabinet agreed that until June 1915 the force in the Mediterranean should be based on Malta and should consist of 4 battle cruisers, 4 armoured cruisers, 2 smaller cruisers supported by a suitable number of destroyers and torpedo craft.

We accepted Churchill's declaration that except in the event of some unforeseen emergency in a war with Germany, the battle cruisers should not be withdrawn from the Mediterranean.

After we discussed the information to be afforded by the British and French War Offices and Admiralty respectively to each other. It was agreed that they might exchange information, but that Ed. Grey should tell M. Cambon the French Ambassador and should instruct Sir F. Bertie to tell the French Govt. 'that it was clearly to be understood that anything which passed between the naval and military experts must not be taken so to commit either Govt. to come to the assistance of the others in time of war as to prejudice their freedom of decision.'

P.S.   The 'unforeseen emergency' alluded to above was defined by Grey and accepted by Churchill as being (a) the torpedoing of our battleships by Germany or (b) a declaration of neutrality by Austria or Italy or both.

Incidentally Asquith declared that 'the Liberal press was written by boobies for boobies.'

1 August

At Cabinet yesterday [31 July] we discussed the old standing alliances with Portugal. She permits her Colonies to be very badly

administered as at Macao and Delagoa Bay, and if any foreign subject is damnified, she drags in the alliance with us to protect her
against the possible consequences of her laches. Grey and Harcourt
are afraid that a quarrel with Germany may so arise. Moreover by the
secret treaty of 1898, Germany & Great Britain have created &
shared a reversionary interest in the Portuguese Colonies. Since the
treaty is secret we cannot tell would-be investors in these possessions
that they must not develop such and such a place since it is *going* to
be German. Germany is similarly embarrassed.

Grey therefore proposed to convert the permanent alliance into
one renewable at 10-year intervals, and to publish the secret treaty
with up-to-date revisions. The P.M. objected that this would look
like pressing the new republican Govt. for sins which had passed
unnoticed under a monarchy.

Lloyd George said that it would hardly do to denounce the treaty
& partition the Colonies. We should get the odium which the Tories
deserved. I suggested that by threatening to denounce the alliance
we could procure some better administration in the Colonies and this
was agreed to. In the course of the discussion Haldane spoke of 'the
nuisance of small nationalities'.

We then discussed Churchill's visit to Canada which he described 'as a duty and obligation and not as a pleasure'. Harcourt
told us the Duke of Connaught[23] was very unpopular with the
Liberal party in Canada whom he totally ignored, and that they were
complaining bitterly. Finally at my suggestion it was agreed that we
should consult Laurier as to whether the construction of 3 Canadian
dreadnoughts for the British fleet would be a party battle there, and
if not that Churchill should go. The P.M. decided that he should
approach Borden, and Borden should communicate with Laurier.[24]

✻ Hobhouse took the opportunity to slip away from London before the
   end of the session to tour the Duchy estates with his wife. They left
   London by car on 7 August and visited various Duchy properties in
   Lincolnshire and Yorkshire, including the ruined castles of Pontefract
   and Pickering and Rievaulx Abbey which provided Nina Hobhouse
   with some fine opportunities for her sketching. They went on to stay at
   Auchen Castle, at Moffat, in Dumfriesshire, and it was from there that
   Hobhouse sent the following letter. It sheds some light on the minor
   frustrations of his traditional office.

13 August [Letter to Walter Runciman][25]
My dear Walter,

I am proposing some changes in the Duchy of Lancaster Council. It is a body largely invented by the late King, to help the Chancellor to do nothing. But since it exists it ought to be composed of people not yet in their dotage.

Two of its members Lord Cross aged 89, and Sir G. Engleheart aged 90, are practically in that condition. I have approached them informally through Sir W. Carrington with a request for their resignation. Lord Cross desires to be addressed formally & Sir G. Engleheart refuses voluntarily to budge. Herewith is my letter to Lord C. Would you criticise language or method if you think necessary? You should know that I have the King behind me, and that if these people prove recalcitrant they will be given notice to quit.

We got 25 brace here yesterday 3 guns walking half a day. It ought to be a record season.
>   Yours ever
>   C. Hobhouse

✳ It was on the same day that he resumed his diary with the following survey of his colleagues.

13 August
After practically a year's experience in Cabinet, I note the following characteristics of my colleagues.

Asquith, the Prime Minister carries naturally great weight, and everybody likes him, and has great admiration for his intellect and for the ease and rapidity of transacting business, and his extraordinary quickness in seizing the right point in any case. On the other hand he has little courage; he will adopt the views of A with apparent conviction and enthusiasm, but if the drift of opinion is against A he will find an easy method of throwing him over. He is nearly always in favour of the last speaker, and I have never seen him put his back to the wall.

Ed. Grey is clear, narrow, obstinate when convinced of the soundness of his case, but convincible up to that point. He carries great weight in Cabinet, and is apt at finding solutions of difficulties, very conciliatory, and with plenty of humour.

Crewe is slow of thought and slower of speech, but sensible and clear headed. Both he and Grey are much more radical than is commonly supposed.

Haldane is a dangerous man, subtle, a good friend to his followers, but tricky and not to be trusted. He carries great weight with Asquith and I think with no one else except perhaps Grey.

Ll. George has humour—great quickness of thought, and a wonderful power of managing men for a short time. He knows no meaning in the words *truth* or *gratitude*. Asquith is afraid of him, he knows it, but likes and respects Asquith. He is a little afraid of Grey —and of no one else, and treats Winston Churchill like he would a favourite and spoilt naughty boy. He has a genuine dislike of plutocracy, some regard for squirearchy and affection for the peasant, but especially the Welsh one.

Morley is useful in keeping us to constitutional precedents, and as both George and Churchill have some veneration for him, he acts as a useful check on them. He threatens resignation twice a week, and will never go till the Govt. does.

Churchill is ill mannered, boastful, unprincipled, without any redeeming qualities except his amazing ability and industry. I doubt his courage to desert during a victorious cruise, but he would, without hesitation, desert a sinking ship.

Birrell is cynical, amusing, a bad administrator, but high principled and with plenty of courage.

McKenna has wonderful quickness of mind, and a remarkable memory. Asquith first petted him, and then treated him abominably over the September crisis. He attempts bonhomie, but is not sufficiently of a gentleman for it to be successful. He was a good and economical administrator.

Burns, Buxton and Beauchamp are except on office questions silent members of the Cabinet.

Samuel is industrious, a good speaker, and clear thinker. His judgement is respected and his advice accepted, but everyone thinks him absolutely self-centred and his whole horizon bounded by his own career. He would never have time to pick any unfortunate fellow creature out of the mire.

Harcourt has many attractive qualities: charming manners when he likes, a temper under good control, a hard worker, but no one trusts him, and everyone thinks that language is only employed by him to conceal his thought.

Runciman is able, honest, hard-working, courageous, but while a good speaker, just lacks that touch of genius which Churchill has got, and that charm which Lloyd George abounds in. He will enjoy and deserve high office, but never I think the highest.

✳ The remainder of the summer recess was spent in Scotland, shooting and walking. When Hobhouse returned to London, the tension in the Balkans was rising. Turkey's weakness had been revealed in her war with Italy. Serbia, Bulgaria, Greece and Montenegro, encouraged at first by Russia and later viewed with alarm by her, had formed the Balkan League, committed to the liberation of the subject peoples of the Balkans from Turkish rule. Once let loose the forces of Pan-Slavism were uncontrollable. Montenegro led the way into war against Turkey on 8 October and was rapidly followed by Bulgaria, Serbia and Greece. Turkish power crumbled under the onslaught. By the end of November the Great Powers viewed with dismay the virtual ending of Turkish rule in Europe and the swift development of aggressive rival nation-states in this sensitive area. Rival claims for territory might well lead to provocation involving one of the Great Powers. To avert this, in December a Conference of Ambassadors, from Austro-Hungary, Italy, Germany, Russia, France and Britain was called in London.

12 October

The Eastern situation is very difficult. The Turkish Govt. are probably sincerely anxious to avoid ill-treatment of Christians in future, but find it almost impossible to punish offenders for past outrages, such as at Kotchana. They will have to surrender Turkish territory to Italy and therefore are not strong enough to make constitutional concessions to Christian populations in Turkey. The Bulgarian and Serbian Govts. desire peace, but are not strong [enough] to hold back their nationals; the King of Montenegro is in the same position. Austria does not want a barrier of Balkan States, between her and Salonika—and will never consent to the division of Macedonia and Albania between them. Russia cannot consent to their absorption by Austria, nor can Italy. Every Govt. therefore wants peace, and nearly every people desires war, without realising the result of it.

The real offender appears to be M. de Hartwig, Russian Ambassador at Belgrade, who openly says he detests Russia's policy of a *modus vivendi* with Austria, and whose private encouragement of

Bulgarian and Serbian hotheads is accountable for the belief that Russia will, despite her present attitude, come to the military assistance of the Confederacy if they come to grief.

The Govts. of Bulgaria and Serbia knowing what they *must* do, have agreed to demand reforms, not territory, from Turkey, trusting that if war occurs they will be able to occupy agreed portions of Macedonia, which later on as in case of Eastern Roumelia will declare for annexation to the 2 countries respectively.

13 October
Talking over foreign affairs at Cabinet this week, Asquith said 'What extraordinary bad luck the Balkan States had in their kings. Montenegro was a savage, Serbia an assassin, and Bulgaria a cosmopolitan financier of the lowest type.' Grey added that of the confederates Bulgaria was the only real item, the only part that Greece and Serbia would take would be to feel a Turkish bayonet in their *backs*. Personally I think Asquith was unjust to Montenegro, anyone would be a semi-savage who was burdened by hereditary invasions from the Turk.

16 October
We discussed today Botha's proposal that the King should visit S. Africa. The King was willing, but declared he must go to Canada first. He was not however willing to go to Continental Courts, but if he had to go, he would go to Austria first. We decided he had much better stay at home, and not teach people how easily the machine worked without a King.

22 October
The Cabinet had considerable discussion as to whether Grey should intimate to Greece and Turkey that they could not be allowed to attack or mine respectively the Dardanelles. Eventually it was decided to say and do nothing unless British shipping was greatly held up.

18 November
Most of the recent Cabinets have been occupied by the Balkan War problems. Nearly all of us are anti-Turk, Grey being perhaps the only one who [would] like to hold the balance even, and that because

he despises the Greeks and Serbians. As regards Austria and Serbia we should all like to see Serbia economically independent of Austria. As regards Constantinople we consider an enclave round it, ample ground to contain all the Turks who ought to be in Europe.

We also discussed a letter which Grey proposed to write to Cambon,[26] in continuation of a letter of Lord Lansdowne of May 25 1905. We are to tell Cambon that in certain eventualities when the peace of Europe is threatened or disturbed, we are to consult together, and if we agree to action, to take into consideration the plans of the General Staff. Vague words which however satisfy Cambon.

After our defeat on Monday the 11th,[27] those of the Cabinet who had been in the division held a meeting in the P.M.'s room. Harcourt, Isaacs, Lloyd George, Wood, myself and Birrell. Churchill came in later. The P.M. took the matter with more concern than most of us, and it awoke him from his lethargic optimism most completely and satisfactorily. No one thought of resigning, only of the delay in time and confusion. Though no one blamed Illingworth, who actually prevented people from continuing the discussion as he believed he had a majority in the House, we were angry at so unnecessary a defeat on a point which on the previous Friday we had carried by 120. While we were talking Grey came in laughing, threw himself down on the sofa at full length, and said 'Well, is it relief?' and then hardly another word. I went to try and find the Speaker for the P.M. while Samuel hunted for Ilbert[28] and precedents.

There was a Cabinet Committee that night till 12 midnight and next day; Lloyd George would have liked to have accepted the blow, gone on with Franchise alone, with subsequent redistribution and dissolution. I agreed, but no one else. The P.M. was for undisguised reversal, which was adopted, cost a great row in the House, a fortnight of time, and final abandonment. I was not present during the row, as I was speaking at the Anchor Dinner.

27 November

We had the usual display of bad manners and bad temper from Churchill. He proposed a fortnight ago an increase of £500,000 for Navy pay. The Estimates Committee cut this down to £300,000.[29] At this he stormed, sulked, interrupted. Like an ill-bred cub. The P.M. treated him admirably and finally reduced him to silence.

We had another curious incident. The Chancellor of the Exchequer said he had been approached by Sheffield University College for a building grant of £9,000. He had been warned by Treasury that if this was granted every other University would demand similar grants, and that it would mean eventually a very large sum. He however pressed the Cabinet to assent to payment, nominally on the ground that Cardiff had received formerly such a grant, really to enable him to grant like sums to the other Welsh Colleges. The Cabinet, save Haldane, were dead against him, it was strange to hear a Chancellor of the Exchequer urging expenditure and resisted by his colleagues. He seems to have no idea that he is the guardian of the public purse.

When we were talking the other day after our defeat, I said that during the debate we were likely to hear grumbling from some of our friends as to the length of sessions; Ll.G. rather pooh poohed the idea of anyone being tired of a session. When someone said 'Well, look in today's *Daily News*', Ll.G. replied 'I never read the *Daily News* now,' at which the whole Cabinet laughed. Then someone spoke of Massingham's[30] article in the *Nation*, and the P.M, looking at Ll.G. said that he thought it a pity that those who gave M. his information did not see that he took care to use the information accurately. Ll.G. said that he had had Massingham to lunch and spoken to him about it, but that he couldn't lock him up in a room till he promised to sin no more. Thereupon Grey said 'Well if the Cabinet will authorise me to lock myself up with Massingham until he repents, I will take on the job willingly.'

9 December

Shot at Canford, large party, mostly family. Geoffrey and Lady Dorothy Howard,[31] Lady Rodney, Freddie Guest—his wife. Oscar and Henry Guest, Mr. and Mrs. Illingworth, Winston and Mrs. Churchill, a Mr. Murphy and Mr. Lewis, Ld. Ashley St. Ledgers—and an American lady. All pleasant enough. I should have added Eustace and Mrs. Fiennes.[32] Very political news. We shall have some serious difficulties over the Disendowment Clause of the Welsh Bill. About 40 of our friends have memorialised the P.M. to say they will not support anything in the shape of disendowment beyond tithe. I agree with them, and am certain that Wales will give way if pressed. She will never have another chance of getting her Bill, for the Irish would never forgive Ll.G. if he resigned, and would not help another Bill of this character.

I am not quite sure that I like the Govt.'s too hasty acceptance of the Canadian Govt.'s offer of £7 millions. The Canadian Liberals haven't acquiesced in methods, and if they withdraw the ships for a Canadian Navy, we may be saddled with Canadian interference in foreign affairs, without the compensation of getting some Canadian money in return for protecting their commerce, educating their children, and training their workmen, which we now do to a most unprofitable extent.

25 December
The position of a Balkan monarch is not enviable. The King of Montenegro will certainly lose his throne if Scutari is not captured on the renewal of the war, or if it is not surrendered to Montenegro on the acceptance of peace. His uncertainty of tenure has no doubt been increased by the return of the Montenegrins from America, where Kings are not venerated.

The King of Bulgaria was forced into war, and dare not return to his capital till peace is concluded on terms satisfactory to Bulgaria. The loss of Salonika by either Greece or Bulgaria will not be pleasant for the King of either country.

31 December
We had a meeting of the H. of C. members of the Cabinet to discuss Carson's amendment to exclude Ulster from the Irish Bill. The P.M. largely on the strength of *The Times* article was convinced that it was merely a wrecking or embarrassing amendment. He had looked up Grey's and Churchill's speeches to see that they had said nothing which would prevent his refusal of the amendment. It was agreed there was nothing, and the matter was nearly settled when I said I thought it was a very important and significant step for Carson to take, and that though he and his co-signatories declared their 'fundamental and unalterable objection' to the Bill, yet they were right in saying the responsibility would be ours if serious distur-bances broke out later in Ulster which could be attributed to our refusal to exclude Ulster; moreover I was certain that we had no means of coercing Ulster, for the troops were not to be relied on, even if we wished to coerce. Then Churchill asked Birrell what

really was the state of Ulster. B. said he had no very good information, but it was impossible to overestimate their real racial, religious and local abhorrence of a Dublin Parliament, that he had received a report of a conversation at dinner at Capt. Craig's house at Craigavon, where Carson, Craig,[33] Lord Londonderry, Sinclair[34] etc. were, and that Carson and Craig were for compromise, Sinclair against. Thereupon Ll. George and Churchill took up the running and advised no banging of the door against Ulster, Ll.G. particularly strongly, and ultimately it was agreed that the P.M. should speak rejecting the actual amendment but hinting that if settlement was in the air, our attitude would be one of meeting them half-way.

V

A Very Disturbed Atmosphere

1913

❋ The first Balkan War resulted in the demoralisation and defeat of
Turkey. Between December 1912 and May 1913, while hostilities con-
tinued, peace negotiations took place in London between Turkey and
Bulgaria, Greece, Montenegro and Serbia. Simultaneously Sir Edward
Grey, at the Ambassadors' Conference, tried to reduce the tensions bet-
ween the Great Powers over the Balkan situation, especially between
Austro-Hungary and Russia. Austro-Hungary sought to establish Al-
bania as an effective barrier to prevent Serbia acquiring an outlet to the
Adriatic and refused to allow Serbia and Montenegro to retain the
Albanian territory they occupied. Russian diplomatic support for Serbia
was followed by her partial mobilisation and counter-mobilisation by
Austro-Hungary. But Russia was forced to concede the inclusion of
Scutari within Albania although she refused to compromise on the
claims of Serbia to territory on the Albanian eastern frontier. Meanwhile, the Montenegrins, who were still besieging Scutari, refused to
withdraw despite threats of a joint naval demonstration against them
by the Great Powers.

Following the successful Second Readings of private members' Conciliation Bills in 1910 and 1911, the Government had had to promise
facilities for further stages of such legislation in 1912. Instead of this, in
November 1911 Asquith had announced the intention of introducing a
Franchise and Registration Bill which would grant manhood suffrage,
remove plural voting, and be so drafted as to allow amendment to
include the enfranchisement of women on the same terms as men. The
Bill had been introduced and passed its Second Reading in July 1912.
Its introduction had encouraged the pro-suffrage Ministers, such as
Grey, who put down the necessary amendment that the word 'male' in
the Bill should be omitted; delighted Lloyd George and others who had
feared the consequences of a 'Tory' Conciliation franchise; and infuriated the militant suffragettes who wanted their 'own' bill and accused Asquith of trickery in proposing so wide a female franchise that

128

it would be defeated. The Committee Stage to discuss the women's suffrage amendments was to begin on 24 January. On 22 January the Cabinet agreed that there should be no question of resignation if Ministers disagreed on the issue. On the next day, Bonar Law, the Unionist leader, asked for a ruling from the Speaker on whether the amendments were in order. The Speaker ruled that the amendment did so substantially alter the purpose of the Bill as to require another Bill to be introduced. This was an unexpected and undeserved blow to the Government. On 27 January the Cabinet decided it could not break faith with the suffragists by proceeding with the unamended Bill and it was withdrawn. There had been no Government 'plot' to defeat women's suffrage, but it is true that Asquith, the really great obstacle to women's suffrage, greeted the Speaker's ruling with no marked sense of loss.

8 January

At Cabinet today we talked of the Aegean Islands, which Russia had proposed should go to Greece on condition there should be no fortifications thereon, and no cession of sovereignty subsequently. This view we agreed to. I am glad that so far there has been no question of ceding Cyprus. We then passed to Rhodes which Italy claims, but only perfunctorily, as we could not assent to her establishment there, as it would close the Adriatic, and command the trade routes from the Black Sea and Alexandria.

We also declined to make a naval demonstration at Constantinople but only to send ships to Besika Bay. It is clear we couldn't bombard Constantinople to prevent them continuing the war, and if the Turks yielded to the force of the Allies without further war, they would pretend they had yielded to the naval demonstration, and every Mahommedan subject we possess would be aggrieved.

Gen Yostof, Chief of the Bulgarian staff, told Seely that they could not, and probably would not attempt to force the Tchataldja lines, but would concentrate on Adrianople.

The P.M. then said a few words in recognition of Grey's skilful handling of the Ambassadorial Conference, and we all 'hear, heared!'

Afterwards on the Franchise Bill, Grey, Churchill, Samuel, Buxton and myself took the view that with the reduction of the qualifying period[1] should go an increase of the age to 25 or 23. Asquith turned to me for my reasons which I gave as being that 23 was the age at which the workman married and settled down, more or less permanently. As the P.M. rather took the line that we could not now alter the Bill Churchill became very excited, declared it was almost tyrannous that a large minority should be coerced by a very small majority, and asked for the absence of Govt. Whips when the question came on. As Asquith pointed out such a course had not been successful re the women's suffrage, and would put an end to Cabinet Govt.

10 January

We were talking of Mason's[2] last novel, *The Turnstile*, at dinner and saying how little knowledge of H. of C. Mason showed in spite of his five years therein. Birrell gave us another example in Mr. Warmington, Q.C.[3] who surrendered his seat in Monmouthshire to Sir W. Harcourt, and a month or so afterwards remarked to Birrell that it was very strange that he had not received a line of thanks from Rosebery, Morley, or Fowler for his disinterestedness.

I had a luncheon party at H. of C. to meet M. Venizelos the Greek Premier. John Morley, Lady Lovelace,[4] John Seely, Miss Farquhar, Sydney and Mrs. Buxton, and Mrs. McKenna.

On Monday I gave a little dinner for M. Vesnitch and his wife he being the Serbian Minister in Paris.

23 January

We had a very disturbed atmosphere at Cabinet yesterday. Churchill came up from Windsor and reported that M. Cambon had said to him that the state of Europe was 'infiniment plus grave' than at any time since 1875. Much more so than at the time of Agadir when France and Germany could at any moment arrange the whole dispute.

Then Churchill began to talk about Woman's Suffrage and said that the Cabinet ought not to be bound to go with the Parl. Bill, if suffrage was put in. Grey *burst* in that much had been whispered in the lobby as to the possible embarrassment and resignation of the P.M. if suffrage was carried but unless there was complete acceptance of the principle that the Cabinet would abide by the free decision of the House, there would be other resignations. His tone and look were those of a man driven into a corner and ready to use any weapon however lethal. Ll.G. told me later that once before he had

seen him explode, with Loreburn, and Derek Keppel[5] who was at
school with him said he was now and then quite dangerous. Ll.G.
and the P.M. each from his own standpoint agreed that acceptance
of the House's verdict was binding, and for the moment the blaze
died down.

24 January

We had a Cabinet this afternoon to discuss the position of the
Franchise Bill. Ed. Grey and Ll. George wanted to drop the Bill
because they said the fate of the amendments was prejudiced by the
fear that they would destroy the Bill, under the Speaker's ruling if
carried. Harcourt claimed that in that case anti-suffragists must be
free to tell Liberals that the Suffrage amendments had killed their
chance of an extended suffrage for men. Grey then claimed that
the Cabinet pledge held good for next year. I said that the pledge
was intolerable and very detrimental to the Govt. and that to drop
the Bill would do irreparable harm to the Govt. Asquith very em-
phatically said that he considered that he had done his best to give
the suffragists a fair opportunity and that he held absolutely absolved
from his pledge after this year. We then after 2 hours' discussion
resolved that the Speaker should be asked what he intended to rule
if the amendments were passed, and frame our discussion on Monday upon that.

27 January

Went to Windsor for the usual 2 nights. We were met by a *carriage*,
pair of horses and postilion at Windsor—and by the Master of the
Household on arrival at the Castle. Our rooms were in the Edward
III tower. The party consisted of the D. of Argyll, and Princess
Louise, D. of Northumberland, Archbishop of Canterbury[6] and
Mrs. Davidson, J. A. and Mrs. Pease, the Italian Ambassador
Marchese Imperiali & his wife and Lord Esher.[7] We had a footman
and a 'page' told off to look after us. Dinner was at 8.30 and both
brief and excellent. Afterwards we talked in groups, those smoking
in one room, the Queen, ladies, and non-smokers in another. About
11 a.m. the Queen went off, and the King sent for me and we talked
for about an hour; he very cheerful and even boisterous. On Sunday
we had a walk round the garden with the Archbishop and Mrs.
Davidson. He made an excellent cicerone having been 9 years Dean

of Windsor and in daily attendance on Queen Victoria. To Chapel in the private chapel at the end of St. George's Hall and then we visited in turn the gems, said to be worth £200,000, the Armoury, and the library where I spent most of the time looking at an illustrated MS of the life of Shah Jehan, of its kind and quality unique. In the afternoon I walked across the park with John Fortescue the librarian criticising the forestry which was very bad. Then had an examination of the original Holbein drawings—dinner at 8.45, afterwards, talk with Queen and King, who gave us a graphic account of the attack in Australia on late Duke of Edinburgh.

On Monday [27 January] Pease and I came up early for Cabinet where we agreed unanimously that we should drop Franchise, take Plural Voting early in March, and give the suffragists full opportunity for a private member's Bill next session.

✻ The suffragette reaction to the failure of the Franchise Bill was violent. Over the next few months hundreds of thousands of pounds' worth of damage was caused by window-smashing, cutting telephone wires, arson and even bombs, to both private and public property. Partly to try to deal with these new excesses, and partly to try to avoid the forced feeding of prisoners bent upon martyrdom through hunger-strike, McKenna, the Home Secretary, asked for powers to re-arrest prisoners released on grounds of ill health. His Prisoners (Temporary Discharge for Ill Health) Bill was to become known as the 'Cat and Mouse Act'.

17 February
At Cabinet on Tuesday [11 February] Pease told us that one of the students had come to him and confessed a suffragist plot to destroy all the china and pictures in S. Kensington Museum. As a preliminary the suffragists had induced some of the [? students] to point out to them the most valuable cases and pictures. Grey and Morley said that at the Museum they had been warned to take precautions.

We then settled the King's Speech, and passed to Scotch temperance and the question of disinterested management. Lloyd George, Haldane, and Isaacs were strongly for giving facilities; McK., Wood, Burns and the P.M. were as firmly against. The last-named saying it was a fad of doctors, professors, etc.

It was curious to see how when we all dispersed Ll.G. stayed several minutes at the table, evidently deep in thought. I am sure he wanted to bring on the land question, and yet didn't want to incur a rebuff from the P.M. or the Cabinet.

6 March

Cabinet this morning. The King is much exercised as to what he ought to wear on his head at the opening of Parl. His father started the F.M.'s cocked hat, but he wishes now to revert to the Crown of the Sovereign. As we none of us cared what he wears, we agreed to the Crown.

We had some discussion over the suffragettes. The public think that they are defying the law and the Govt. with absolute impunity, but McKenna was able to make out a good case to the contrary: 51 have been sentenced, of whom 29 have completed their sentence, 15 are still in prison, 7 being forcibly fed and only 7 have had to be released because in the process of forcible feeding, they have shown heart or other trouble which has brought them to the gates of death.

13 March

We discussed today McKenna's Bill for permitting short-sentence prisoners to be released on licences, as penal servitude prisoners now can be. Such a system will prevent suffragists being freed from a long sentence by means of starving themselves for a short time. Pease said there would be great objection to the Bill in H. of C. The P.M. for some undeclared reason didn't like it, criticised its wording, but wouldn't actually say he wouldn't have it. Grey made no objection. Lloyd George supported it, no doubt to get rid of the extremists. McK. told us that Miss James, sister to Forbes Robertson the actor, a paralytic, and epileptic, had starved since the previous Wednesday, only eating a piece of toast and drinking a cup of tea on the Sunday night. Eventually after a reluctant agreement from Asquith, we agreed unanimously to the Bill.

10 April

I was away, kept in bed by lumbago from the last 2 Cabinets.[8] Yesterday we discussed how we should respond to the German Emperor's move of sending his Ambassador in America to J. P. Morgan's funeral. It would create an awkward precedent if we sent the King's representative to a private citizen's funeral, and would

cause a little heart-burning if the English did not play up as well as
the Germans. Eventually Bryce was told to be present unofficially.

Then came up the question of purchasing Lord Crawford's[9]
collection of Revolutionary and Napoleonic pamphlets, unrivalled in
completeness. £100,000 to £150,000 is asked for them, and this
Ll.G. was ready to give. The P.M. however was loth to pay any such
price or to propose the purchase to the H. of C. and though I and
one or two others supported Ll.G. the proposal was shelved by a
suggestion that Winston Churchill should approach Sir R. Caird[10]
to thus pay for his baronetcy.

Then we came to National Compulsory Service. Seely asked
what he was to say. Churchill declared himself for compulsory
territorial training, so did Ll.G. and Haldane. McK., Runciman and
I were unreservedly against it, as was Harcourt also. Eventually the
P.M. after we had all talked at once for quarter of an hour said dryly
that Seely would be able to make an excellent speech in accordance
with all our views.

16 April

At today's Cabinet the P.M. told us that for the first time in his
experience a man, viz. Dr. David of Rugby, had refused a Bishopric,[11]
and that he had been searching 3 weeks for a suitable Broad Church-
man.

We then passed to discussing the Budget. The Chancellor of the
Exchequer pretended to be quite surprised that we should expect
to hear the details on Wednesday of the Budget he was to produce
on Tuesday, and that it was much more important to discuss with
Harcourt a detail of £300,000 than to unfold a statement covering
£195 millions of income and expenditure. This the P.M. insisted on,
and we had the whole tale which consisted of reduction of balances,
and the production of death duties kept back.

Haldane told us that Ld. Halsbury was very anxious that the
H. of C. should give Sir S. Samuel[12] a 'bill of indemnity' against the
penalties, amounting to £45,000, incurred in voting after his seat
had properly become vacant, and which penalties would be legally
payable to a man now actually in prison.

✳ On 23 April Scutari fell to the Montenegrins, thereby raising tension
   in the Balkans again.

25 April

At Cabinet yesterday discussed fall of Scutari. Austria asked for European mandate to enable her jointly with Italy to turn Montenegro out, Haldane and Ll.G. spoke strongly for sending an international force to give colour to Austria and Italy's action and to tell France, who in the P.M.'s phrase was hiding behind our petticoats, and Russia that the European powers could not be derided by Montenegro, that if the *Entente* would not act then Austria and Italy must be given a free hand so far as Scutari was concerned. Churchill was vehemently, as always, opposed to the landing of even a single marine. We agreed to give Austria and Italy opportunity to deal with Scutari.

Churchill told us that the dockyard men had refused to work overtime, and were on the verge of a general strike.

26 April

The fall of Scutari has upset a good many calculations. The Serbians who have been offering help to Montenegro when they knew it was unacceptable in order to tell the Serbs' world that they were the champions of Serbdom, and who withdrew that help, as they said, only under the pressure of Europe and when they were assured that the Montenegrin dynasty would suffer grievously from its inability to take Scutari, have been completely disconcerted by its capture by Montenegro single-handed, after the public and ostentatious withdrawal by Serbia.

M. Tosheff, Bulgarian Minister in Belgrade, has expressed himself to Sir R. Paget as astonished at the Serbian capacity for falsehood and that they were a people without conscience who murdered not only Albanians but Bulgarians! He spoke of the Bulgar-Serbian alliance with profound contempt as an ephemeral affair, and that when the Serbians having refused payment for the *guns*, not men, lent for the siege of Adrianople, had asked for territorial compensation—the Bulgarian Govt. had rejected it *sans phrase*.

Turkey is going through a purely revolutionary crisis. The Sultan is a prisoner in his rooms, cut off even from his family. The heir apparent is almost imbecile; the next heir, Vahiheddin is subject to strict espionage; the ostensible Cabinet is run by an Occult Committee who though hybrid Jews and Caucasians, and Cretan Mahommedans, are arbiters of an Asiatic and Ottoman Empire.

22 May

Nina, Sir Matthew Nathan and I went to Holland to see flowers, architecture and pictures. The latter were delightful, the flowers were rather over, and the architecture disappointing until one remembered that the Spaniards, French and Dutch themselves destroyed up till 1600 nearly every building in the country—and the French after 1800 defaced what little was then untouched. We stayed a night at Dortrecht, another at Amsterdam, and a week at Leyden.

Nathan went on to Berlin, Nina returned to London, and I went to Hamburg, staying with Consul-General Hearn. A beautiful city, well laid out with spacious gardens, streets well lined with trees, often in double avenues, and a general air of prosperity arised from its being both a shipbuilding and trading centre. The workpeople are however much given to senseless acts of sabotage of which the recent damage to the *Imperator* is an example.[13]

✳ Since the previous autumn the 'Marconi affair' had cast its shadow over the Government. Lloyd George's career nearly foundered in a welter of accusations of contractual malpractice and ministerial corruption. Herbert Samuel, the Postmaster-General, was alleged to have awarded an unduly favourable government contract for the construction of wireless stations to the Marconi Company, whose managing director was the brother of Rufus Isaacs, the Attorney-General. Three prominent Liberals, Lloyd George, Isaacs, and Murray of Elibank, the former Chief Whip, were accused of speculation in Marconi shares, using their knowledge of this contract. In October 1912 a Select Committee had been set up to inquire into these allegations. Amidst more rumours of peculation, in January Lloyd George and Isaacs admitted that in April 1912 they had purchased shares in the American Marconi Company. In October they had denied buying shares 'in *this* company', i.e., the English Marconi Company, but now they offered their resignations to Asquith. They were refused, the Prime Minister regarding his Ministers as foolish but not corrupt. The Liberal Party closed ranks against the campaign of rumour and innuendo intensified by blatant antisemitism. Isaacs and Samuel were irresistible targets. So too was the Liberal M.P. for Whitechapel, Sir Stuart Montagu Samuel, about whose involvement in government dealings in Indian silver questions were asked in Parliament in November 1912. Under the 1782 Contractors' Act no M.P. was allowed to sit or vote while holding a

government contract. Messrs. Samuel Montagu & Co. had purchased
large amounts of silver on behalf of the Government. It was argued that
under the Statute Sir Stuart was liable to a penalty of £500 for every
occasion on which he had voted, a total amounting to some £46,000!
The Judicial Committee of the Privy Council ruled that he had to vacate
his seat. After he had fought a successful by-election in Whitechapel
and been re-elected, Asquith announced that the Government would
introduce an Indemnity Bill to exempt him from these penalties. There
were precedents for such a Bill, but in the heightened 'Marconi' atmosphere Opposition pressure forced the Government to withdraw. Fortunately for Samuel, two actions by 'common informers' to recover the
penalties had already failed. It was in this atmosphere of rancour that
the Select Committee, bitterly divided on party lines, produced a majority report in June which cleared the peccant Ministers. To the Opposition it was a 'whitewash': to Liberals it was an embarrassment.

29 May
Yesterday the India Office sent Rufus Isaacs a paper which they had
had since Dec. 4 1912 showing that Franklin, partner in Samuel
Bros., the silver merchants, had acted as buyer as well as broker,
written on the same day that Franklin gave evidence before the
Select Committee without disclosing the fact. The F.O. permitted
the Cabinet to embark on the Samuel Indemnity Bill without saying
a word on subject and now Samuel's will have to be told that they
must ask for the Bill to be dropped.

6 June
Borden has sent Churchill a telegram, which he read at Cabinet
[4 June] asking us to build the 3 ships which the Canadian Senate
will not give him, and saying that we might do so on the condition
that when he gets his way in Canada he will buy them back from us.
W.S.C. was much inclined to get us to adopt this course, but we were
unanimously against it as a direct interference with Canadian politics
on behalf of one of the contending parties. Borden also telegraphed
that he would get his way in the Senate in 3 years, which as the
Senate is appointed for life is a curious anticipation of the probability
of life of its members.

Churchill advanced fresh claims for naval expenditure to the tune
of £600,000. Pease has also issued a memo showing how we cannot

get off for less than an increase of £1½ millions. Seely wants £200,000 for aviation. Ll.G., who has a doubtful balance of £180,000 estimated, practically made no attempt to resist any of these claims. He expressed himself as certain to be defeated next year if he continued to impose the sugar and tea taxes, but offered no alternative taxation or reduction or even maintenance of expenditure. If the P.M. were not afraid of tackling Ll.G. or of doing the work in H. of C. which Ll.G. now does for him, he would make a drastic change in his Offices.

13 June

Ll.G. last night had a council of war. McKenna, Walter Runciman and Alfred Spender. They discussed his attitude towards the Marconi report which they had been assured would exculpate *him*. Ll.G. gave them to understand that having had the resignation which he tendered to Asquith in January refused, he had no intention of resigning again. Starting from that basis his three councillors, under McKenna's inspiration, advised him to say that he saw nothing wrong about his Marconi transactions, he did now see that they were open to misrepresentation, and if he had realised that it *was* possible to misrepresent them, he would certainly not have engaged in them. Apart from this there was to be no 'white sheet'. McK. put it to me that Ll.G. being the greatest platform asset the Liberal party possessed, we could not allow him to say anything that would damage *that* reputation by quotation of words, torn from their context, which would be twisted into an admission of guilt. That so far as his value as a public statesman with serious people was concerned that was gone for ever. His value as a demagogue was retrievable, and it was the business of the party to pull that out of the mire.

I disagree entirely with this reasoning. It may be true as Lord Northcliffe says that Marconis don't sell an extra copy of the *Daily Mail*, but first I am certain that the bulk of the Liberal Nonconformists are shocked at his levity and his speculating at all, and will not easily be won back to allegiance. Secondly the Tory newspapers will not allow this to be forgotten. It is unnecessary to penalise a man for ever for a single mistake, but if Ll.G. had the courage to now resign, I believe he would come back in less than a year universally admitted to be purged of 'error', of which alone he is charged.

22 June

We had a Cabinet today on Marconi. The P.M. apropos of Cave's motion said he thought that Ll.G. and R. Isaacs ought to indicate the line they intended to take.

Ll.G. then said he intended to regret that he was silent in the House as to American Marconis, but he expected to be a very early witness before the Committee and therefore to make his statement to them at a very early date and he proposed to throw a few stones at their discursiveness. Next he would declare that it was far more innocent to invest in Marconis, which being an American Co. could have no contracts with the British Govt. than in a British Railway Company which did have some, and the value of whose shares and property could be influenced by Ministerial legislation; lastly he would justify the use of term investment, because he had never desired to sell any Marconis until his broker had over persuaded him, and because he still held the major part of the shares.

Rufus Isaacs said he would admit being the originator of the whole action, and as to the indiscretion, but would repudiate vehemently any want of frankness.

Burns said that it was much better to admit to an error of judgement in the original purchase, regret any apparent reticence, and ask the House to believe it was a single mistake never to be repeated. This view would be generally and generously accepted—and the whole question would fall to the ground.

Asquith curiously said that while at the Exchequer it had never occurred to him that he was not free to buy Govt. or any other stocks, although he never had even a single transaction as a matter of fact; but he went on to add that when Mr. G. appointed him Home Secretary the first thing he did was to sell his B.S.A. shares.

The debate on Marconi was very unreal. Everybody on Conservative side knew that they had expected and hoped to prove improper, as apart from indiscreet, dealing on the part of Ll.G. and Isaacs. They had never absolutely formulated such a charge. They were not therefore obliged to offer an apology, and didn't wish to state exculpation. We did not think Ll.G.'s and Isaacs' explanation satisfactory and considered their dealings to have been certainly indiscreet and very nearly improper, and their 'regret' hardly adequate. At the same time we were unwilling to record formal censure. Balfour's speech to read was excellent, but marred in deliverance by hesitation and repetition. Asquith perhaps not so good subsequently, but immensely effective at the time. Grey was not on form, and B. Law a repulsive party hack.

Lord Loreburn with whom I had a long talk blamed, and not unfairly, the P.M. for not seeing from the first how serious the matter was; he said every kind of evil rumour *had* been in circulation about Marconi, and *was* being said as to oil.[14] Quite untruly, I am certain.

24 June

Very long Cabinet yesterday. We were favoured by addresses from Churchill on Education, Finance, Navy, Aviation and Electioneering and finally there was a general revolt summed up by the P.M. remarking that his views were pure 'cynicism defended by sophistry'. We then commented on the increasing cost of administration but the only result of our talk was that before the Cabinet was over we agreed to spend £150,000 on Education, £490,000 on Naval and Military Aviation, and £210,000 on Uganda!

Ll.G. said that actuarial calculations recently made revealed the fact that there was not a single one of the Friendly Societies which was solvent, i.e. which could continue paying its present benefits for 5 years.

26 June

A long cabinet at H. of C. It was proposed by the King to give Poincaré[15] the G.C.V.O., a thing which the P.M. truly said 'was hawked about all the stations and back gardens of Europe', and after some playful remarks of J. Morley as to the distinction conferred there the P.M. said he would suggest the Order of Merit which 'none of us are likely to attain', and which would put the French President on a level with the German Emperor.

Afterwards I had some talk with the P.M. who suggested my taking charge of the administration of the Insurance Act, the Development Commission and Road Board, and I went to the Treasury to see whether it would require an Act or could be done by administrative order. It will not please Ll.G.

9 July

Considerable talk over the Russian demand on Turkey for the

acceptance of scheme of 'reforms' in Armenia which would practically make it an autonomous province which could when the time was ripe be swallowed at leisure by Russia. Grey was inclined to yield to all the Russian demands on the ground that the regeneration of Turkey is impossible, and that though it was inexpedient now to partition her, yet the sooner in decency it was done, the better for everyone. The P.M. agreed and took Crewe rather sharply to task for saying that Mahommedan India would be profoundly moved and dangerously so by the dismemberment of the Caliphate. They had never resented the severance of Tunis, Tripoli, or Egypt, why should they revolt over the partitionment of Asia Minor? The Turk was impossible anywhere as a dominant race and should go. Crewe made little reply, but it should have been that it would be very unwise to force the Indian Mahommedan to regard Kabul as the centre of Mahommedan orthodox sovereignty, as it would be if the Turkish regime ended. The greater part of the Cabinet took the same line, save Churchill, Seely and myself. I remarked that if under the German Portuguese arrangement, Germany could be astride our W. African trade at San Thomé, and under an Asian Minor partition Germany, with Anatolia, and France, with Syria, could be astride our Black Sea, Indian and Mediterranean trade, we should have to face responsibilities which would be far greater than would fall to our share by resisting Russian ambitions. Winston was not so verbose or vigorous as usual, but spoke in same sense.

15 July

Came to Knowsley for attendance on the King during his visits to Liverpool and Manchester. The house is red brick faced with white stone. The centre part was rebuilt by the present earl's uncle, but pulled down and rebuilt again by the present man about 2 years ago and is now in keeping with the general structure. The S. wing is of stone and looks like Early Tudor work inside. The park lies to the east of the house, and contains a good sheet of water. The place is well kept up, the pictures have been rearranged, and are in good order. But the whole place is too near Liverpool, and must sooner or later be engulfed. We are to be 53 to dinner, and about 40 people in the house. These were Lord and Lady Derby, Lady Victoria Stanley, Arthur Stanley, George Stanley and his wife, R. Molyneux, R. and Lady Moyra Cavendish, Ld. and Lady Gosford, Ld. and Lady

Inverclyde, Bonar Law, Ld. Revelstoke, Lady Ampthill, Mr. Hansell, Col. Cook and officers of 1st Life Guards.

We left the house at 11 a.m. 11.7.13 drove through streets *really* lined with sightseers, eager and interested and warm-hearted, to the Town Hall, where the crowd was very dense. There were the usual street decorations, garlands hung from pole to pole, flags, wreaths, Venetian masts, and with northern caution, made of waterproof paper. It seems that Lord Derby has personally worked out all the details himself of the routes to be traversed, the time to be taken, and has rehearsed the presentations to be made of various Mayors, Mayoresses and Councillors to the King and Queen. The police were spread over a great distance of ground but there were only single men every 30 yards in the town and as the crowd was exceedingly patient and orderly they were quite sufficient. I saw no pushing—not a single drunken man, and all the people were well dressed and tidy, the men shaved, and all had *good* boots and stockings. The people stood from about 10.30 until 5 p.m. when we left the *Mauretania*.

On Sat. 12th trained to Ashton near Manchester, and motored by Bolton, Middleton and Heyworth to Bury. Long lines of houses the whole way, but seemingly only one house thick on either side and in front of each house the whole family had turned out. Most of them were rather more than friendly, the women enthusiastic and all respectful. In fact it looked as if really the whole population had turned out. We visited Platt's works at Oldham, and lunched at the Estate Offices at Bury which practically belongs to Ld. Derby.

My duty is confined to receiving the presentations made to the King, giving the answers and standing at his right hand during all the functions, and writing to the Lord Mayors of Manchester and Liverpool a letter upon the success of the visit.

On Sunday 13.7.13 the King inspected 7,000 territorials in Liverpool, came back in time for lunch and I wrote letters. John Morley joined the party yesterday. Ld. Stamfordham told us the King was much perturbed at the thought of having to sign the Home Rule Bill, but would do so if necessary. His attitude has been exactly reproduced socially by the party in the House, which is one of perfect civility, but of unfriendliness, with the exceptions of Lady Beatrix Stanley and Lady Ampthill.

I had a walk round the greater part of the park which is 14 miles round, not very interesting, but some good recent plantings. I got close to a party of stags 2 of which had 14 points—so tame that while we were looking at them they walked into a pool to cool.

On Monday we trained to Manchester, where the official preparations were not much, but the people were present in even greater numbers than elsewhere. The various local notables were presented, and the City gave the King two gold plates which had belonged to the Duke of Cambridge with which the Queen was delighted. Then after lunch we drove to Salford, where practically the whole population was visible along the line of the route.

On Sunday night we were 200 people sleeping at Knowsley including servants. I slept with my friend Bishop Rawstorne at Croston. He said that he had lately married 2 parishioners. When the woman reached the 'love, honour, and obey', she mumbled the words indistinctly. Rawstorne insisted, and eventually she pronounced the 'obey' distinctly. As they were going into the vestry he heard the man say 'Eh lass I told thee parson would maak thee say obey', to which she retorted 'Aye he did, but ar'll not black thee boots.'

We were discussing the utility of international congresses, which were really inaugurated to give permanent officials an opportunity of visiting other countries at the expense of their own. And I tried to summarise by saying 'They talked of sciences, but thought of sauces.'

16 July

At Cabinet today we had some discussion about the employment of Imperial troops by the Gov.-General. Haldane and Harcourt tried to argue that they were subject only to the Secretary of State at home, while Crewe and the P.M. held that whatever might be the technical position, everyone would consider the Gov.-General the person to sanction or refuse their use.

Then Birrell put forward his Irish Land Purchase Act with that wonderful mixture of sentiment, irony, sarcasm, and cynicism which makes his expression of opinion different from all other men's. McKenna worked out the details of the half-cash half-stock payment which would enable the selling owner to get a stock at a better price, or the cash when the stock was lower.

Then we talked about the Navy. The German Emperor had been

telling Capt. Watson, our naval attaché, that he wanted to hear no mention of 'a naval holiday' and that any reference to it would be taken very much amiss. At the same time Bethman Hollweg had in the Reichstag invited us to explain what we meant. The Emperor thinks that we had tricked him over the Canadian ships, and wanted to be nasty. Haldane, as usual wanted us to accept the German point of view, forgetting that we must state and maintain our own case just as the Germans took care always to state theirs.

20 July

The King a few days ago wrote through Ld. Stamfordham, and as I gather at his instigation and Ld. Derby's, to say that he wished his health to be drunk in Lancashire as the 'Duke of Lancashire'. I at once had a memorandum from Mr. McCall K.C., the Attorney of the Duchy, pointing out that it was extremely doubtful whether the King was Duke of Lancaster. I found also that Ld. James of Hereford had left a memo in the office dealing with the same point, showing that the King enjoyed the revenues of the Duchy by hereditary right and ordinance, but that the *last* Duke was Henry VI, and as the present royal line is descended from Edward of York, and not from John of Gaunt, they cannot claim a title which came through the latter alone. No English King has ever claimed or used the title, though all have enjoyed the revenues. Accordingly I felt bound to write to the King pointing this out to him, and, as I also reminded him, Queen Victoria when travelling abroad incognito was careful to call herself '*Countess* of Lancaster'.

I got a civil letter back to say that all this was a surprise to the K. which he would have to consider. That it was very disagreeable was evident, for when I met him yesterday, I got a *very* cold bow indeed.

✳ Of far greater import was the King's position regarding the Irish problem. By the summer the Home Rule Bill had passed the Commons twice and been rejected by the Lords twice. Under the Parliament Act it would become law automatically when passed a third time by the Commons, provided the King gave the Royal Assent. In Ulster, arms running, military drilling, the threats of army officers to resign their commissions, and the declared intent of the Unionists to establish a Provisional Government rather than submit to Home Rule presaged civil war. George V became more and more uneasy about his position, in which, as he complained to Asquith, 'Whatever I do I shall offend half the population.' He was under pressure from many Unionists to insist on a dissolution and require Asquith to resign, enabling a Unionist Government under Bonar Law to go to the country on the issue of Home Rule versus the liberties of Protestant Ulster. In August, therefore, the King suggested a conference between the party leaders to seek a compromise solution. In September Lord Loreburn, no longer Lord Chancellor, published a letter in *The Times* advocating separate treatment for Ulster. In October, after a visit to the King at Balmoral, Asquith agreed to open negotiations with Bonar Law, to see if there might be the basis for a settlement. At the same time talks with the Irish Nationalists tried to establish how far they were prepared to compromise on Ulster.

8 August

At Cabinet discussed the position of the King *vis-à-vis* to Home Rule. Churchill had 'heard rumours that he intended some unconstitutional action'. The P.M. said that in all his dealings with him he had seen 'no sign' of any such intention. Everyone lamented the loss of Knollys, and the influence of Stamfordham whose wings the P.M. earnestly desired should be clipped.

Then Churchill burst out about the Channel Tunnel which he said was the wish of the Board of Admiralty and of every well-informed person. Thereon the P.M. asked him to name one adding that as far as he knew or remembered no one of eminence had ever advocated it, and quoted as if he attached the greatest weight to it, the opinion of Campbell-Bannerman which was very antagonistic.

11 August

We spent the weekend at Nuneham, 20 people in the house—Francis McLaren,[16] R. and Mrs. Harcourt, Ld. and Lady Abingdon, H. Sturgess, M. Thierry of the French Embassy etc.

Today we had John and Mrs. Ponsonby[17], Lady Lovelace and Sir S. Edgerly to stay at The Ridge. Edmond Fitzmaurice came over but was very uncommunicative.

19 August

Cabinet on 13th. The reverse in Somaliland was discussed. Churchill gave us the usual lecture on the country, and ended up by urging the withdrawal of all forces, and the substitution of an airship patrol, 'which would terrify the Arabs beyond conception', as if they should not be habituated to it after the second appearance. Then we discussed Royal Commission on Venereal Disease. It was apparently thought necessary to put on some divines, one Church of England, and one Nonconformist. In debating one name as Chairman of this far too large and heterogenous assembly, the P.M. remarked that he was reminded of Parnell's refusal to have Healy as one of his counsel because 'he had left too much wool on the hedge.'

Then Haldane came forward with a proposal to start and endow a British University at Hangkow, which the P.M. denounced as a monstrous proposition; and an impudent Cecilian proposal, for it emanated from the Studd[18] and Cecil group of missionaries.

Ll.G. produced a letter from Bryan, the U.S. Secretary of State asking him to persuade the Govt. to be officially represented at the Panama exposition. Grey declared against it on the ground that the Yankees were always asking and never conceding. Buxton put the cost at £250,000 and we were unanimously against sending anything.

The P.M. then said that he hoped nothing would be said during the holidays about a land campaign. We should meet in October for Cabinets, and till then we ought, if we spoke, to find other topics of interest. Ll.G. said that he thought he could hardly refrain from reviewing the land problem early in October and to this the P.M. assented, provided no policy was enunciated. For this latter purpose a Cabinet would be held on October 14, before which time papers should be circulated.

17 October

We have had 3 very long Cabinets. They were friendly, harmonious, unanimous, and as the P.M. afterwards remarked, the most business-like proceedings he had ever seen at Cabinet.

We opened with Ireland, the P.M. was very emphatic that no concession was due to Ulster threats, and none should be given. He said he had seen the King who was at first much inclined to press for negotiation and hinted at royal intervention. He had then read to H.M. a memorandum in which he drew attention to the stability and regard for the throne being based almost solely on its abstention from political quarrels, and to the unfortunate results for English monarchs when they broke this rule. As H.H.A. said 'these rudimentary truths in plain language' had a marked effect, and at the end of his visit, the King used very different language. Loulou Harcourt had also had a long interview during his wait, in the course of which the King had said he would never go to Dublin to open a Home Rule parliament, and that if he signed the Home Rule Bill he would be hissed in the streets of Belfast. To this L.H. replied that if he didn't sign the Bill he would be hissed in the streets of London. (L.H. showed me a few days later at Nuneham a memo of this interview which lasted 2 hours.[19]) Birrell then told us that Loreburn's letter had had an irritating and disquieting effect in Ireland, as everyone thought it originated from the Cabinet: instead of being the output of an always disgruntled ex-colleague who in earlier days had said the Govt. should unhesitatingly shoot out disobedience. He said there were many rifles in Ireland but no ammunition; and that credit was due to Devlin and Carson for restraining their partisans in Belfast. We had considerable discussion, but were all agreed that if the Tories wanted concessions, and would in exchange offer a permanent settlement based on an Irish Parliament and Executive, we would go any lengths to meet them.

We then went to Land. George unfolded his proposals. They were to create a Ministry of Land which should have large powers to deal with the following subjects: A. Registration and transfer of land; B. Valuation; C. Afforestation; D. All purchases of land required for public purposes; E. Settlement of disputes between rural and urban owners and tenants both as to conditions of, and renewals of, leases; F. Consideration of schemes for betterment of properties by state assistance. This would be a charge preferential to family charges, and perhaps even to mortgages; G. Compensation for damage by game whether of the tenants or of adjoining owners; H. Undercultivation of land; J. Hours of labour and wages; K. Notices to quit for capricious reasons; L. Rent and conditions of tenancy in cases of minimum wages being raised, or increase of rent, or a change of agricultural condition.

These matters were to be handed over to a Commission of agricultural experts with full powers of prompt decision and action.

Housing was our next consideration. This was to be dealt with by another central authority which should assist landowners to build provided economic rents were paid for cottages; labourers whose cottages were tied to farms should be entitled to 3 months' notice.

Burns at this point gave us half an hour's lecture, from notes, against the Irish system of doles, and suggested acting through Local Authorities, this advice we rejected as we thought them bodies opposed to and incapable of progress.

These proposals of Ll.G. were all agreed upon. The talk on details was conducted by Crewe, Harcourt, and myself, Runciman coming in on the third day.

The latter who was at Brodick[20] in the beginning of October gave me an account of the P.M.'s strange dislike of business. He was asked especially to talk Ireland and land, and when Ll.G. suggested that land would best be begun, the P.M. said he couldn't speak until Runciman was present. So R. was sent for, and as he entered the room, the P.M. said 'Oh Margot is keeping tea for you upstairs,' and though she knew nothing of her supposed desire for R.'s presence, she kept him, a willing prisoner, till it was too late to discuss anything. Next day they were driven into land discussion, but Ll.G. could wring no assent to any of his schemes till after the Cabinet met. (Hence the length and tedium of the Bedford speech.) Next evening Winston Churchill tried to corner the P.M. for naval estimates, but was put off by being told that the sea passage to Ardrossan in the *Enchantress* was the proper time and place for such things. When however he got on board he locked himself into his cabin and refused to see anyone until they landed!

11 November

Asquith opened the discussion this morning by saying that of the two recent elections, Linlithgow was the most adverse.[21] Ll.G. thereon produced a copy of the *Freeman's Journal* with a verbatim report of Larkin's trial in Dublin, and pressed on us that Larkin had had but scanty justice at the hands of our Attorney-General in Dublin.[22] Birrell repudiated this idea and said that Dublin had been living in a state of terror under Larkin, and that his trial was fair, and his conviction and sentence necessary to restore peace. I said that it was necessary to say that the industrial classes in the U.K. were angry and rightly angry, with the Govt. for prosecuting, convicting, and sentencing Larkin when they ignored the violent and illegal language of Carson; and that we should regain the confidence of our supporters, not by pardoning Larkin, but by dealing with Carson. Crewe, and then Morley, said that Moriarty's conduct reminded them of Irish Law Officers' actions and vindictiveness in Unionist days. Birrell replied that Dublin was made up of tradition, but as he admitted that he had been at Sheringham during the whole of the Dublin riots, it seemed to me he could, had he had the wisdom, have stopped the tradition. Eventually it was agreed that Larkin's sentence should be reduced, the P.M. saying in the tones of absolute contempt, 'The Lord Lieutenant can easily be dealt with.' Pease added that he had been severely heckled by his constituents over Larkin and Carson. Churchill, half-laughing, half-serious, said that if Larkin's language was open to indictment it would be impossible 'to carry on decent political controversy'—McKenna, Runciman and Burns confirmed my views.

The P.M. then said that he had recently proposed to Bonar Law that they two should meet privately for the purposes of talking over Ireland, making it clear that he had brought no proposals with him. Law agreed and they met near London. Law was friendly, ready to come to a compromise if possible, intimated that Carson, alarmed at the excited condition of Ulster, which he could no longer control, and perhaps not direct, would gladly come to a reasonable arrangement. The real difficulty would be a revival of the 'diehards', not in the Lords which he *could* control, if he could not get agreement amongst the leaders, but amongst his young men in the Commons. Asquith made it plain that he could only treat on the understanding that eventual agreements must be based on an Irish Parliament and Executive—Law agreed, but said his minimum was the exclusion of Ulster, and the reservation of legislation relating to it, to the Imperial Parliament, and not even to an Ulster Assembly. He claimed that Antrim, Down, Armagh, Derry, Fermanagh, were beyond question to be held as Ulster, and that Donegal, Tyrone, Cavan and Monaghan should also be so reckoned. Asquith said that as to Donegal, Monaghan and Tyrone the Catholics were in large majorities and must be left out. Cavan might perhaps be kept in to strengthen the Catholic element in Ulster. Law asked that the Post Office should remain British, Asquith agreed. Law then spoke of a general election, Asquith pointed out that if the result was a Liberal victory with a small majority the Tories would be pledged to neutrality or even to help carry through Home Rule. If the Tories came back victorious they would be faced with the rebellion of three-quarters of Ireland. Law undertook that if there was a Home Rule measure by agreement, that it should not be upset by any subsequent Tory victory.

Churchill said that Arthur Balfour told him at Balmoral this autumn that, if an arrangement was come to amongst the leaders of all 3 sides, much as he disliked Home Rule and little as he believed in the capacity of Southern Ireland to rebel, he would not personally stand in the way of a settlement.

18 November

We have had this week 2 gloomy Cabinets, the first I have seen. The P.M. began by saying that Cabinet Govt. was impossible if *The Times* was to be able to give a shorthand report of all our proceedings and proposals as it had done yesterday. Morley said that with the P.M.'s assent he had seen Buckle[23] late of *The Times* but had said nothing as to Ireland, and in his conversations as with Robinson[24] on the previous weekend, he had talked very general politics. Crewe and Buxton who had also been with J.M. at Lord Rothschild's gave similar assurances. Ll.G. was most vehement in his *un*spoken denunciation of this indiscretion, which he never is when he is guilty, and there is little doubt that Morley is the culprit, though unintentional.

I should add that McK. said to me as we were leaving that Winston Churchill was the culprit, and that he maintained regular communication with Lord Northcliffe. The P.M. finally kept silence as to his interview with Redmond, only imparting its tenor to Birrell —but I gathered Redmond was hostile to any concession.

We talked a great deal about expenditure and future taxation but no one put the real question which was whether we were going to agree to the vast increase on Navy expenditure, as well as a substantial rise of £800,000 for Army.

21 November

We went to Canford for the weekend. A large family party of Guests. Lady Rodney, Ivor, Ashby St. Ledgers, Henry and his wife, Sir G. Prescott,[25] Lady Randolph and Lady Gwendoline Churchill,[26] McKenna and his wife. Captain Spencer Holland, a Scotch agricultural professor, and Mr. Horner of the Labour Exchange. Most people played bridge the whole time—but varied it with political talk.

6 Herbert Louis Samuel in 1893. Hobhouse: 'Very able, not liked or trusted by anyone, but much used'

7 Lewis 'Lulu' Harcourt. Hobhouse: 'Subtle, secretive, adroit'

8 History repeats itself. This cartoon depicting *l–r* Macnamara, Hobhouse, Runciman and McKenna is based on one published in 1838 entitled 'The Age of *Leetle* Men', which includes Hobhouse's great-uncle, Lord Broughton

9 The Ridge, Corsham. In Hobhouse's day it had five guest bed-rooms and only one bathroom (for gentlemen)—ladies had to make do with pitchers of hot water in their bedrooms

Sydney Buxton wrote me that it was settled that he should succeed Gladstone as Gov.-Gen. of S. Africa. I shall regret his departure very greatly. He has been my most intimate political friend for 20 years. He is a bad speaker, and a devotee of compromise which never satisfies anyone, but he works very hard, and is quite honest and straightforward, and possesses a considerable fund of wit and humour. He and his wife ought to do well in S.A.

25 November
At Cabinet on Monday [24 November] the P.M. told us of an Ulster deputation which came to see him secretly on Saturday, some Home Rulers, some Unionists, and equally diverse as regards religion. He said they seemed solid and representative. He did not give all their names, but mentioned Mr. Henry, an Ulster notable, and Mr. Campbell, Chairman of the Belfast Trades Council. The latter gave most distinct assurances that the greatest pressure had been put on the workmen by the employers to 'volunteer', and that all except a small residuum would do nothing actively to revolt. The deputation put the Volunteers at about 20% of the Protestant males of man's age—and the turbulent at about 10,000 to 20,000 all told. Seely said that the difficult element to deal with would be the 2 battalions of 'special reservists' who were 90% violent Protestants officered by men who were taking a leading part in drilling the Volunteers.

The P.M. then read us Redmond's written reply to the interview he had had with him. This was largely written by Dillon, for it used phrases and voiced opinions identical with those which he used in separate conversations he had had with Ll.G. and Runciman. It was very uncompromising—no arrangement as to Ulster was thinkable, any suggestion of such a character would rend the Irish party in two. England was enthusiastic. Why spoil a unique opportunity? But the last few words gave the key. *At present* negotiations were harmful and undesirable. At the interview Redmond had said *he* was prepared for an Ulster autonomous in all respects within the Irish Parliament, and for an enlarged Senate, but it was plain that he had been overborne by his colleagues.

John Morley said he was to see Dillon that night, and would remind him that every Irish leader—O'Connell, Smith O'Brien, Butt, Parnell—had died in turn of a broken heart, his task unfulfilled and that Redmond should not also be left 'suspended between two hells'. For his own part he would give up Home Rule rather than witness its inception with bloodshed.

The P.M. gave an outline of what he would say at Leeds, and would in no case close the door to conciliation.

Here we separated to take up the subject anew this morning. Dillon came at 9.30 to see J. Morley at Wimbledon, and stayed till 12 midnight. He was, said J.M., a Tammany manager, with grandiose language, always one eye on the electorate. He was very critical of the suggestions made by Grey and Churchill; they were uncalled for and inopportune, and should not be repeated. He agreed that any serious bloodshedding would render Home Rule impossible. Now however was not the moment for compromise, though he would not be hostile to it later on.

Birrell then casually remarked that he had heard from Liverpool that 1,500 rifles and 95,000 ball cartridge had been just sent to Belfast, apparently on 21st. He had taken no steps to delay them at the Customs, and was not sure how many had been delivered to the consignees. I suggested that a telegram should be sent to Dublin to stop delivery. Winston was prepared to raid the Customs, carry them out to sea and sink them. Simon told us that the Customs gave us power to prohibit export of arms etc. or import, into or from the U.K. under penalty, but no power to seize or destroy them. McKenna, W.S.C., Runciman and I urged that with or without legal power, they should be detained and destroyed. It was finally agreed, after a foolish speech from Burns that both crowds would run at the sight of a machine gun, that a proclamation should be issued, saying that in the interests of *all* Ireland arms traffic was suspended.

✳ As the year ended the Cabinet faced a major crisis over the naval estimates. In November Churchill had infuriated Radical opinion by an
impolitic speech in which he boasted of British naval power. Then on 5
December he presented his estimates for 1914–15. He asked for
£50,694,800, an increase of nearly £3 millions over the total estimates
for 1913–14, compared with £44 millions estimated by McKenna for
1911–12. Churchill argued that the increase was necessary because of
German naval expansion, because of the increased size, speed and armament and therefore greater cost of maintenance of new ships, the cost of
new developments such as oil, wireless and aircraft, and the overall in-
flation affecting prices. Later he pointed out that the loss of Borden's

Canadian ships could only be made good by a supplementary estimate of £2½ millions. It is evident that it was not just the sums involved which provoked the violent reaction to his proposals. Partly it was a question of personality, but more important was the suspicion felt by many Liberals about Churchill's views on Ireland. It was thought that he might well sell the Home Rule pass over Ulster. Such suspicions were exacerbated when Churchill attended a dinner to discuss Ulster with F. E. Smith and Austen Chamberlain on 8 December—and Morley's presence on the same occasion did nothing to allay the doubts of his colleagues. The estimates crisis soon roused the Liberal Party at large, and on 17 December Asquith faced a deputation representing 100 Liberal M.P.s protesting against the estimates. Then on 1 January Lloyd George in an interview for the *Daily Chronicle* called for a reconsideration of the whole question of armaments and denounced the current naval proposals. It has been suggested that Lloyd George was bidding for the leadership of the old Radical 'Little England' Liberal Party at this time. Hobhouse's account makes it clear that this was not so. Hobhouse himself, on this occasion, was a protagonist in the events he described. Lloyd George was regarded as an unreliable ally by the Cabinet 'economists', who could not, for that matter, be considered as particularly Radical. But the naval estimates crisis did provide an opportunity to defeat Churchill and possibly remove him from the Cabinet.

20 December

We have had a succession of Cabinets [8, 15, 16 December] dealing, for far the largest part of each sitting, with the Navy estimates.

It was pretty clear from Winston Churchill's opening statement that he had contemplated much larger expenditure than the £50,694,000 he presented to us. We had the usual lecture about the 'selected' moment of the Germans as opposed to the 'average' moment of our preparations, which must always have a dangerous amount of truth in it. All this was coupled with voluminous papers of calculations very difficult to refute, and still more so to verify. Samuel opened the ball by pointing out that the average excess of strength of the British fleet over the German was much above the 60% agreed to by the Govt. and the H. of C. Then I produced Churchill's estimates of Feb. 1912 by the figures of which it was clear that his forecasts of expenditure necessary to meet the German *Novelle* was in this year being exceeded by £5 millions although our diplomatic relations were much happier now than then. As no one else had kept these estimates which covered the years from 1912 to 1917, their effect was considerable. Churchill answered them by producing a letter which in July 1912 he had written to Ll.G. but which neither of them had communicated to the Cabinet, and in which for that period of years he had increased the Feb. estimates by £10 millions.[27] At our next sitting he produced more papers by which under cross-examination he was forced to admit that he had in order to make his percentages even presentably small, excluded from the British fleet 2 Lord Nelsons as too old and slow in 1915, while including in German fleet 10 ships of less speed and gun power. He had also excluded the *Malaya*, the *Australia* and another, though the Germans would justifiably reckon them when adjusting their relative strength to ours. Eventually, since courage like fear is contagious, everyone took up the running, even Beauchamp and Buxton joining in, and the P.M. as usual crossed over to the winning side. We could get no decision as to the reduction for '13–'14 beyond the £728,000 agreed to privately between Lloyd George and Churchill but as regards '15–'16, it was decided to cut 2 ships out of the building programme. Churchill therefore protested his inability to carry on and went off characteristically *banging* the dispatch box and door as he went out as loud as he could. An interesting feature of these discussions was Ll.G.'s repudiation of the bargain, which had evidently been come to between Churchill and himself, as soon as he saw others were prepared to fight Churchill; the P.M.'s equally unblushing agreement with Ll.G. as to the construction of some words which had passed between Ll.G. and Churchill; and his desertion of the latter as soon as the Cabinet were seen to be adverse to him. This is the third important occasion on which the so-called minor members of the Cabinet have beaten the more prominent ones since I have been there.

Ll.G. has *since* then got the Treasury to read their own with the Admiralty papers sent to him, and to prepare for him a memo, showing the naval position in all its exaggeration: a memo which with other Chancellors would have preceded the discussion.

VI

Churchill and Crisis

January–July 1914

23 January

We have had an interesting week. It commenced with the return of
the P.M. Ever since our last Cabinet Ll.G. has been hardening to
the view that he and Churchill must part and that W.S.C. is only
waiting to choose between Home Rule or Navy before he quits a
sinking ship. This view is held by nine-tenths of the Cabinet.
Accordingly Ll.G. has with McK., Simon, and H. Samuel, made a
detailed examination of the Naval memos for the first time for 3
years. These 4 agreed that W.S.C. (who had concealed from the
Cabinet and the Treasury the *amounts* of his retardation of *payments
and* acceleration of *construction,* while basing our acceptance of his
programme on our knowledge that there would be some of all three)
must have the full Admiralty programme conceded. This course
would prevent his engineering the resignation of the Naval Lords;
but the acceptance of the programme must be the accompaniment of
a reduction of expenditure to that of 1912–13. If Churchill would
agree to this reduction he could stay, if not he *must* go.

On Wednesday [21 January] I saw the P.M. I told him I could
not well accept the Second Chamber decisions of the Cabinet,
pledged as I was by inclination and statement to an elected body.[1]
He replied the subject was still open, and till a final decision was
taken, no difficulty need arise. We then spoke about naval estimates.
I pointed out that Churchill's memos would permit of 5 separate
totals, varying from £48 millions to £50½ millions and of 6 different
statements as to the number of ships we should have ready by April
1915. He was rather taken aback at my figures, and asked me to
speak to Churchill about them; that for himself however large the
sum to be paid, the whole facts must be stated to the House, and that
the whole bill must be paid, and that reductions must be made thereafter as steep as the original increase. While I was speaking to him,
Ll.G., Simon, Samuel, and Beauchamp had come over from No. 11
for an interview. They repeated to the P.M. what I have already

narrated, and added that the party would never be contented to pay ordinary estimates of £46 millions or according to other figures £47 millions, plus additional estimates of £3¼ millions of arrears and extras, for this year, together with an increase to £54 millions next year, unless as a guarantee against such future events—Winston Churchill retired, certainly from the Navy, preferably from the Cabinet. 'Oh,' said the P.M. 'this is a personal question.' 'No,' replied Simon, 'a question of temperament.'[2] This revelation of differences clearly surprised and distressed the P.M. very much. Crewe, who came in afterwards, confirmed our views. Churchill was seen by the P.M. and asked again I am told to produce his programme for 1915–16.

On Thursday 22nd, I lunched with Beauchamp. He had been asked by Ll.G. to tell me that Churchill had produced not a steep decrease, but a bill for 1915–16 of £53 millions. This we felt to be a direct challenge, with but one ending. We met at 3 p.m. to discuss as we knew Ireland. The P.M. had conversations with B. Law on Dec. 10 and 16 and had also seen Carson. The former was very pessimistic, but the latter much less so, but both agreed that the exclusion of certain counties in Ulster was the only settlement their Orangemen would accept. The conversations led to nothing. Finding moreover that the 2 leaders would propose or suggest nothing, on Dec. 23 the P.M. wrote to *B. Law* proposals which he said were unknown to his colleagues, and which he did not even know whether they would approve of. The terms of the proposals were these, as well as I recall them. While there would be a general devolution of powers to the Dublin Parliament as in the Irish Bill, the Post Office and Customs would be retained under Imperial control; and as an entirely new point, any individual citizen who thought himself injured in person or pocket, or oppressed in religion or politics could appeal to judges appointed by the British Parliament.

A statutory Ulster, i.e. the 4 N.E. counties, was to be created to be represented in the Irish Parliament but with a veto on any Irish legislation concerning finance, police, education, patronage, and Local Govt., and with an appeal to the British Parliament against generally oppressive legislation.

On Dec. 27 *Carson* replied that these proposals were useless to his friends in Ulster, but if Ulster could be left out he was ready to accept Home Rule for the rest of Ireland.

On Jan. 2 the P.M. met Carson and said he greatly regretted these 'valuable concessions' should be rejected, but then and later in a letter of Jan. 7, Carson while declaring that the proposals were 'veiled exclusion', said the sentiment of his friends would prevent his accepting them.

On Jan. 8 the P.M. wrote to Carson, and on the 9th heard from B. Law, reiterating regret at the failure of the conversations and on the 10th Carson sent a final letter saying that for him and his friends Ulster exclusion meant Ulster as it was at present from the legislative and administrative standard.

On this statement we had considerable discussion. Grey thought it put an end to all further conversations, until after the Bill had passed—he said that pressure was being brought to bear on the King not to sign, which idea was being taken rather seriously by the Palace.

Lloyd George wanted an early announcement of our offers which he thought the Irish would accept. Devlin[3] had said he would take anything which would stop short of permanent or formal exclusion. McKenna said an envoy from Redmond had reached him with the same message. Birrell declared the Irish said one thing to him and quite another to his 'conversational colleagues'. This was probably true, that they were stiff with a weak man, and pliant to strong ones. It was finally agreed to settle *times* with the Irish, but to declare as *we* wished.

26 January

On coming to London on Monday I found a message asking me to the Treasury. I found there McKenna, Simon, Ll.G. and Masterman. Ll.G. said he had a most satisfactory meeting with Churchill, who would give every guarantee that expenditure was down in 1915–16. We said he could not, with the best will in the world, give such a guarantee—internal and external events or pure accidents might upset all calculations. In any case large increase in maintenance expenditure this year is not a good prelude to reduction next year. Ll.G. got rather hot. We parted at 5 p.m. McK., Simon, and I dined in McK.'s new house in Smith Square, largely the work of Lutyens and Sir H. Jekyll.[4] We sat till 11 p.m. when Simon and I agreed to write a note each to Ll.G. expressing our views. My own ran thus 'I served under you so long that I feel I must let you know at once that I find myself unconvinced by Winston's figures. If I get a chance at Cabinet I shall express my dissent from, and distrust of them. My fear is that between him, and them, the Labour party and the Tories, we shall come to hopeless grief.'[5]

27 January

On reaching the office I found I had been urgently asked to the Treasury several times—so had McK., Simon, Beauchamp, and Samuel. We severally showed reluctance, but urging becoming correspondingly severe we turned up in driblets about noon. Ll.G. received us shaking letters over his head: our two and a note from Churchill written at 8.30. In effect it repudiated any possibility of a guarantee by the Admiralty, though claiming one from the Treasury. 'This', said G., 'justifies all your doubts of Winston's sincerity. I was defending it and almost at that very moment he was writing this letter, which fully upholds your contentions and fears. I had parted yesterday in heat with my best defenders and I was absolutely wrong.' He then showed us a vigorous reply to Churchill, and sent copies of the correspondence to the P.M. While we were waiting back came a messenger from Churchill acknowledging Ll. G.'s note and saying that if they were to part company, it was most agreeable to think that there was no severance of personal relations. We parted just before lunch in the hope but not the fixed belief, that Ll.G. had decided finally to walk the path of economy. At Cabinet it soon became evident that a reconciliation had been effected. Lloyd George began with a lecture on the desirability of economy, to which Winston replied with a dissertation on National Security, and we examined in detail some fresh papers circulated by the Admiralty put forward to show that his expenditure had been pre-announced and was inevitable. McKenna took him to task over details, but he got no effective help from Ll.G. and practically our entire sitting was taken up with a real attack on the Admiralty by McKenna, Simon and myself, with occasional interventions from Runciman and Beauchamp. Churchill defended himself with what Simon afterwards described as wonderful fecundity of mind, and with the vigorous though ineffectual support of Haldane to whom no one seemed to attach much importance. We broke up on the understanding that the following day we were to have a general statement from Lloyd George as to financial policy. On returning home from the office I found an urgent invitation to dinner from Illingworth with an intimation that Ll.G. and Simon would also be at his house. Accordingly I got there about 8.30 p.m. and we had a late dinner during which we had an interesting discussion on poetry in which Ll.G. revealed a much greater knowledge of English literature than I had credited him with. He made himself vastly agreeable in explaining the system of Welsh poetry which seems to depend for its rhythm on a double or even triple system of alliterative effect. After dinner we got back on the old subject. Ll.G. tried to wean us, and Simon in particular from the view of our group but we went home unseparated and unconvinced.

28 January

We met at McKenna's at 10 a.m. and found no new reason to trust Winston's ability to reduce estimates, nor Ll.G.'s sincerity in asking for reduction. When we had moved on to Cabinet we found the P.M. had personally circulated a print of his suggestions to Bonar Law. This led us on to speak generally about Ireland, the Ministerial position and difficulties. Grey, Churchill and Haldane, who had been lately in touch with the King's entourage all agreed with the P.M. in believing the King had considerably altered his position lately. He now took the attitude that he was by belief a Home Ruler, and was even ready to grant that the country had supported Home Rule at the last general election. He contended however that it was a Home Rule based upon agreement or acquiescence, and not on Home Rule as the result of civil strife, to which the country was agreed. He was, as the P.M. described him, in a state of moral and intellectual tumult. He declared that one of Asquith's replies to a heckle showed that Asquith himself was not prepared for civil strife. It seemed clear to us all that the Tories would refuse to come to any agreement on Home Rule trusting that if Ulster made noise enough they would be able to frighten the King into offering the Ministry the alternative of dissolution or dismissal before the 3rd reading of the Bill in H. of C. In that event the power of Parliament Act to carry the bill after a dissolution lapses—and the whole of the work of the last 3 years on Home Rule, Disestablishment and Plural Voting would disappear— and whatever the result of the coming election it would be a complete practical triumph for the Tory Party. Simon, Runciman, Beauchamp and I dined with McKenna. We were all clear that our one chance of success was to let the P.M. know that we were determined to resign rather than vote Churchill's extravagant estimates. We drew up a letter to the P.M. accordingly, setting out our reasons for being perturbed at the proposed Naval Expenditure and dealing with the figures themselves.[6]

29 January

We sent Beauchamp and Simon to present our letter to the P.M. signed as it was by Beauchamp, myself, McKenna, Runciman, Simon and McKinnon Wood in the order named. He received them very well, thanked them for having put their case to him and said he would give the fullest consideration to our views. At Cabinet Winston Churchill explained to us, and it needed no explanation, that the Admiralty estimates and figures had frequently differed and that the proposals for any one year could be made to equal any sum. I attacked him on the totals, McKenna on the details—we had a fierce wrangle for more than two hours—Lloyd George gave us no assistance and both he and Churchill endeavoured to get the Cabinet to assume that £52½ millions were the estimates agreed to. We separated having come neither to this nor any other agreement.

✳ But on 11 February Asquith was able to write to the King that agreement had been reached. On that day the Cabinet agreed to total estimates of £51,580,000 and Churchill in turn promised that there should be substantial reductions in the following year. In addition the building of two battleships was to be accelerated in order to make up for the delay in the Canadian ships, although Parliament was to be told that there was no commitment to supply three extra ships if Borden was ultimately unsuccessful. With these difficulties resolved, the Cabinet turned its attention to the last act of the Irish drama. The prospect of Home Rule or civil war over Ulster dominated 1914 until the outbreak of European War in August. In late spring tension had come to a head with the Curragh mutiny, but the Government's authority was precariously reasserted. The long golden summer was dominated not by impending European catastrophe but by discussion of what Churchill called 'the muddy byways of Fermanagh and Tyrone'. Once again, too, in this extraordinary period of constitutional history, the Crown became involved in proposing the Buckingham Palace Conference of party leaders to discuss Ireland. Only as that conference ended, on 24 July, did attention swing dramatically to the European situation, and the Austrian ultimatum to Serbia which precipitated general war.

For Hobhouse, 11 February was significant as the day on which he was appointed Postmaster-General, thereby acquiring departmental responsibilities for the first time.

3 February

Cabinet began by a statement from the P.M. that he had seen Redmond, had pointed out to him the difficulties with which the King thought himself beset, and the consequences they would have on the fate of the Irish Bill. He said that Redmond was much surprised, and disturbed at the information. He promised to think the matter over, discussing it with but one or two of his most intimate colleagues, and would give us an answer before the House met. The P.M. said he could quite understand that Redmond would have to denounce our proposals, the important point was, he should not oppose them. Redmond himself did not wince at any of Asquith's suggestions. He was prepared to concede anything the effect of which was temporary, but the permanent exclusion of Ulster he would not however consider for a moment.

25 February

Today the question arose as to a Petition said to have been presented to H.M. by a number of Peers bidding him to dissolve Parliament. Inquiry from Stamfordham direct to Buckingham Palace led to a statement by him that no such Petition had been presented to, or even heard of by the King. It was decided that the arms seized in Belfast should be handed over by the Customs to the Police Authorities and by them broken up. This was to apply to all future seizures.

Birrell and Lloyd George were deputed to state to Redmond and Dillon the attitude of the Govt. which was this:—it was necessary to make concessions to legitimate fears in England and Ireland, which were thought quite groundless but recognised as sincere; that permanent exclusion of any part of Ireland was undesirable in itself and undesired by any part in England or Ireland; that temporary exclusion of the four North-Eastern Counties either singly or *en bloc* would be considered by the Govt. if it would be accepted by the Opposition, an acceptance which for political reasons they would probably not concur in; that it would also be necessary to come to some fresh arrangement about the Judges, the fears of reasonable Ulstermen about an inefficient and pliable Justiciary being very real and in our eyes not unreasonable; it might be necessary, and was perhaps in itself desirable, to repeal the Post Office Clause and we would certainly do so if any desire was expressed for any such repeal. Beyond that we were not ourselves prepared to go and should not ask them to yield further. It was probable that the action of the Opposition would take this course, they would tell the House of Lords to reject the Third Reading of the Army Annual Act except upon the condition that men enlisting and paid under it, were not employed in the Province of Ulster, and that, if this condition were not accepted they would run the risk of the Govt., taking no notice of their action and of the whole armed forces of the Empire having to be disbanded, that they hoped the Govt. would not face this contingency but would be driven to an election some time in the middle or end of May.

The P.M. sketched his statement to be made in the H. of C. on Monday night. The only difference between what had already been considered was that exclusion should be possible after a plebiscite of County by County, not in Ulster alone but all over Ireland, this would give the Protestants of the west and south who might be supposed to feel strongly upon the matter a chance of expressing whether their feelings were as strong as they were said to be. Both Lloyd George and Birrell said that they found Redmond and his friends quite prepared to meet the views of the Govt. so long as they were not actually asked to vote for them in the H. of C. The procedure they contemplated was that if the proposals of the Govt. were acceptable to the Opposition there would be no necessity for them to do more than accept them under protest. If they were unacceptable to the Opposition it was clearly not their duty and they supposed it would not be the duty of the Govt. to require them to vote for things of which they disapproved personally and for which the Unionists expressed no desire. Redmond reiterated his earnest opinion that he could make any concession short of permanent exclusion of Ulster in order to meet the wishes and fears of the Unionist Party. The P.M. indicated that he had knowledge—though he mentioned no names—that the leaders of the Orangemen were seriously alarmed at the position into which they had led their followers and into which their followers had pushed them, that they were all desirous of a settlement, but each feared lest his fellows should brand him with having gone back on the Covenant.

Since I last wrote, I have been to Berlin on Post Office business, stayed at the Embassy with Sir Ed. Goschen, who was pleasant and exceedingly astute. He told me that the Kaiser wished me to lunch, and so on Sunday March 1st I went to the Palace. We had a strong detachment of some Guard Regt. on duty, marched in with the absurd parade step which they affect. The interior of the Palace was like a glorified Clapham villa, neither taste nor space being shown, the pictures very indifferent, and the decorations gorgeous without beauty. There was however a charming picture of the Empress by Lazlo, in the room in which we smoked after lunch.

The Ambassador being ill I found my own way to the Castle, and was presented to the Emperor and after a few minutes' talk with him to the Empress, to whom I sat next at lunch. She seemed unaffected, and was charming in manners. Goschen liked her much better than the Emperor.

After lunch he talked to me for about $1\frac{1}{2}$ hours, rather to the astonishment of his suite, aeroplanes, Zeppelins, the Hamburg-Amerika and Herr Ballin, his brother Prince Henry,[7] Mexico, were in turn our topics. He was vivacious, restless, buttonholed me, well informed, uncertain, a remarkable individuality, but not a commanding personage. I was very glad to have had the interview, but he seemed to be only dangerous because he was unstable.

✳ On 9 March Asquith introduced the Second Reading of the Home Rule Bill for the third time in the House of Commons. At the same time he proposed that the Government should introduce an amending bill which would give the Ulster counties the chance to opt out from Home Rule for six years, by referendum, although, unless Parliament meanwhile decided otherwise, at the end of that period they would be included. The Liberals hoped to win over public opinion by labelling the Unionists as obstructionist if they rejected the offer, and such a compromise also went some way to reassure the King. George V was particularly concerned about the position of the Army in Ulster. There were fears about possible Ulster Volunteer Force attacks on arms depots. The Cabinet were doubtful of the loyalty of some Army officers if they were ordered to take action in Ulster to enforce Home Rule. On 11 March a Cabinet Committee was set up to consider how to deal with any U.V.F. attack. Three days later, in a forceful speech, Churchill sternly warned the Unionists against any direct confrontation. On 17 March the Committee decided to reinforce the garrisons guarding certain depots. In the Commons on 19 March there was uproar as Carson accused Churchill of a Government plot to coerce Ulster. In these circumstances General Sir Arthur Paget, the General Officer Commanding troops in Ireland, received orders in London to take these precautionary moves. When he briefed his commanding officers on 20 March Paget described these orders in inflammatory terms and gave them the apparent choice of obeying orders or resigning their commissions. Sixty officers based at the Curragh, near Dublin, forthwith resigned rather than take part in 'active operations' in Ulster. Paget's folly was matched by that of the War Secretary, Seely, in the following week, when he allowed General Gough, leader of the resigning officers, to extract an unauthorised declaration that the Government had no intention of using the Army to crush political opposition to Home Rule. The Government's embarrassment was heightened by the revelation of Churchill's naval preparations in ordering the 3rd Battle Squadron to Lamlash. This gave further credence to what *The Times* called 'the plot that failed'. The account which follows shows clearly that although the Government itself may not have conceived a scheme to provoke an Ulster rising which could then be put down by superior force, many members of the Cabinet, including Hobhouse, were increasingly exasperated by the defiance of the Unionists, and believed, in the end, that the authority of the Government would have to be upheld by force.

23 March [24 March]

We had two difficult Cabinets on Monday and today [23 and 24 March]. On Saturday Henry Guest came to me at 9.30 a.m. to say that Gen. Wilson,[8] D.M.O., at the War Office had a dinner on Friday night at which he formally stated that Gen. Gough[9] in Ireland had resigned, had telegraphed to his brother at Aldershot to do the same thing, and that half the Cavalry Brigade at the Curragh were involved. Guest added that his friends told him that in the Quartermaster-General's Dept. some officer had refused to prepare plans for movements in Ulster. I took him to the P.M. to tell his tale. The latter was neither credulous as to the unrest among the private soldiers, nor encouraging to Guest's statement, which he had learnt at midnight the day before. He declared to Guest first and to me later that it was only a cavalry subaltern's tale not worth notice. As to Gen. Wilson, whom Guest said had more influence in and more knowledge of the Army than French, and who was very pessimistic, Asquith more than hinted that he was at the bottom of a good deal of the trouble. At the Cabinet on Monday, the P.M. produced a letter from B. Law and another from Lord Lansdowne, asking for information to be given in Parliament. Seely with much jauntiness of manner gave us his version of what had occurred. He had sent Paget to Ireland to see that garrisons were provided for 3 or 4 stations where large stores of arms existed unprotected. He had not taken the precaution of writing down his orders to Paget, and so could not give us exact language. He declared that Paget reported that soldiers marching in the south and west of Ireland were very subject to insults from Nationalists, and quite as much disaffection was to be found amongst the rank and file as among the officers. If Paget had done more than ask officers to prepare for the increase of these petty garrisons, he had misunderstood his orders.

Churchill said that whatever might be the indiscipline in the Army, the Navy was prepared for anything. Bayly, the Admiral at Lamlash had called his Captains together, and told them roundly that the first officer who hesitated to obey would be court-martialled on the spot.

Grey said that all this only showed him that unless Ulster refused to take the 6 years' offer, it would be impossible to coerce her without a previous election.

Just as we were breaking up I asked that the Cabinet should see the note to be given by the Army Council to Gen. Gough in accordance with Seely's explanation to him that Paget had misunderstood (and exceeded) his orders. The P.M. agreed. Churchill telephoned to W.O. for the memo which was sent over by Seely's private secretary, Seely himself having gone to see the King. Churchill in giving over the envelope said to P.M. 'You'll take the responsibility of breaking open the envelope?' It was opened by the P.M. who read it aloud. When he had done before we could express dissent he ran his pencil through the bulk of it saying there was only one paragraph which could possibly remain. We all said, even Haldane, that terms with mutinous officers were impossible. We broke up and as we did so, Seely came back.

25 March

On Tuesday at dinner time, just as I was starting for the St. Aldwyns, McKenna said he was told Seely had altered the Cabinet memo as to Gough. On Wednesday Seely, still buoyant and breezy, said he had been pressed to give Gough some more reassuring statement than the one proposed, had rewritten the Cabinet's draft of the Army Council order (with the aid of Morley who provided the necessary literary graces) and given it to French, and Ewart[10] the Adjutant-General who with himself initialled this new document and gave it to Gough. Seely said that he only saw Gough's letter to Ewart after Monday's Cabinet rose, didn't realise its importance, didn't realise that the Cabinet had deliberately cut about Ewart's draft, for Seely, of the Army Council memo. He was in fact in a state of great excitement and disturbance, his wife's death was a blow he never recovered from, and he missed her steadying influence. No one moreover can say what pranks Churchill had been suggesting to him.

Ll.G. intervened by asking whether the Prime Minister or Lord Chancellor knew of Gough's letter to Ewart, before the Army Council memo was sent to Gough; or of the memo being revised, and both said they were in absolute ignorance.

I put it to the Cabinet that the only point *we* had to consider was whether the Govt. would repudiate the Army Council memo, *as Gough and the soldiers would interpret it*, or whether they would adhere to it. If the latter course was taken I would not remain an hour longer in the Govt., as the soldiers would clearly be entitled to think they were at liberty to choose whether they would or would not go to Ulster, and my belief was that the Govt. would be out and deservedly so in less than six hours.

The P.M. refused to accept Seely's proferred resignation (Churchill having suggested reasons why it should not be accepted, a curious proceeding seeing that it was purely the concern of the P.M.), asked me to telephone for French, who was seen by Seely and Churchill who reported he was desirous of going, but only because the soldiers would be entitled to claim his promise that they

10 Winston Churchill with Lord Northcliffe at Hendon in 1911.
Hobhouse: 'Really a spoilt child endowed by some chance with
the brain of a genius'

11 Rufus Isaacs

were free to choose. He was for coercing, and drastically, any insurrectionary movement in Ulster, and taking very strong measures with indiscipline among the officers.

27 March

Today, 27 March, we heard French and Ewart had resigned definitely, not because they differed from our policy, but because their initials to Seely's document were a pledge to the soldiers at the Curragh that they would not be asked to initiate proceedings in Ulster. A mistaken, though honourable point of honour. Haldane had seen French who said he would stay on if P.M. would read or give him a statement that the Govt. intentions were in accord with declarations made by P.M. in H. of C. and Haldane in Lords. These were found on examination not quite to tally, and we repudiated Haldane and with Haldane his offer, for it was his suggestion, to French. Ll.G. suggested issue of new Army Order as help to French and a guide to the Army, and this was drawn up at once. Seely amongst other things said its terms should be such that it should be 'clear to all that the Cabinet was not on its knees to French or Ewart, or to me'. The P.M. saw French between the Cabinet which broke up about 1 p.m. having met at 10.30 a.m., and the second gathering at 3, when he told us French was immovable on his punctilio, but on nothing else.

30 March

On Sunday afternoon the P.M. decided, as Harcourt says on his suggestion, but really on his own reflection, to take the War Office, on Monday he so declared his acceptance and received a spontaneous tribute to the respect and regard in which the whole House holds him, which I have not seen shown to anyone before by or in that assembly.

1 April

I find some notes on a previous Cabinet which I can't date but which must be about 15th March. [17 March]

There were 23,000 troops in Ireland. Seely would want about 13 Battalions, 2½ Regts. Cavalry and 12 Batts. of Artillery as his force with which to maintain order: this would be increased to 20,000 men if the Ulstermen turned out in large numbers.

At the same meeting a letter from Col. Repington,[11] *The Times* military correspondent, to Asquith was read, pointing out the military value of the Ulstermen, and the vulnerability of Gleichen's Brigade in Ulster. Seely repudiated, as his information went, any intention on the part of Ulster to attack the troops, but said he was told police barracks would be rushed, and the police would not resist. Churchill declared the coastguard would fight in defence of their arms to the death. Morley reminded Asquith that in '93 the Irish Govt. had consulted Wolseley[12] who had counselled a swift descent on and coercion of Ulster.

Asquith declared that if the Lords rejected, as seemed probable, the Annual Army Bill, he would not advise creation of Peers, but in the certainty that this action would disgust not only the country, but the Army, he will instantly dissolve Parliament.

At the Cabinet of 31st March which I could not attend, the P.M. stated that though he had telegraphed to Paget to state categorically what he had said to his officers, no real information could be got from him.

Grey in speaking of the rewards of political adherents, remarked that honours acted as aperients to the purse. While Morley reminded us that William Harcourt used to call the small Bills mentioned in the King's Speech the 'Choral Service'.

I was told by my Dept. today that last August Birrell was warned by the Post Office and Customs jointly that 1,500 rifles complete were being sent to Ireland, but he refused to take action or inform the Cabinet.

✻ There was an interesting sequel to the Curragh incident. On 16 April Bonar Law denied in the Commons that there had been any communication between the dissident officers and him. When these remarks came to Hobhouse's attention he wrote to Law, pointing out that an unsigned telegram had in fact been delivered to him at the House of Commons at 5.46 p.m. on 20 March. This said Hobhouse, 'presumably reached you. . . . An unsigned message may not have attracted your attention or slipped your memory, but in either case you ought I think to be told of the fact of the message even by a political opponent.' The next day Bonar Law replied that he received many anonymous communications, that they were never kept and that in any case he paid no attention to them. 'I do not recall the particular message to which you refer, and if it is of any interest or importance I should be obliged by your sending me a copy of it.' Ever-helpful, Hobhouse obliged. The telegram, sent at 5.40 p.m. on the fateful 20 March from the Curragh Camp, read simply 'General and all cavalry officers Curragh Division resigned today.' Thus did the Army inform their political allies, the Unionist leaders, of the fateful event.[13]

1 May

This last week we have had 5 Cabinets. The last 2 were chiefly taken up with the Budget, but the first of those 2 on Thursday were partly on the attitude to Ulster Volunteers and partly on my Postal budget. We thought we ran a good chance of defeat on this so strongly had the Postal associations been canvassing all parties, and so little moral courage have M.P.s when an election is in sight. I am told by Buckmaster[14] that, *pace* Ramsay MacDonald, the Labour Party would have ignored the Postmen's Federation, if the Tories hadn't succumbed to him. As to Ulster Churchill said he had come round to the P.M.'s view that he should take no action except send a squadron of destroyers to patrol the Irish coast. Burns and I stuck out for the dispatch of several regiments to Dublin and the Curragh, and Ll.G. joined us saying we were apologetic beyond wisdom to the Tories. Personally I would have sent troops to Ulster, and if they would not go, I would disband them, and re-enlist only those who would not hesitate to shoot.

Eventually the P.M. deleted the sentence which said he did not intend to move troops. The Irish party were very strongly against 'prosecutions', there was a good deal of personal sympathy with Carson for having successfully defied the law, even when the law was on their side and they wanted troops moved to Belfast. This would not be wise, as they would be there some time, there would be much discriminating hospitality, and ultimate fraternisation, à la Louis Philippe.

The Cabinets earlier in the week were taken up with the same subject of the consequences of gun-running.[15] The first person really to dismiss is Birrell, who until he was sent over by the P.M. had not been near Dublin or Ireland for months. As this isn't done, no one else ought to be blamed for mischief caused. I suggested the removal of Neville Chamberlain, the Chief Royal Irish Constabulary official, who is incompetent and disloyal: as an alternative

Gen. N. Macready[16] was sent as dictator to the Belfast district. He began by reporting that the secret service of the R.I.C. was non-existent and that most of the Postal Officials were active Orangemen. This I had told the Cabinet 2 months ago, but as no one seemed to mind, I could only make departmental arrangements for removing them all in case of emergency. Accordingly I sent Mr. Ogilvy to Belfast with orders to pack off any official suspected to another office in England.

22 May

I have made no entries for a long time, and my recollection may be at fault in details but the minute notes I made at the time make the main facts accurate, but the dates are uncertain.

After the Speaker's rebuke to B. Law which the bulk of the Tories thought justified though a very noisy minority were very angry at, Harcourt and Illingworth saw him and found him desirous of resigning as having seriously damaged his authority with the House.[17] The P.M. thought he had been very maladroit, but he was in a most difficult position created by Law's absolute lack of generosity. The Cabinet agreed that any amending Bill should be Asquith's offer of March 9th if agreement were not first reached, but of that even the P.M. had given up hope. Masterman made his acceptance of Ipswich conditional on his retention of the Duchy, successful or unsuccessful.[18]

At Cabinet today [?13 May] the P.M. very confident that exclusion of Ulster would be insisted on by diehards. Simon put forward a proposal which had been suggested to him by Glyn-Jones[19] who had also made it to me that the provisions of the Home Rule Act should as far as Ulster was concerned remain suspended at the end of 6 years unless Parliament renewed their operation. By this means *this* country would be forced to reconsider the Irish question which otherwise she might be inclined to overlook.

Redmond sent us a letter making some very foolish proposals about the redistribution of Ulster. Birrell said he was informed that the R.I.C. had come to some private understanding with the Ulster Volunteers that the latter should take charge of the greater part of Belfast, parting the two spheres of influence by a vast wire fence. Neither he nor the police seemed to think that there was anything unusual in such a division of authority.

Macready wrote that the Ulster Volunteers were tired of drilling, and wanted to be either allowed to fight or else to be disbanded. I tried to induce the Cabinet to consider what actual steps should be taken if the Ulster Provisional Govt. was actually set up. But no one felt inclined to move until the trouble actually arrived. History if it concerns itself with us at all will write us down as either the most patient, wise, foreseeing Govt. this or any country ever had, or else as the inept, blind, and cowardly crew that ever disgraced Downing St. No middle judgement will be possible.

On May 26 [misdated: this discussion took place on 27 & 28 May] we seem to have discussed foreign affairs. Grey told us the French had no desire for a formal alliance, they preferred a flexible *Entente*, but the Russians were very anxious for it. In particular they were anxious as to the growing naval strength of Turkey, which the English instructors reported as being very marked. W. Churchill admitted today for the first time that the Russian naval force in the Baltic was a quantity which Germany could not ignore, and which would allow us to reduce our Rosyth fleet.

He and Harcourt went on to advocate aeroplanes in Somaliland as to which Burns remarked that a dusky native with a box of matches would put an end to them all in five minutes.

✳ At the end of May Hobhouse took advantage of his official duties to combine a cable inspection tour with a short cruise. He recorded later rather blandly:

22 June
I went for a cruise on the *Monarch* telegraph ship with Nina, Matthew Nathan, S. Coke and Dorothy C. and my niece Evelyn Thornton; our most northerly point was Gairloch in Ross-shire, we also visited Island of Coll, Mull and Skye, being away about a fort-night. As the *Monarch* is 30 years old, and has only one screw she was not very handy for cable work. We laid one near Rothesay, and repaired one at Coll, and inspected a wireless station in Mull.

✳ But on his return to Parliament he faced a series of pointed questions about the provision of accommodation for his friends on the *Monarch*. It was alleged that officers of the ship had had to give up their cabins for these unofficial passengers, and it was also implied that another ship had had to be chartered to carry out work which the *Monarch* was therefore unable to do. The questions were patently mischievous, and there had been no extra public expense or interruption of cable work, but it was an embarrassing episode for the new Postmaster-General. He explained, with dignity, that he had only realised the accommodation arrangements necessary once the voyage had started, that it had been the practice of his predecessors to so use the vessel, and that he had tried to recompense those who had been inconvenienced by his friends' presence.[20]

Meanwhile the King was at the centre of the political stage. He was desperately concerned to achieve some compromise on Ulster which would avoid his having to give the Royal Assent to a Home Rule Bill which would alienate his Unionist subjects. He seized upon the Amending Bill, introduced in the House of Lords on 23 June, as a solution. When the Lords wrecked that prospect by their amendments, he pressed for an inter-party conference. After a variety of other indirect approaches to the other parties, Asquith finally agreed to resort to the so-called Buckingham Palace Conference.

22 June

We had a Cabinet yesterday at which the P.M. read a letter from the King in which he rather hinted that he considered the Home Rule Bill and the Amending Bill interdependent propositions. The letter was apparently written to place on record his expectation that the Amending Bill would exceed the proposals of March 9. Both Crewe and Morley had seen the King and told him quite plainly that whatever happened to the Amending Bill, Home Rule would not be scrapped. Then we went to Finance and Education. Ll.G. said he had 'a little doubt' as to the time necessary for his Finance Bill, to which P.M. rejoined that he had 'none'—then Ll.G. suggested that an adjournment for Sept. would enable us to get the measure in Oct. I said I would rather retire from Office and the H. of C., the others joined in, and an autumn session was stillborn.

1 July [? 7 July]

Today we talked about the Lords and Wales, and the attack on the India Council Bill.[21] Crewe was not very anxious to proceed with it, and feared lest Courtney's intervention might lead to an Inquiry by a

Lords Committee into Indian affairs. Winston Churchill wanted to agitate against Lords for improper interference with the Govt. whereon P.M. broke in that 'a reasoned speech by a great man like Curzon' could never be improper!

18 July
On Wednesday and again twice on Friday we practically discussed nothing but Ireland.

(I forgot to say about the Lords inquiry into the Welsh Church Bill that the P.M. said we ought not to ignore their Committee but should put Lord Bryce and Sheffield on it, for no one on their side could know so much or talk so long as both of them and so they might confuse the others.)

On Saturday 11th inst. the P.M. saw both Redmond and Dillon who were very grumpy and impracticable on the point of any 'area' concession, but quite amenable on the time limit. He had not seen Carson, but told us almost as we were going away that he had had a message from him to the effect that if the P.M. could make a *'firm'* offer, he (Carson) would get over 2 or 3 friends from Ireland who would be willing with him to accept as a settlement the division of Fermanagh, and Down and Armagh between Ulster and Ireland if Derry City were ceded to Ulster, but they must keep Tyrone intact. The P.M. replied by saying Tyrone would have to be divided.

The King was anxious to get Redmond and Carson to meet personally and his latest idea was to assent conditionally only to Home Rule Bill. He would make signature dependent on an election, to which the P.M.'s comment was that the King could dismiss us, but that we should not resign before an election, a course always fatal to the outgoing Ministry.

On Friday 17th the P.M. said he had seen B. Law who was very anxious for settlement, and angry with Carson for the 'clear cut' speech, but was not prepared to come to a conference. Carson would not refuse to attend if his sovereign summoned him to one, but he would yield nothing. Thereupon McKenna and Ll.G. said that our best and indeed only course was to go forward with the Amending Bill, leaving perhaps Ulster outside Home Rule but allowing any Ulster County to vote itself into Home Rule and say to the H. of C. that we had made concession after concession and got nothing from Carson since March 9 in return and we would now budge no further.

Carson was in all probability bluffing and would begin to consider terms the moment he found we had come to a real stop. Thereupon P.M. said B. Law had told him that the Ulster Provisional Govt. would be set up at the *end of the week* if the Govt. had not come to some agreement. Then Churchill said that here was a willingness of both sides to yield so much that only the division of County Tyrone stood between a settlement and a civil war, and it was criminal to plunge Great Britain into strife for so trivial a difference. Why was a conference impossible? Crewe declared that the force of public opinion should be employed to force the 2 sides in Ireland to get over this last obstacle: to which McK. said yes, but as the admission of mutual concession is private and as each will in public deny that he has budged an inch, public opinion cannot be informed that the difference is so small. I said that if it hereafter became known that the King had desired a conference, that Redmond and Carson were willing to attend, and that we had put any hindrance in the way and that civil war had broken out, we should rightly be held responsible as the authors of it—and we were bound to try and bring about a conference, and especially at Buckingham Palace, the publicity of which would force the negotiators to reveal the slenderness of difference. Harcourt spoke strongly to the same effect. While we were talking a note came from Alick Murray of Elibank to say that Max Aitken,[22] B. Law's financier and jackal, was with him to say that Law had desired a conference. I went out of Cabinet and telephoned to Murray asking if Aitken had definite authority from Law to say that a conference would be accepted by the Opposition. Murray replied that Aitken was in his room and authorised him to say that Law would agree to a conference if one was proposed. We then broke up to meet again at 3. Ll.G. had seen Law meanwhile and confirmed that agreement, though characteristically trying to show that Carson would go there very defiantly. The P.M. also saw Law for a short time, to the same effect, so we carried our point. Capt. Craig, our people agreed, would be much the best Ulster negotiator, because himself an Ulsterman he could accept conditions and make conditions which Carson a Dublin man could never accede to.

23 July
The P.M. gave us an account of the Conference at our meeting at H.

of C. this evening. The tone was amicable though not hopeful, for the only two people in complete agreement were Carson and Redmond and they only as what the other could not be expected to accept. Two things emerged: one was that the exclusion of what was technically Ulster could not as a whole be asked for, and Carson in his most expansive humour only now demanded the six plantation counties. Redmond was on the other hand quite ready to give up the time limit, and was quite indifferent as to the exclusion of any part of Down or even Armagh, but on Tyrone where the Protestants and Catholics are inextricably mixed up, he was as immovable as Carson. Derry City he acknowledged to be the ark of the Covenant, but on Tyrone he derided any compromise. Lansdowne and Dillon took little part in discussion, Law was pacific, and Craig reasonable and helpful. Then the P.M. and Ll.G. suggested division and concession in the debatable counties by Poor Law Unions, as these gave truer geographical and religious boundaries, but Carson wouldn't accept these, though Redmond said that he would accept any division based on a decision of a reasonable majority of the inhabitants whether Papist or Protestant. As to the proposed reference to the arbitration of British opinion, Carson would not agree to abide by any British opinion or decision. The P.M. said that Carson's opening speech was the most moving he had ever made, or that he himself had listened to.

We agreed that if the Conference broke down we should send back the Amending Bill to Lords with county optional return to *Home Rule* tied on their Clause I and give them the responsibility of rejecting it.

Grey was very anxious to let the country see that the British Govt. had views of their own about the settlement of Ireland, but the fact is that the Liberal members will suffer no proposal to be made if Redmond is not in agreement with it.

24 July

At today's meeting from which Harcourt and Burns were absent, the P.M. gave us an account of the last two days' conference, and read us the very jejeune statement of its termination by the Speaker. The members of the Conference had agreed that the Speaker should publish a statement which any member should be free to revise by another published statement. He went on to add that throughout the whole 4 days Lansdowne and Law gave no helping hand towards settlement though the latter had pacific intervals. As the Irishmen made no progress towards settlement the P.M. and Ll.G. on their own responsibility offered Carson that half of Fermanagh, a quarter of Tyrone and the 4 Ulster counties should be allowed to vote as a block on inclusion. Thereon both Carson and Redmond joined quickly in rejecting the proposal. Then the Speaker, appealed to by Asquith, proposed that Tyrone should be treated as a separate enclave, and excluded for 2 years, and then allowed to vote itself in or out of Home Rule. Carson interjected 'But they will vote themselves in.' Whereon the Speaker, as if at last awake to their intentional obstruction, asked 'Are you proposing that the people themselves should never be consulted?'

The most interesting and instructive part of the conference was the complete understanding which grew up between the two sections of the Irish. When all was over Dillon and Craig shook hands with cordiality and almost affection, the latter saying, 'You and I have sat many years in the House together, and you may have found [me] offensive and troublesome, but today I hope I have only shown myself as a foeman worthy of you.' Redmond and Carson parted from each other almost in tears, so the P.M. told us.

The King had an interview with Redmond at the end of the Conference and told him that he himself was not to be regarded as an enemy of Home Rule which he knew must come. He was only concerned that it should come peaceably. He left Redmond an enthusiastic royalist.

We then discussed our next step, and it was decided to go on with Amending Bill, in spite of the threats of Carson to call out the Covenanters to seize Derry. Simon's view was that if only we made known our intention to go on with Home Rule without dissolution, there would be no provisional Govt. and no Ulster Volunteers but that these would be used to drive us to dissolution. McKenna agreed. I am certain that neither our own people nor public opinion would permit us to ignore the Provisional Govt. when once started, however wise it might be to do so.

Grey broke in to say that the Ultimatum by Austria to Serbia had brought us nearer to a European Armageddon than we had been through all the Balkan troubles. He had suggested to Cambon, and was going to do so to Lichnowsky[23] that Germany, France, Italy and the U.K. should jointly press Austria and Russia to abstain from action, but he was certain that if Russia attacked Austria, Germany was bound to come to the latter's help. Italy had already asked him to pair the U.K. off against herself in case of a general row.

27 July

Spent Sunday at Lord Farrer's at Abinger Hammer. Amongst others Sir Thos. Barlow, the physician, and Dominic Spring Rice, a son of Stephen Spring Rice, and a very capable young man.

We had a Cabinet at 5.30 at H. of C. to discuss the Dublin riots and Serbia. Birrell gave us the most lame and unconvincing account of Mr. Harrell's action.[24] In the first place Birrell had not, save for a few days, been in Dublin for months, nor did it occur to him to go there now. Secondly, he had made up his mind on an *ex parte* statement of Doherty that Harrell was wilfully guilty. The whole of the present difficulties of Ulster and Dublin are due to Birrell's own negligence of his duties, and his habitual absence from Ireland.

As to Serbia Grey said that both the groups are waiting for England's decision. If she kept aloof from France and Russia we should forfeit naturally their confidence for ever, and Germany would almost certainly atttack France while Russia was mobilising. If on the other hand we said we were prepared to throw our lot in with the *Entente*, Russia would at once attack Austria. Consequently our influence for peace depended on our apparent indecision. Italy, dishonest as usual, was repudiating her obligations to the Triplice on the ground that Austria had not consulted her before the ultimatum.

Our fleet fortunately was mobilised after manoeuvres which gave us a pretext for retaining them in that state.

VII

War-lords under Strain

July–December 1914

✳ The First World War erupted dramatically from a period of relative diplomatic calm. On 28 June the Austrian Archduke Franz Ferdinand, heir to the Austro-Hungarian throne, was shot by Serbian nationalists at Sarajevo. Within a month the Austrians had issued a punitive ultimatum to Serbia, Russia had come to the Slav kingdom's aid, and Germany and France came hastening to support their respective allies. The suddenness of the crisis took the British Cabinet by surprise. Preoccupied by the violence of Howth rather than of Sarajevo, the Cabinet were startled into awareness by Grey's dire account of the European situation. Eventually the issue of Belgian neutrality provided the legal fiction and popular excuse for British intervention. In fact, closely tied diplomatically and strategically to France as she was, and facing the age-old threat of an expansionist Continental enemy to the Low Countries and the Channel Coast, Britain reverted to her traditional policy in such circumstances and went to war to redress the balance of power.

The scale of this war dawned slowly. It is obvious from Hobhouse that 'business as usual' remained the dominant sentiment despite the attempts of a few more belligerent—or far-sighted—spirits to seek radical changes in administrative, governmental or commercial practice to meet the new demands of war. Day by day, whether in the technicalities of 'cable' warfare, the supply of munitions, the recruitment of manpower, the disposition of the Navy, or the search for allies, the complexity of the problems and the unparalleled demands on resources increased. The mosaic of cares and responsibilities and the strain on Cabinet Ministers which followed, is faithfully reflected in the diaries. So too were the inevitable tensions which resulted from clashes over policy, not least from the mercurial Churchill, the growing stature of Lloyd George and the looming presence of 'that great poster' Kitchener. These three were the dominant figures in the Cabinet. By contrast Asquith himself was already assuming that quasi-judicial role which was soon to be so heavily criticised as a failure in real leadership. But at least until the end of 1914 the Liberal Cabinet were able to weather the storm. For the moment they muddled through. Despite the tensions, in most areas of policy the old answers still seemed adequate for the new questions the war was posing.

August [undated]

We have had daily Cabinets since Thursday last [30 July] with two on Sunday and Monday. At each we discussed what should be our attitude to France and Germany. We had and have no engagements to France and Cambon in an interview he had with E.G. never suggested that we in any way were bound to her. But he pleaded hard for assistance. Grey had from Lichnowsky the most definite assurances that as Germany and in particular the Emperor were working hard for peace, we ought to remain neutral, which Grey was inclined to do. But on Thursday despite the telegrams of Henry of Prussia and the Emperor William, . . . it became clear that Germany meant to invade France and violate Belgium and that to hoodwink us, she had kept Lichnowsky deliberately in the dark as to her real intentions. From that moment Grey who is sincerity itself became violently pro-French, and eventually the author of our rupture with Germany.

At first Ll.G. was very strongly anti-German, in memory no doubt of their attempts to Delcassé him in 1909 [sic], but as the Liberal papers were very anti-war, he veered round and became peaceful. Churchill was of course for any enterprise which gave him a chance of displaying the Navy as his instrument of destruction. McKenna was for war if Belgian territory was violated, but against the dispatch of an expeditionary force. Harcourt, Beauchamp and Simon were for unconditional peace. The P.M., Haldane and I for war if there was even a merely technical breach of the Belgium treaty. Pease and Runciman were strongly against war but not for unconditional neutrality. Burns on Sunday morning was saying that this meant either unconditional neutrality or (leaning over the table shaking his clenched fists) war with both hands, naval and military. He was interrupted by McK. and Ll.G. saying 'But *which* is your policy?' He hesitated, they repeated the challenge, and with a gulp said 'Neutrality, under circumstances', and turned very white. John Morley then said 'You all know my views, those of a lifetime, I cannot renounce and if you persevere in intervention, I cannot return to this room.' As he had said the same thing about once a month for 3 years, no one took this very seriously. At the end of our meeting J.B. lent forward and in a few words of deep feeling said he must separate himself from his colleagues with whom he had lived in friendship for 9 years and from a P.M. whom he loved. He was moved to tears. J. Morley said he too could not continue. The P.M. begged them to wait at events till our evening meeting. When we met at 6.30 to continue the pros and cons of neutrality or intervention we the majority came to an understanding that E.G. should tell the H. of C. that we could not stand aside if Belgium were invaded, and that we would give France maritime protection, and so inform Germany. The minority—Burns, J. Morley, Beauchamp, Simon said they could not agree and they must retire. On Monday Aug. 3, after settling what Grey should say, the P.M. said he had the painful duty of telling us he had received the resignations of J.M., J.B. and Simon. Beauchamp leant forward and asked to be included. The P.M. whose eyes filled with tears, said it was the first time in his 6 years of leadership; they were men for whom he had regard and friendship; the party was still hesitating; the country was in danger and unity of counsel was essential. So they agreed except Burns, who had undoubtedly been trapped by Ll.G., to stay, until after Grey had spoken and the H. of C. had indicated its opinion— not very brave conduct. In Simon's case almost despicable because he pretended to a special and personal abhorrence of killing is any shape.

Grey made a very remarkable, moving and powerful speech presenting his case as I think no one else could have done. Its simplicity and sincerity, exhibiting the depth of the feeling of the speaker, contributed greatly to the effect it had on its audience.

He told one or two of his friends afterwards that the sight of the double row of chairs up the floor of the House recalled to him the Home Rule Bill of '86. He ought to have said perhaps of '92 for I saw them similarly in that latter year. The recollection brought back the fact that while he stood in Mr. G.'s place, hardly another person was now present who had been there. His friends, leaders, wife, most of his private life had disappeared and he was so overcome with emotion that if he had been called on at once he could not have spoken. Redmond's few words had an immense influence in steadying our people, and perceptibly affected the Tories, while taking the wind out of the sails of the Orangemen.

Our meetings on subsequent days were to discuss questions of detail, financial or military or social, and the measures decided to be taken were handed over to Committees for management. Our work in the Post Office was very heavy before the outbreak of hostilities, the numbers of telegrams being in excess of any previous record, and some of the staff working for 36 hours continuously. Ten thousand of the Postal Staff were mobilised as reservists, 6,000 as Territorials, and about 500 for postal work. I gave orders for the reduction of postal facilities all over the Kingdom and particularly in London, and stopped any recruitment for the staff, so that after the war we might have as many places as possible vacant for discharged soldiers.

12 August

Yesterday, Aug. 11th, Cabinet determined to incite Japan to declare war against Germany. Harcourt was doubtful of the effect on the Colonies. I was alone in saying, whatever others may have thought, that I thought to bring Japan in would bring us greater trouble than she would remove. She would be a greater rival than Germany to our Eastern trade, she might arouse fears of Colonials, she would certainly enable German press in U.S.A. to arouse considerable feeling against the power who actively allied herself with a yellow race which Americans hated and dreaded. I urged that the *casus foederis* had not arisen, and that if Japan wished to come in she ought to do so on her own account. No one took my views, though the previous day the P.M. had expressed himself strongly against using a Japanese alliance.[1] While we were discussing a telegram came to Grey from the Tokyo embassy saying Japan was going in anyhow and that no Govt. could withstand anti-German clamour, much heightened by threats of German ambassador.

Birrell then asked that Irish National Volunteers should be recognised. Kitchener who made his second appearance at Cabinet said he thought recognition should be the vehicle by which arrangement should be reached. His idea of arrangement being the postponement of Home Rule Bill. He professed himself unable to comprehend that a majority of the House would not permit this arrangement, and that unanimity depended on 2 sets of conditions being complied with. After some struggle with him and Churchill, the P.M. in reply to a direct inquiry by myself agreed that recognition of the Volunteers in Ireland could not be made conditional, but must be immediate and complete.

14 August

Cabinet yesterday and today were occupied by the question of food and raw material supply, the mining of the North Sea, and the reopening of trade with Norway and Denmark. This last despite opposition from Churchill was agreed to. The W.O. censors have held up telegrams from the U.S. Ambassador, and if it was not for Mr. Page's good sense, there would have been trouble with this very sensitive nation.[2] Then we got on to the subject of Rotterdam as a depot for provisioning Germany. Grey, who has never forgiven Germany for attempting to play with him, is the fiercest of us all to destroy her once and for all. He looks on her as the reckless author of war and its attendant miseries, and wishes to prevent her ever again indulging in the same cruel game. He proposed to institute conditional contraband i.e. that Holland should be entitled to unrestricted entry of the same quantity of supplies as she took from year to year, but that everything over that should be held to be for Germany and should be captured. Haldane thought a case for doing this could be sustained before our Prize Courts, the P.M. and Simon thought the contrary, an admirable testimony to the impartiality of the British Law Courts which foreign nations would perhaps not credit. It was eventually agreed to offer Holland coal and cotton, which she badly wants, if she would facilitate our restriction of her other imports.

* It was soon apparent that this would not be simply a war of armies. Economic and diplomatic considerations were of paramount importance. The Allies hoped especially to prevent Turkey from joining forces with the Central Powers, and to attract Italy away from her allegiance to the Triple Alliance with Germany and Austro-Hungary.

21 August

Cabinet yesterday and today. Ll.G. away with bad cold. He has been much overworked of late. Runciman says that the way he has picked up financial questions is marvellous. He knew nothing originally of commerce and trade, and bills of landing or of exchange, holders, drawers, acceptors had no meaning for him. Notwithstanding all this he has mastered these problems, and captivated the bankers and the measures taken have been wise, prudent and farseeing. Discussion occurred as to the action of Japan, which Grey finds cannot be circumscribed as he desired and thought possible. They claim and intend to exercise a free hand in dealing with Germany. Italy has put forward her claims if she is to take part in the war on our side. They will, if they are or have to be granted, make her independent of Austria and strong enough to stand up to a reduced Prussia, but their demand will damage any possible reputation she may have hitherto retained. . . .

The last 3 or 4 meetings have been occupied by consideration of the position of neutrals. Churchill jumping about from consideration to consideration, 'backing and filling' without rhyme or reason, but with incessant talk. First telegrams of congratulation to Enver Bey through Admiral Limpus,[3] then orders to the Fleet to seize all Turkish ships. Grey very angry about the *Goeben* but recognising the Turks had legitimate grievance over *Osman*[4]. He told that there was an unceasing struggle between pro- and anti-Germans. He thought the pro-Germans would win because while the others threatened Enver performed assassinations. The P.M. said that Enver had received Churchill's telegram and was reported to be much pleased at it adding 'a very queer set of people these Turks', which remark W.S.C. did not respond to. The latter said that we had captured 35 German ships in distant waters; they had accosted, without taking, only one of ours. Today, however, they took the *Hyades*, and sank her, though she had a German cargo, paid for and insured by Germans.

The Turks have dismissed Limpus—so W.S.C. would attack Turkey, without giving a thought to what Bulgaria would do, and ignoring Rumania. Ll.G. was equally violent and heedless. Greece having made us an offer of 250,000 men, her fleet and harbours, W.S.C. propounded a Napoleonic plan of forcing the Danish passage with the help of the Greeks, and convoying Russian troops to the coast off Berlin and making a *coup de théâtre*.

Belgium came to us for rifles, preferably Mausers, so we gave her those captured from the National Irish Volunteers and recommended her to try for those of the Ulster Volunteers. Carson and his friends however refused, unless the Govt. would undertake, should Home Rule Bill be passed, to replace those given to Belgium by rifles from Govt. stores, truly a drôle proposition producible only in Ireland. Eventually Redmond gave the Belgians all his Volunteers' rifles. . . .

✳ By 20 August the British Expeditionary Force of five divisions had
landed in France and moved into position on the French left. On 23
August they faced the German attack at the Battle of Mons two British
divisions facing General von Kluck's six divisions. But on the same day
the Germans entered Namur, and the ensuing French retreat forced the
British to retire also.

25 August

Monday's news was uncomfortable. Kitchener whether from personal
recollection of 1870, or from knowledge of or prejudice against the
French has always been pessimistic. When Gen. French's telegram
came to say that he had had a hard day's fighting, held his own, but
owing to the fall of Namur had to abandon his position and fall back
about 12 miles, K. was of wrath and some despair. He and the
Cabinet jumped to the conclusion that 'Namur' meant the *forts*, I
said it might mean only the town, and with great difficulty got our
official statement confined to Namur. Kitchener wanting to add
'Fort'. Ll.G. was for 'taking the people into our confidence', in
other words scaring them out of their senses. If things go wrong he
will try to cut us adrift of our allies, and make terms at almost any
price. Kitchener took the opportunity to unfold a scheme, with foreign
garrisons, colonials, territorials etc. which would give us 29 Divisions
in all. The 5th Div. having gone on Friday, the 6th he desired
to hold back in case the French had to be extricated. For this purpose
Cherbourg peninsula might be fortified and held by the British.

On Tuesday came confirmation that I was right and Namur forts
were holding out 'au bout' which alas also confirmed K.'s doubts as
to the qualities of the French troops. These he said as in 1870 were
always being drawn back for a fresh spring until they reached the
time and place where forward movements were impossible. The
120,000 men of his new army were reached last week; we have arms
apparently for 750,000, and can turn out 4,000 a week. Horses are
very short. Guns can apparently be got. Ammunition is being got
from the U.S.A. through Canada.

W.S.C. brought up Conscription as an immediate remedy. The
P.M. asked why we should discuss it now, so did [?] and most of the
others. W.S.C. said truly that if not now we should never speak of it,
for Germany if victorious would annex us politically, and if defeated
would depart with her system of militarism into limbo.

I said that a proposal of F. E. Smith to explain, through M.P.s, the reasons for, and the necessity for maintaining, the war should be accepted and put into force now. If it caught on K. would get a second 100,000 voluntarily—and *then* we could fall back on conscription. However the P.M. was determined that only his eloquence and that of Grey could rouse the country to a sense of duty and peril, and that neither could spare time for speeches.

26 August
Our difficulty is that the French War Office don't tell their Military Attaché or even Ambassador what they are doing, perhaps not even their own Govt., and least of all Sir John French. We think their movements show indecision and lack of judgement. We know nothing of their gains or losses, so we have asked K. to telegraph to Sir John French and to Sir J. Maxwell[5], our General attached to the French Army H.Q. staff to represent our desire for complete information. We gather from our own people that the 1st Army is being moved up from the south to *our* right wing. . . .

31 August
Sir Horace Rumbold, Councillor of Embassy at Berlin, dined with me a few days ago.[6] Up to the last there seems to have been a struggle between Von Jagow and Zimmerman of the German F.O. for peace, and Tirpitz, with Stumm of the I.F.O. for war. Goschen's dispatch gives the important details and facts. The footmen of the Embassy set their Kaiser an example by pulling off their livery, and stamping on it in the drawing room. The better-dressed part of the crowd attacking the Embassy was the most violent. In Holland Rumbold saw a Russian lady whose face was cut open by a blow from a stick given by a German officer. He himself had to leave his house with all his pictures, furniture, plate, clothes, without a single person to look after it of any nation or age.

It appears to be thought that we are not getting enough recruits; as a matter of fact they are coming in at the rate of 10,000 or 11,000 a day.

French's report of the French troops is not satisfactory. Gen. Joffre[7] gives him no information as to plans or dispositions; left him to bear the brunt of the 4 days' fighting from Sunday to Wednesday, and forced him to retire as the only alternative to being left 'in the air'. Meanwhile we only know of about 700 wounded. French has reported only 5,000 to 6,000 losses, out of 148,000 in the field, and yet today he proposes to retire behind the Seine, resting on Compiègne-Clermont. He also has lost 27 guns, but none was abandoned save those who were injured by shell fire, or whose horses were all killed. The Germans can't ride, shoot or face the bayonet, but their artillery fire has been overwhelming, directed by a cloud of aeroplanes.

Joffre and French do not seem on the best of terms. The latter does not like the former's plan of constant retreat; while Joffre said to French he would not advance 'owing to the inability of the British to go forward'. French proposes to retire S.W. behind the Seine and base himself on Le Mans. This seems to us to be cutting himself adrift from the French plan, whatever that be, and as we cannot reconcile 3% losses with a necessity for retirement to 'reorganise', especially after 4 days' rest, we telegraphed to him to give his reasons and his losses. Gen. Joffre sent Gen. French a portmanteau of Légion d'honneurs for distribution!

The P.M. saw some of the wounded yesterday. One, an Irishman, whom he closely cross-questioned, declared most succinctly that he had seen the Germans driving before them to the attack troops of Belgian men and women, and when any of these were wounded, they were thrown aside, and others dragged forward in their place.

1 September

French's difficulties may easily be of his own making, if he is as reticent to the French military authorities as he is to us. Consequent on our telegrams of yesterday he telegraphed last night a casualty list of over 4,000 for less than one-half of his army, and that the least heavily engaged. He now explains that twice his force saved the day for the French armies during the continuous 4 days' fighting, and on each occasion was little supported or relieved by the French Corps adjacent. He thinks that Joffre is badly supported by his Generals, some at least of whom owe their rank and command to political influence. He believes the soldiers to be admirable, but the higher leading to be defective. Of the Germans he has a poor opinion. Their cavalry unless 3 or 4 to 1 fly before ours, the infantry can't shoot or stomach the bayonet, and it is only the astonishing volume, not quality, of their artillery which saves them. He told Sir F. Bertie[8] to inform President Poincaré that he intended to draw off his troops to the S.W. and to recruit them for a separate campaign. In face of the two telegrams summarised above, the P.M., W.S.C., Pease and Grey authorised the dispatch of K. to Paris to meet French Military authorities with Poincaré. They met at midnight and K. left at 1 a.m.

From the casualty list it would appear that the whole of the Cheshire Regt. has been wiped out. The Cavalry would appear to have suffered little.

We are told to expect Zeppelins over London at any night. W.S.C. has sent 100 aeroplanes to Dunkirk to watch for them. In the last resort the officers in charge of aeroplanes will charge the Zeppelins, but in view of the certain death have arranged to draw lots for the task.

3 September

Two Cabinets today, the second being to hear what K. had to say. I undertook to lay a cable to La Rochelle to take the place of that which is (or are) likely to be cut to or in the north of France. I got the engineers to pick up the German cable from Emden to Vigo, added 30 miles to it in the Channel, and led the new end into New-haven, and 280 miles to the Atlantic end to bring it into La Rochelle, our new naval base with France.

W.S.C. elaborated a plan for combining with the Greeks to seize Gallipoli, and thus dominate Constantinople before the Germans have armed the forts. The whole country has seen, spoken to, and cheered a Russian force traversing the U.K. from Rosyth to Southampton! As a fact, though we discussed the feasibility of such a plan of bringing Russians from Archangel to France, we found there were no troops quartered there and the line of rail to that port from Russia was a single one, and incapable of transporting any appreciable body of men. . . .

The co-operation of Japanese troops and ships in Europe was pressed by everyone. If we are to utilise this dangerous ally, we may as well make full use of his powers, but I don't like the alliance.

Kitchener returned at 6.30—and came straight to Cabinet at 7. Though he went in uniform he escaped report. He saw M. Millerand, French Minister of War, and Gen. French whom he clearly con-sidered distraught, but between whom and Gen. Joffre there had been no quarrel, only misunderstanding. Owing to bad training Gen.

French did not comprehend that he must himself see that his army was refitted, and that he could not depend on others—Gen. Robb had not done his work well on the lines of communication. The men, transport and guns we sent him had not been forwarded to him, and his force had undoubtedly lost value. The Germans had concentrated against the British troops who had not been too well supported by the French on either flank. They had now resumed their place in the front line, and were fighting a successful action. French was however very reluctant that K. should either visit his troops or see Gen. Joffre.

W.S.C. proposed to us today that he had authority from the Cabinet to capture or sink every vessel which appeared in a given area round the Dogger Bank; regardless of nationality or occupation, or cargo. He even declared that he had instructed his ships to sink without examination, or boarding any vessel so found and all this because the Germans had employed, as he supposed, Dutch trawlers to lay mines.

No one was proceeding to object to this until I told him such a course was a declaration of war on the world, and that though it might be fair to hang people caught laying mines, he himself would deserve to be hung for sinking fishermen or seamen following a peaceful or lawful calling. He retaliated that my opinion was of no value. But the P.M. suggested we should require all fishermen to carry a British licence. He was not pleased when I reminded the Cabinet that it was precisely this requirement which made the Dutch declare war on us in 1660.[9] Eventually W.S.C. declared he would bring forward 'a more reasonable proposal' tomorrow. . . .

7 September

Kitchener asked us today to sanction the departure of the 6th Div. and it goes at 3.30 p.m. Dick Wortley who is the second in command in the Q.M.G.'s Dept. being Director of Military movements asked me today at lunch why the Cabinet had refused to let it go before. I told him that K. had recommended to us that in the first instance he could only let 4 Divisions go as the German plans re a raid were not developed. Later he came and proposed the dispatch of the 5th Div., still saying he could not part with the 6th Div. In each case, including today he got immediate and unquestioning sanction to his demands. Wortley replied that the W.O. had been urging the earlier dispatch of the 5th and 6th Divisions, and K.'s reply had been that the Cabinet would not sanction their dispatch in spite of his insistence. In fact K. had been at his old tricks. As we walked back to work, Wortley told me quite casually that French had wanted to fix his base at Le Mans, and K. had tried to place it at La Rochelle, but that eventually French had prevailed, and the bases were fixed at Le Mans and St. Nazaire. I asked him was he certain about this, as K. had told us La Rochelle was to be our sea-base and I was bringing a special cable there. Wortley insisted he was certain. So I made him go to Sir J. Cowans, Q.M.G., and very soon I had a message to say that St. Nazaire was to be our base, and not La Rochelle. I am writing for confirmation of this, but the above doings do not increase my confidence in K. . . . .

8 September

War news more encouraging. Joffre's strategy is approved by Kitchener who reports that Gen. French writes that since the G.O.C. of the 5th French Army was dismissed the morale of the French troops have improved wonderfully. He is sending us his *first* dispatch on Wednesday—tomorrow.

Kitchener contemplates 46 Divisions in the field within 12 months from now, i.e. 8 regular Divs., 3 Colonial, 2 Indian, 7 Territorial, 24 of the 4 'K.' armies: 3 Municipal and 1 Marine. We have already sent 6 complete Divs. *and* 26,000 reinforcements.

W.S.C. then proposed to take the Dutch Govt. 'by the throat', and force them to allow us to use the Scheldt to revictual and rearm Antwerp, to which violation of the neutrality of Dutch waters, he assured us the Dutch would not object. He offered no evidence in support of this assertion, while all our evidence is the other way. Eventually at Grey's suggestion we agreed to put the foodstuffs openly in the cargo, and carry what we could secretly. I thought and said that I saw no difference between the Germans violating their guarantee of Belgian neutrality, and our violating the neutrality of the Scheldt, if we had guaranteed it. It would bring down on us 250,000 Dutch, and the certain loss of Antwerp.

9 September

The P.M. presented us with the Home Rule alternatives which he thought Redmond should choose from. Suspension of the Home Rule Act for 12 months or the end of the war whichever might be the longer period, or an arrangement to bring Ulster in afterwards. Birrell agreed that the second was the best, but doubted if Redmond had authority to carry it in S. Ireland. B. Law on the other hand asked for, but did not expect a moratorium for Irish and Welsh legislation, but wrote that he would acquiesce in our first proposal.

Kitchener said, and as I know truly, that there was so little recruiting from Ireland outside of Ulster, that he had to fill up the gaps in the Irish regts. with English reinforcements. . . .

The French Govt. put out a feeler as to whether we should consent to their flotation of Treasury bills in London. As they have £160 millions sterling tucked safely away somewhere, and we have to finance our own expenditure, and that of other countries, we thought we could only agree to the extent of money required to pay for orders placed in this country.

13 September

Neither of the Cabinets of the 10th or 11th were very interesting. On Friday K. tried to defend the employment of Church agencies, parsons, curates etc. as the purveyors of separation allowances etc. He seemed to be astonished at our opposition, and eventually agreed with me that P.O. should take over payment of pay, pensions, or allowances, leaving charitable donations to look after themselves.

He was very angry at Ivor Herbert's[10] exposure of the recruiting arrangements for the later recruits, which Henry Guest, now in that Dept. of the W.O. tells me are very bad. To shield his own reputation he threw the blame on Lord Middleton's Committee, and wrote him as insolent and untrue a letter dissolving the Committee as could be conceived.

16 September

Our last 3 meetings [11, 15, 16 September] have not been very informing. French's telegrams are very brief and indicate a recurrence of nervous tensions. He lets his army waste *matériel* as if we were at the end instead of the beginning of the war, and his letters, so K. says show that he and his staff really think that this battle on the Marne is going to end the campaign. We think that it is only a prelude to a winter campaign, which the Germans will conduct on the banks of the Meuse.

. . . French is asking continuously for fresh officers who must all be experienced soldiers. We have sent him out 630 officers, besides those of the 2 extra Divisions. But as the troops have had 21 days' continuous fighting, it is not surprising if French is a little over-wrought.

W.S.C. tells us that the German cruiser *Emden* which has been lost for 3 weeks has reappeared off the Hooghly,[11] where she is coaling at her leisure, having sunk 5 ships, one of 7,000 tons. The *Gneisenau* and *Scharnhorst* have also arrived off Samoa, but finding the place in British occupation cleared off. His Admiralty expect that these cruisers will make for the straits of Magellan, but we don't understand how they get their coal. W.S.C. says that until his con-voying duties are over, he is quite unable to capture these cruisers. Russia asks us to float a £10 million loan, which we are not ready to do unless she will spend the money here. Bulgaria also wants money, but offers little value for it. News from E. Africa is not good —poor Grey is much cut up at his brother's wound and amputated arm. No one ever deserved better, and had worse, fortune in his domestic life. McKenna has investigated 8,000 'spy' cases: in none has he found any actionable treason, although a few individual aliens have been found in possession of arms.

A very circumstantial statement that a soldier in the British infirmary had been found mutilated by retreating Germans was specially inquired into, and found to be quite untrue.

It was agreed that until they had proved their worth, the Cana-dians and other Colonials need only be received by Ld. Roberts[12] and the local Mayors, for whom K. said they seemed to have a strange regard.

We agreed to pay enhanced separation allowances to dependants of wounded soldiers up to 16/9 p.w. to those with 4 children. I under-took to *pay* these for both W.O. and Admiralty. Crewe naïvely told us today that Graham, the Clerk of Parliament in H. of L. had gone to *Lansdowne* to tell him something of the procedure necessary under the Parliament Act and he himself had then written to Lansdowne asking what Graham had said. It is a further example of the power of Tories in Lords, that Opposition should settle procedure, to which Crewe is so accustomed that he did not even notice it as a strange method of doing Govt. business.

Cabinet on recommendation of W.O. and Admiralty, agreed to abandon the wireless chain of stations round the Empire.[13]

18 September

I attended H. of C. today. As I was in the middle of answering a question put by Sir J. Rees, Black Rod arrived. We went off to hear the King's Assent to various ordinary Bills. After them, and separately came the 2 Parliament Act Bills, Home Rule and Welsh Church. H. Samuel and I were the only two Cabinet Ministers present in the Lords behind the Deputy Speaker at the Bar. Next to me stood John Redmond, behind him his brother, and 50 or 60 members. There was a large party of ladies on the right-hand side, but only two peeresses—Lady Pirrie and another a little way off. When the Clerk of Parliament came to the 'Govt. of Ireland Bill', the Commons present cheered loudly, an unprecedented event, and again but less heartily for the Welsh Bill. H.S. and I shook Redmond by the hand, he displayed no emotion *here*. Afterwards in the Commons, when Whitley[14] reached the Bill there was some subdued cheering, and later on Crooks[15] starting the National Anthem, some very self-conscious and shy singing in which the Irish members joined heartily. It is almost 20 years ago exactly that I attended as M.P. for East Wilts. the contemptuous rejection by the Lords of Mr. G.'s. measure.

24 September

The three last Cabinets have been tolerably peaceful, thanks to Churchill's absence. He has made up for it today by talking without cessation, interrupting everyone, even the P.M. and K. and Ed. Grey on their own Depts. . . . The P.M., K., and W.S.C. on Friday put their heads together and under the latter's inspiration sent 3,000 Marines, and the Oxford Yeomanry under Gen. Aston to Dunkirk to demonstrate with some 18,000 French territorial troops as if they were the vanguard of a large British force towards Douai and the German right. The British Consul at Dunkirk reports the French territorials to be brave and efficient, but their officers to be incompetent, their generals to be jealous, and the whole scheme to be fraught with extreme danger. K. is very nervous at the continuance of the Aisne battle for so long. He fears the Germans will outstay the French and will bring up reserves. Sir John French is not very easy either. The heavy waste of men upsets the latter, and of *matériel* the former. . . .

W.S.C. was very brief in his references to the 3 lost cruisers,[16] his comment was 'very provoking'. If his observations on other occasions were equally short, we should get through business much easier. He seems to have run across to Dunkirk and there met Seely who had come up from Gen. Sir J. French to arrange for this foolish adventure. While he was talking one of our own airships came over Downing St. and we all turned out on to the terrace to look at it, not being more than 300 ft. up.

28 September

I came to stay with Birrell at the Chief Secretary's Lodge, where he has not stayed for 2 years. The party was Lord Crewe, Percy and Mrs. Illingworth, Ld. Lucas and Miss Herbert, Sir Harry Verney and John Simon. A most comfortable house, and a beautiful view over the Wicklow Hills. We went to the P.M.'s meeting in the Mansion House. The Lord Mayor said he would admit no ladies, whereon the P.M. said if there were no ladies, there was no speech. So eventually the female belongings of the 7 Cabinet Ministers were admitted. The audience was friendly, very curious as to possible results, and sufficiently appreciative. The P.M.'s speech was admirable, but much of it they could hardly understand, and when at the end they sang 'God Save the King' most of them could only guess at the time. We supped at the Viceregal Lodge, a most dismal affair.

2 October

It appears that though the Belgians have 60,000 regular and 80,000 territorial troops in Antwerp, and the investing Germans are only 50,000–60,000, yet the former are in great trepidation. They have asked us to send 1 Division and we have agreed, if the French will also send 1 Div. of *regular* troops, they want to send only territorial troops. We have also sent naval big guns and gunners. As we are housing thousands of their homeless people, and lending them £10 millions sterling, they ought to be grateful. It will be interesting to see how soon they will forget their debt.

The Portuguese are very insistent on entering the *Entente*, and solicit us to use their guns and troops.

Dr. Seaman has established the fact that many, perhaps all, German soldiers are provided with discs of compressed benzine which on being lighted will flare up, and set fire to any building, and it is with these that they fired Termonde and Louvain.[17] There is little doubt according to Dr. S. that the Belgian people are in close danger of actual starvation, so we agreed to provide them with food, to be bought if possible in Holland, and to take over all their German prisoners.

One result of the *Emden*'s activities is that the Indian cavalry transports are detained at Calcutta, and since it takes 7 ships to hunt for her, and 2 parties of large ships to look for the *Scharnhorst* and *Gneisenau*, I think the Germans have reasons to be proud of their cruisers.

Meanwhile the Turks threaten us with an ultimatum because the gunboat *Odin* is anchored in the Shatt-al-Arab.[18] Grey means to reply that so long as the Turks shelter the *Goeben* in the Dardanelles, so long shall we do what we like in other Turkish territorial waters.

With McK. I met a deputation of Manchester merchants who desired the resumption of code telegraphic messages. He and I are agreed to this but the W.O. are very obdurate, and he will only be successful by threatening to withdraw the warrant under which alone the W.O. can censor letters. We have picked up over 300 miles of German cable wire, given some to the French and utilised some to lay a fresh cable between Dartmouth and Brest.

5 October

At Cabinet today K. announced the decision of Sir J. French and Joffre to gradually withdraw the British Army from its positions near Soissons where it has worked up to a salient in advance of its French neighbours, and reorganise and concentrate it near St. Omer. The German movements on their right seem to have brought Castelnau to a standstill, and he has permitted them to entrench in front of him. Meanwhile in Antwerp there was nearly a débâcle. On Friday at midnight E.G. and K. were told that the Belgian ministry had decided that the King[19] and archives and field army should embark for England. Mr. Van der Weyde, the socialist deputy, and the King were alone resolute in opposing this decision. Our 2 Ministers were convinced of the fatal nature of this step, they stopped the train in which W.S.C. was going to one of his jaunts, got him back, and eventually sent him off helter-skelter to Antwerp. Meanwhile K. got together the 7th Division 18,000 infantry, 4,000 cavalry with Gen. Aston and 8,000 men of a Naval Brigade and sent them off to Antwerp. The French agreed to send 15,000 Territorial troops, 6,000 Fusilier Marines, 2,000 details with 24 guns. Making a total force of 53,000 men. As the Germans are credibly reported to have only 50,000–60,000 of second-line troops mainly we ought easily to relieve the city.

Meanwhile W.S.C. telegraphed to P.M. that he thought he ought to place his resignation in P.M.'s hands, and to offer to take military service. Such service to be in command of the expedition to Antwerp with appropriate military rank, and a full staff. This generous offer was declined together with his advice as to his successor. He appears to have promoted during his stay in Antwerp several officers to be generals.

By a diary found on a German officer, that army has certainly crossed the Dutch frontier at Maestricht, and we have heard of no remonstrance by the Dutch Govt.

With the dispatch of the 7th Div. to Antwerp disappears the last organised body of regulars in this country. Such a situation is dangerous, and if we can withdraw them from Antwerp we shall send them to the front and withdraw one of the Divisions that has suffered most, and when we have organised and dispatched the 8th Div. withdraw a second war-worn Division.

On the Russian frontier the Germans have 19 Army Corps and the Russians 19½ Army Corps and 4 Siberian Army Corps. The Russians report through the French Ambassador that the German troops are of the second line, and their guns of an old and inferior pattern.

6 October
This morning K. told us that one of 3 transports sent out from Dover by mistake, had come right through the mines outside Zeebrugge by night uninjured, a great piece of luck. The Admiralty have sown their mines in the wrong place, and almost blocked us out of Belgian ports. The French Minister of War wrote that Joffre begged that when Gen. French was concentrating at St. Omer, he should as each Division refitted push it up into the firing line, without waiting for the whole Army, at this moment the presence of one division might decide the battle and the campaign. We agreed with Joffre, but as French dissented we thought it only fair to ask his reasons. He seems again to be in difficulties with the French authorities. K. complained a great deal at the lack of information sent home by Gen. French. He had however asked to have Calais and Boulogne

entrenched and garrisoned by our Territorials. K. preferred a base at Dunkirk. W.S.C. is still away. The P.M. grumbles a good deal at having to do First Lord of the Admiralty as well as of the Treasury. Churchill has had an *audience* of the King of the Belgians 'with the result you might expect'; has deprived the Oxford Yeomanry of their horses, and otherwise made himself felt. I got Ll.G. to agree to finance my tube railway for mails between Paddington and Liverpool St.

8 October

Antwerp despite the enthusiasm which we were told would be and was aroused by W.S.C.'s visit is in great danger. The field army is shattered and worn by incessant conflict and the so-called garrison troops have no arms.

The Expeditionary Force is being gradually withdrawn from the centre of the French line and being again concentrated on the left with its base at Le Havre and its headquarters at Abbeville. In view of the Belgian weakness in Antwerp and the conflicting reports from Generals Parish and Aston we decided to send the 7th Div. to Ghent and attach it to Gen. French. We expect to be able to give him 14 complete Divisions by Xmas. We shall have great difficulties with the supply of guns, arms and rifles, and gun ammunition. The W.O. and K. seem unable to look forward more than 6 months in the matter of requirements. They were only prepared to order 400 guns, and it was all Ll.G.'s insistence alone which induced them to say 650, and even this is not half enough. K. refused to take the extra 20,000 Canadians, and is very unwilling to order any military supplies from America. Today he was absent from Cabinet very unfortunately as he and W.S.C. have issued contradictory orders to their respective generals, and the P.M. said (apropos of Cabinet Committee to see that the W.O. should order sufficiently in advance) that K. was always very reasonable, his first opinion on any subject was almost always bad—but he would always listen to arguments and be open to conviction.

The Cabinet decided that prosecutions for simply failing to report the existence of a wireless installation should be before a civil court, but any overt action should be referred to a court martial.

9 October

The French military authorities have for good or bad reasons refused

to send their troops to the rendezvous behind Antwerp. Consequently we cannot single-handed tackle the German Antwerp troops,
and the city must fall. It will become a centre for aircraft attacks
against us.

K. is still very obdurate about the sufficiency of supplies. He is
most difficult to persuade that they are now likely to be short next
July, and then will not be able to improvise. Ed. Grey and Ll.G.
accordingly combined to force him to agree to an investigation.

E.G. told us that the U.S.A. were getting very restive over contraband. Foodstuffs they were bent on procuring freedom for, and
would make a bargain over oil, rubber, and even copper. Oil being a
Republican interest, and copper being Democratic. They were also
bent on the doctrine of 'continuous voyage', which they had bitterly
opposed at The Hague.

14 October

I attended Ed. Fuller's funeral yesterday and missed Cabinet.
Today's was the most depressing meeting we have yet had. The
rebellion in S. Africa, the fall of Antwerp, and the rumoured
abandonment of Warsaw damped the volubility of Churchill and
affected all our spirits. As to Russia either our attaché is a very
incompetent person, or else the Russians don't let him send us what
he knows, at all events we are in complete ignorance of the situation
there, and so it appears are the French. As to Antwerp the P.M. and
K. are very anxious to block the entrance to the Scheldt by mines on
an extensive scale. W.S.C. objected very strongly, nominally because
he had only 2,500 mines and couldn't, as he said, get any more, but
really because he thought a mine-field would block in the German
fleet, and prevent or postpone the *réclame* of a naval victory. It is
obvious that a German occupation of Antwerp, which could have
easily been prevented if the Belgian troops or people had any spark
of valour left, renders us open to air or land attack comparatively
easily and deprives us of a jumping-off ground for air attacks on
Germany. K. is very apprehensive as to a German attack in force,
the P.M. as representing the C.I.D. very scornful of its possibility,
and Churchill quite certain that he could destroy the fleet and transports before they had landed 15,000 men.

One of my officials brought me today a letter which he had found
in the post, bearing the Admiralty seal, addressed to Herr Ballin by

W.S.C.[20] I sent it to the F.O. Runciman tells us that the Germans have in Hamburg 250,000 tons of shipping on which they could embark an expeditionary force. By this evening French will have concentrated the British force at St. Omer, with his left resting on the Belgian frontier. The 2nd Indian Division also landed in France today, and the Canadians at Devonport. A German submarine was seen off the Isle of Wight. The result of the Cabinet Sub-Committee at the W.O. has been to greatly expedite and expand supplies. We are promised by the trades concerned 66 new field-guns by April, 500 by May and 2,500 by July 1st. We had a long discussion as to the rate of payment to soldiers' widows and for the second time in my 3 years, a formal division of the Cabinet by votes was taken. Ten including the P.M., Haldane, Pease, Churchill, Beauchamp, Kitchener voting for 6/6 pension per week; 8 including Ll.G., Lucas, McK. Wood, McKenna and myself for 5/-. Birrell and Runciman were away.[21]

15 October

I was informed yesterday that one of the telephonists in the office had while speaking to France to our troops actually heard the orders being conveyed by Von Kluck's staff to his divisional commanders; and this afternoon they brought me in the actual cipher numbers being telephoned at Ghent. One of the military telephonists at the H.Q. in France heard on his telephone the shells whistling at Hazebrouck 20 miles off. One of our wireless operators tying a piece of wire to a metal bucket and his bedstead and connecting it with his electric light read off in bed the signals sent off in Madrid.

We had some sharp discussions on the Navy. W.S.C. told us in most pompous manner that a German submarine had been seen off Isle of Wight; the Admiralty could no longer guarantee the safety of transports, and he thought the W.O. should send troopships to St. Nazaire. K. objected strongly whereon W.S.C. developed his theme and said that it was impossible to block in the German submarines at Heligoland, and impossible to shut them out of our harbours and we should have to bring in our big ships. The P.M. said 'You mean we have lost command of the sea.' To this bald and true deduction from his remarks W.S.C. took great umbrage. However he had looked again into the mine question, and now told us that 2,500 a month could be procured and also undertook to let us have 100 real air-guns in 4 months. Ll.G. was absent having gone to France. Runciman said that 187 ships had entered British ports today, almost a record for any period.

16 October

W.S.C. came in with a very long face to say that another cruiser, the *Hawke*, had been blown up at 11 a.m.; only 50 people reported to be saved. Her sinking was so sudden there was not even time to send a wireless. Another German submarine had been sighted off Cherbourg, probably the same that was off the Isle of Wight. It is not reassuring to know that the Admiralty have at present no scheme of dealing with submarine attacks.

K. gave us the recruiting figures to date: 26,000 officers; 429,000 soldiers with previous experience; 678,000 recruits, raw; with 235,000 men at the front this gives us 1,360,000 under arms.

We can get no real news from Russia. Hanbury-Williams[22] telegraphs more fully, but gives us little real news. But it seems as if some of the Army Commanders had not reached their places in time, and been dismissed. The forward movement had come to a standstill, and the reorganisation commenced. Meanwhile Przemyśl is besieged by the Russians employing the Japanese siege train and gunners who took part in the attack on Port Arthur.

20 October

. . . Ll.G. and Simon have just been over to France. The former brought back a vivid and useful account. He got within 1,500 metres of the German trenches, which now only fired two bombardments a day at 11 and 2. Foch[23] and Castelnau told him that their troops had been 79 days under fire. They had imagined that the course of the war would be big battles with intervals of quiet: nor had they understood the resisting power of trenches, but now they did, there would be no more French retreats. Ll.G. said the spirit and morale of the French troops was now excellent, but it had been restored by drastic methods. The troops who ran away at Namur, were taken out into the open and drilled under heavy shell fire. The Nicois contingent who ran away in Lorraine on the ground that the war which was no concern or quarrel of theirs were made to stand with their backs to the enemy in front of their own trenches under shell fire. Many were court-martialled and shot, but courage was created and discipline restored. As to the stories of gains, reported by the French staff, it only meant a kilometre or two, behind they found a fresh set of entrenchments awaiting them.

The French could not praise our transport arrangements too highly, nor our aviators. The latter however were much hampered by an air-gun, almost automatic, which burst shells on every side which gave off deadly fumes and paralysed their nerves. The French were making a new and very deadly gun, but were short of steel for shells which we promised to give them.

After some harmless recrimination between K. with W.S.C. and McK. we agreed to arrest tonight every German and Austrian of military age, in all about 23,000 persons.

The attitude of Botha and Smuts[24] in S.A. is magnificent. Buxton telegraphs that burghers are coming in large quantities, the local commandants are determined 'to remove the blot on the honour of the O.F.S. and Cape', rebellion is 'a sin against God, and a breach of the treaty of Vereiniging' and Maritz's treachery is making enthusiasm amongst those who were apathetic or even hostile.

21 October

Grey has today seen an American correspondent of *The Times* who has been in and out of Berlin. He says the Germans are in good spirits, well found in everything which the troops want and they are keen and eager for the war. On the other hand one of yesterday's prisoners was a hunchback which may point to some exhaustion of numbers. The submarines sent to the Baltic have got through, attacking by mistake a Danish submarine on the way. They are to be based on Libau and agitate German naval movements. We are doing what we can to accelerate submarine's construction, as the work is done by either firms or workmen distinct from ordinary naval constructors, we ought to make good. . . . K. and W.S.C. had a duel over the safety of the country from German invasion, from which the Navy could guarantee us so far as the landing of dangerous numbers went. K. was alarmed: the Germans meant to try it, they had a plan seriously framed for the purpose, plenty of shipping for transports, and plenty of aeroplanes. We had no organised regular force at present, and only the trained Territorials were armed, and but few of the 4 new armies. The Germans had concentration rails to Emden, we knew nothing of what was being done at Kiel or

Wilhelmshaven. Positions had been prepared round London. Positions had been prepared on the East coast, and we had done what we could, but a large force could be disembarked in a few hours.[25]

Harcourt read a telegram from S. Buxton saying the Union Govt. were very short of arms and ammunition, and the position was neither clear nor satisfactory.

22 October

This morning no news from French but a message from Col. Bridger, with the Belgians, who are again fighting bravely. The monitors who use special ammunition have been supplied with fresh shell and again been put into the firing line, and with some old training gunnery craft performed most useful service, firing 11,000 shells. A French military mission seeking supplies of steel and iron has come over. K. describes them as very able and intelligent. They told him that the waste of ammunition is beyond belief. In one day 200,000 shells were fired, and 4,000 guns have to be kept going. A new shell of high explosive powder is of frightful power. It ricochets and has a fuse which is set in motion by the first impact with the ground. It supersedes shrapnel. They recommend a battery of 2 guns only, instead of 6 or 4, as being quite equal to the existing German battery of 4 guns, and think the war must be ended by the exhaustion of *matériel* by one or both combatants. H. Samuel brought forward proposed regulations for the East coast population if the enemy landed. He stated the W.O. view was that the population should retreat taking away horses but leaving cattle. K. asked what part of the W.O. held this view, for himself he thought everything should be swept away. He is always unfair to his departmental chiefs and branches. He doesn't consult them, ridicules them to us, and throws them over perpetually. Samuel, like a true Jew, threw out his report in a tentative way to see which way the Cabinet was going to jump, and when he found that we would not accept his view that the civilian population should abstain from fighting, withdrew it without a murmur. We thought that the people should use every or any weapon, fight to the very last gasp, and accept and give no quarter. Every German soldier landing here should be exterminated.

We had a long dispute as to whether we should permit the entry of food into Holland or Germany under the guarantee of the Spanish and American Ministers that it should be used solely for the refugee

Belgian civilian population. K., W.S.C., McK., W.R., Lucas, Ll.G., I myself were of opinion that the Germans would use these supplies as enabling them to consume the Belgian supplies proper. Masterman for humanitarian, Grey, Haldane and the P.M. for diplomatic reasons would have sold or allowed the import of food from this or neutral countries to Holland or Belgium. We compromised the matter by giving a Govt. grant for the purchase, in Holland of foodstuffs by the Dutch Govt. or the 2 Ministers. A harmful decision, as the German garrisons will only requisition more largely and more freely from the Belgians, and Von der Goltz can quite safely guarantee the consumption by the Belgians only of these special imports.

23 October

Buxton's telegram saying that Generals Beyers[26] and C. de Wet[27] were on the point of breaking out into rebellion to set up an independent South Africa republic, and that many of the commandos would go with them, and that as these commandos had been given all the available arms in the country, he and Botha could not arrest them, was decidedly embarrassing. Harcourt proposed that the Australian and N.Z. troops should be sent via the Cape instead of the Canal, and stopped at Cape Town to be disembarked there if Botha needed them. The P.M. objected very strongly as the Colonials all hated each other cordially and would take assistance or even coercion by England which they would not accept from each other. He however got no support, and Harcourt's proposal was agreed to as the only possible course.

Turkish action against Egypt cannot well be delayed more than a few days. They are apparently waiting for money from Berlin to pay their troops with unless indeed they are playing with Germany, but the German officers sent in considerable numbers to all the Turkish frontiers will certainly see that some irrevocable step is taken. In that case Greece may join us, but more probably will keep out to prevent Bulgaria coming in.

Germany has great need of copper, rubber and petrol. Her expenditure of ammunition has been prodigious, and we are told that she searches her battle ground rigorously for cartridge cases. We are short of rifles, and unable to make them, guns don't give us the same trouble, and the French have sent us 60 German ones. The King

insists on opening Parliament in his absurd glass coach. We want
him to do so in uniform, riding down to H. of L. on his horse with
a military staff. The P.M. has argued long and vigorously to this
effect, but the King says 'coach or nothing'. The news from Belgium
was fairly satisfactory. The French have at least sent Gen. Foch
with a division of first-rate troops to help the Belgians.

28 October

French telegraphed today that in spite of the heavy losses—600
officers and 13,000 men in the battle of Armentières—he was very
confident of the result. Grey said that a Belgian officer of some
standing called on him chiefly to tell him that the visit of W.S.C. to
Antwerp had been the means of reviving the spirit of the Belgian
troops and inducing them to renew a struggle they had determined
to abandon. Churchill told us that yesterday the *Audacious* was sunk
by a mine off Tory Island, she took 8 hours to sink, and only 1 life
was lost. We discussed the advisability of publishing her loss. McK.,
K., and W.S.C. were vehemently against it. So was I, but I said that
it was impossible to conceal it. A thousand people were on board the
Olympic who tried to tow her to land. Letters were being sent to me
daily from persons receiving uncensored letters from Germany via
Genoa, and letters were returning that way. Ll.G., Crewe, Haldane
and Grey thought the withholding of bad news from the public
would shake their confidence in our good news being correct, and
would make foreign countries incredulous. The P.M. advised the
delay of publication. We discussed and decided against the formation
of an entrenched camp at Calais. The French military authorities
were opposed to it, and Sir J. French now thought it superfluous.
The *Evening News* learnt from a correspondent at Harwich yesterday
of the disaster to the *Audacious*, which he could only have learnt
from being able to read the Admiralty cipher. We told W.S.C. to
send for the Editor and say he would be court-martialled if he did
not reveal the name of the correspondent.

Buxton sent better news from S.A. We have obtained from
Portugal 12,000 Mausers and 12,000,000 rounds of ammunition and
can get them to the Cape in about 15 days. We have also got 500,000
Crag-Jorgensen rifles and ammunition complete from America.
Lloyd George raised the recruitment of the Welsh Army Corps; the
W.O. had only left Lord Plymouth and the Committee raising it

some 5,000 men out of 16,000. About 40,000 Welsh recruits, enlisted before the W.A.C. was mooted, had been formed into 30
new units incorporated into other Divisions, and the balance had
been taken to maintain the 3 Welsh Regts. at the front. K. refused to
form any of these units into the W.A.C. and was obstructive as
possible. Ll.G. argued his case with skill and patience. K. saw no
reason in grouping the Welshmen together etc. At length Ll.G. told
K. that he forgot he was not an autocrat but only one out of a body of
20 equals, that his attitude showed his sterility of ideas, and ignorance of British conditions and that he must expect and would
certainly get criticism of his doings. K. retorted that he was ready to
be criticised and to retire if necessary, but he would tolerate no
interference with the plan of the W.O. Everyone, even W.S.C. and
Grey sided with Ll.G. and K. made us very angry by trying to laugh
aside the argument. He got a great rebuff, which surprised and disgusted him, but did him good. The P.M. sat very silent.[28]

30 October
. . . Geoffrey Robinson had just previously been to tell the P.M. that
it was impossible to keep the loss of the *Audacious* secret any longer.
I showed the Cabinet a letter which passed the Censors' test by
containing an innocent letter, but which sent the real message under
the flap of the envelope, an ungumming process which would cost
an impossible amount of time. However it was eventually decided
that our policy should be announced as publishing nothing which
would encourage or advantage the enemy. Then we discussed S.
Africa. Harcourt wanted to stop the Australian troops; W.S.C. said
it would be difficult to coal the escorting ships at Mauritius, Cape
Town could be protected for the war, and the country recovered at
our leisure after it. The P.M. and Crewe thought the S. Africans
would resent strongly the use of Australians, for their 1899 record
was not very good. We agreed finally, after I had suggested that
Botha should settle their use or rejection, that they should be con-
voyed to Colombo, and by the time they reached there, the other
question of employment could be decided. Meanwhile Botha should
be asked to say whether he could tackle the rebels single-handed . . .

1 November
French's telegrams have been less optimistic than before, and he far

better than the French H.Q. staff seems to have realised the vital importance of winning this battle. The Germans have brought their Kaiser to Courtrai to exhort his troops to a supreme effort, and Dutch information tells us that the Germans have brought up at least 500,000 men for reinforcement. K. crossed to Dunkirk to see the French President and Ministers who were quite assured that the Germans could not sustain their attack, would go back quite quickly, and under pressure from Russia would make peace on fair terms at an early date. K. was not impressed by Joffre, but thought Gen. Foch a particularly brilliant man. He saw a good many Belgian infantry, strong, healthy, well-fed men strolling back from the front who told him they were not inclined to go fighting that day: and they had absolutely declined to capture certain German guns abandoned on account of the inundations. In a word they are 'journaliers'. Then Turkey's last coup came up for debate as to which W.S.C. said 'It was the best thing since the outbreak of war.' To which E.G. replied that Churchill was always wanting to drag the whole world into the quarrel. It was agreed in face of the German reinforcements, and the inability of the French to provide new troops for 2 months, and our men becoming as K. described them, 'pinched by strain not hunger', to ask Japan indirectly to consider the dispatch of quarter of a million men, for whom we should pay. It seemed to be agreed by K., E.G. and W.S.C. that Japan would agree to this and would be content by being thereby entitled to attend the post-war congress on an equality with the Great Powers. The P.M., Harcourt and I thought differently, and that she would probably demand a Pacific post in return for such help.

4 November

The news from S.A. is very unsatisfactory. The Cape Colony is held fairly well by Botha, but C. de Wet, Beyers and Wessels[29] have a largely preponderant influence in Orange Free State and Transvaal. Until we can get the arms from Portugal, the Union Govt. cannot arm such followers as they rely on. Botha has telegraphed that except in the direst need he does not wish for the Australians, or indeed for troops from anywhere else.

13 November

We have had a succession of uneventful Cabinets. On Friday 6th we discussed the advisability of court-martialling *The Times* and *Daily Mail* for giving, no doubt merely to spite the Govt., information criticising our preparations. This information has no doubt been made specially available to *The Times*, and K. has winked at this. Both he and W.S.C., who has an eye on future political movements, have no intention of offending these rags and they refused to take any action at present, though not denying the damage done by or the malevolence of *The Times*. Then we talked of Gen. Aitken's failure in E. Africa, where 30 officers and 1,300 men have already been lost. Neither Crewe, Harcourt, nor K. would own to have given him any instructions, and he appears to have been under the guidance of a subcommittee of the C.I.D.—a very bad expedient.

On the 9th we agreed to raise a million more men. K. and McKenna had a sharp difference of opinion. K. who is a coward when it comes to a tight place wants as many aliens out of prison as possible, but tried to make McK. responsible for their non-arrest. The fact is that McK. went on arresting aliens till the Adjutant-General asked him to stop saying he had no place to concentrate them in, or any means of guarding them. He declared it was a great pity he had not a seat in H. of C. so that he could tell them some home truths. It would be interesting to know how long he would keep his seat, and refreshing to hear him for once speak the truth.

On the 11th, I brought up a stupid act of W.S.C. for which I could in private get no redress. Last Friday his Admiral, Stanley Colville,[30] arrested and imprisoned in the local gaol without warning the whole of the postal staff of Lerwick, on the ground that some of his letters had been tampered with. They were kept in prison for 7 days and then released, a committee of experts having decided that the wiseacre of an Admiral had accidentally cut open his own letter which was enclosed in 3 envelopes. The Cabinet decided that the Admiralty must pay compensation, but Churchill would not consent to consider such cases jointly with the P.O. until I threatened to cut off all his own and the Fleet's postal or telegraphic communication. He behaved like an untruthful and spoilt schoolboy, which leavened by genius for speech is what he really is.

[On 13 November] Ll.G. and W.S.C. had some high words. Buckmaster had attended to explain he could not maintain the authority of Press Censor unless the W.O. and Admiralty supported him fully. K. as usual tried to control the exercise of censoring the press, but would not incur the odium of restraining much less prosecuting the press. Churchill supported him in what Ll.G. truly called a mean and shabby attack on Buckmaster. W.S.C. became white (or green) with anger, denounced Ll.G.'s 'insolence' which he would not tolerate from anyone. Ll.G. responded equally hotly, and the P.M. intervened.

25 November

Luckily the frequency of our meetings diminishes, for the strain tells on the tempers of the most equable . . .

We had some discussion as to asking aid in East Africa from the French in Madagascar, or the Belgians in the Congo. W.S.C. and K. thought that each or all would demand compensation in the form of a grant from German East Africa. Ll.G. hoped that it was not intended at the final settlement to strip Germany of her colonies, an issue everyone avoided replying to. K. quoted a letter from Beauchamp Duff saying he hoped they would waste no men taking the *Königsberg* whose crew would speedily rot in their trenches from fever. The Admiralty have reported to the W.O. that the sinking of the collier at the mouth of the Dar es Salaam would create a bar which no ship could cross. This W.S.C. has *not* told the Cabinet. It now appears that the *Königsberg* has no coal. She therefore cannot move.

27 November

The scare last week [of invasion] seems to be due to some wiseacre at the Admiralty having discovered that a very high tide synchronised with a new moon. Consequently the W.O. were persuaded to run troops all over the East coast. The Fleet were brought down from Scapa Flow and made an advance to Heligoland itself which shelled them from a safe distance, but nothing happened. One thing is certain and that is that 'command of the sea' can no longer be assured by number, speed, or size of your battle fleet. Large ocean-going submarines will render any fleet unsafe and unreliable. K.'s reluctance to face the public was again shown by his extreme unwillingness for a W.O. prosecution of the seditious Irish papers. Nathan writes that he thinks the S. and W. of Ireland very disloyal, but he has heartened himself up to taking action.

✳ Attempts to win over uncommitted nations to the Allied cause continued. Italy had remained neutral, claiming that the Triple Alliance did not apply to this conflict. A long campaign to woo her support for the Allies continued into 1915. Bulgaria, also neutral at the outset, appeared likely to move into the enemy camp.

4 December

K. had got an unusually long telegram from Russia and provided a map to explain it. We gathered round to listen, and looking round I saw E. Grey had climbed up on a chair to follow the places just as a schoolboy would have done. K. professed to have no knowledge whatever of the French plans, and very little of their movements. W.S.C. asked to be told well in advance of any advance of the Allied left in order that he might co-operate with the Navy, but he didn't wish to keep any ships at sea an unnecessary minute for fear of submarines at Zeebrugge.

We had a long discussion on Bulgaria. Ll.G., W.S.C. and Masterman wanted us to offer the whole of Macedonia to Bulgaria as a bribe to maintain neutrality. Sazonov had telegraphed to Grey suggesting that if Bulgaria maintained a whole-hearted neutrality, then the *Entente* powers would, at the settlement provide Bulgaria with 1. the Enos–Midia frontier; 2. an equitable readjustment in Macedonia; 3. the withdrawal of Greek troops from Serbian Macedonia at the end of the war. And to Greece if she came in now with 80,000 men to Serbia's help: a guarantee of freedom from attack by Bulgaria, and after the war, W. Albania less Vallona which must go to Italy. Grey agreed to second this offer, but our 3 colleagues moved by the sentimental Masterman wanted Bulgaria to get the whole of Macedonia plus Enos–Midia for *doing* nothing while Serbia, who whatever her morality may be, has fought valiantly is to give it up, and Greece is to risk her army and integrity for half Albania. Grey justly remarked that Bulgaria would not be bought by the size of the promise, but would consider which group would most probably be in a position to redeem its promises.

Until I supported E.G. vocally and asked the trio if it was likely that Greece and Rumania would accept that enlargement of Bulgaria now which they fought the second Balkan war to prevent, no one would back Grey; then others took up the running. The Cabinet agreed to give me £125,000 for a cable via Cape Clear to Archangel, wanted for strategical purposes.

8 December

... Ll.G. told us that Italy had now come for a loan of £8 millions. It was agreed that we should say to Boltons, the Italian agents, that we could only supply our *allies*. We have as a fact no guarantee that Italy will not come in against us. Denmark also asked for £1½ millions and gets the same answer.

Belgian requests are more difficult. We have agreed to finance the Congo, but it now appears that France is paying for the whole of the Belgian Army, which fact the Belgians did not disclose last week. We believe that France would like to get the Belgians in her pocket—but we have not resisted a German protectorate over Belgium in order to establish a French one.

We then had considerable discussion over the Balkans. W.S.C., Ll.G., and Masterman pressing for concessions and appeals to Bulgaria. Grey said Sazonov had suggested getting Serbia's consent to the transfer of Macedonia and the Enos-Midia line for Bulgaria, but he himself thought Bulgaria didn't mean to come in, she would pocket the offer, and wait to see who *could* deliver the goods. Greece would be disgruntled, and Rumania uncomfortable. The P.M. as usual started by supporting him, as did Haldane and myself, the rest of the Cabinet was silent, and then as usual the P.M. gave way to the insistence of the trio. E.G. much against his will and judgement agreed to support Sazonov's proposal.

✳ In December Hobhouse had his first opportunity to see for himself conditions on the Western Front.

On the morning of Monday Dec. 14 I crossed from Southampton to Le Havre to see how the postal service to the front was conducted. We took over about 80,000 parcels and 500,000 letters, and these occupied the whole of one of the 3 trains which are dispatched daily from Le Havre for the Army. We reached Le Havre at 3.30 p.m. where I found the General, Bruce Williams R.E. and his staff waiting for me, which was not what I expected as I had told F.O. I was making a private visit. He, however, very kindly took me all round his stores and supplies. There are now about 310,000 British soldiers in France, of whom about 55,000 are on the lines of communications, 20,000 being at Le Havre where they stay a short time *en route* to the front. A great part of the cotton sheds and wharves have been let to Gen. Williams at a rate equal to £10,000 p.a. for each shed, and though they give magnificent and indispensable shelter yet Le Havre Chamber of Commerce might remember that we are in Le Havre chiefly to defend France. The people of the town were busy with ordinary life and cares and seemed quite unconcerned with the outward show of war, and troops arriving or departing attracted only the most perfunctory notice. General Williams told me that Admiral Charlier, the Port Admiral, was a most tactful, obliging and energetic officer, but that hardly any subordinate French official or officer had any initiative or would take any responsibility. They were unable to free themselves from the meshes of prearranged plans or schemes. The recruit training in war was the recruit training of peace, and the area assigned under a pre-war scheme for detraining troops could not be occupied by stores however urgently space was wanted, and even though troops were not being detrained. In these depots were collected everything that an army could want: rifles, about 16,000 recovered from the battlefields; guns; 3,500 horses, of whom 2,000 were sick or disabled; 100,000 tons of Canadian hay; barrels of sugar and oil; clothing etc. literally in miles; portable engines; gifts from the various colonies, while in corners of the sheds were camped labourers, and battalions of territorials passing through. Amongst the recruited labourers were some of the most expert thieves in Europe—but the detective force had identified 38 who were herded together and made to work double hours.

I have about 800 postal servants working on purely postal business at the front and on the lines of communication under a Col. Price and 25 officers. Many of these during the Mons retreat were thrown into the firing line, but as a rule they only distribute to the Regt. headquarters. After dinner and sleep at the hotel where the service seemed to be normal, we motored on to Etretat, and thence to Fécamp. Here I visited a hospital started by Lady Guernsey and a Miss Nelson. The doctor, a man in good practice in London, said he had 60 patients all French, some bad wounds, but many badly frostbitten, he had 8 or 9 nurses and 15 Red Cross ladies whom he would gladly exchange for a quarter of their number of half-trained nurses. Here the French municipal authorities had been very helpful and requisitioned the hotel and casino for them. From there to Dieppe to meet General Maxwell and his posse of Brigadiers at lunch. The whole way from Le Havre to Bailleul the fields were fully tilled, the harvest of beets was in operation and the whole process of agriculture seemed unchecked, and many who ought to have been fighting were busy farming. I did not notice any unusually large appearance of mourning amongst the women, and scarcely any widows' weeds until I reached St. Omer. At first Gen. Maxwell was very shy of a politician, especially one in the Cabinet, but he warmed up and became very friendly. *He* had found the French easy to get on with, but unmethodical, never having much staying power, but brave and always ready to return to the attack; much readier indeed to first leave and then retake a position than to endure the discomfort of a night in the trenches. It was the chief trouble of all allies that since the Commanders-in-Chief had the temperament of their men the requirements made by each upon their men based upon different principles of attack and endurance. In particular the French had no 'six o'clock in the morning' courage. Their hospital arrangements were primeval, no trained nurses, no use of water, few sanitary arrangements no anti-tetanus serum, but the Doctors very skilful and sympathetic. The truth of these hospital criticisms I realised later. We, Evelyn Murray and I, reached Abbeville, the headquarters of the line of communication about 4, found Gen. Capper, settled in an hour's talk to move back some of my sorters to London and do the bulk of sorting in London. My wretched Col. Price was horrified that regulations should be discarded, but my plans will save the constant labour of keeping 400 non-combatants in France. We dined with the Brigadiers' Mess in the house of a German who had lived for years in the town keeping note of all things, but unluckily for himself got a new set of furniture just as war broke out. Our officers gave us an excellent dinner, and all seemed cheery and confident of holding their own against any reasonable number of Germans. Next morning we left at 7.30 with Col. Price as conductor in a car supplied by Gen. Capper. We raced to St. Omer in just under 2 hours, a good road. Many of the villages had detachments of British troops, at one was parked a full day's supply for the whole army in case anything went wrong down the line. I went straight to Sir. W. Robertson,[31] Q.M.G. of the Army whom not a few officers would like to see in Chief Command so great is the confidence he inspires. Self-educated, his 'h's are not certain, but he has a wonderful eye, which he turned very directly on me at first, but as I met him equally directly he soon looked at me normally. We had half an hour's talk on general matters, then he gave me a staff officer and I went off to find Gen. Morland,[32] G.O.C. 5th Division. From St. Omer to Bailleul was most interesting. The road is *pavé*, about the width of a motor and a half. Consequently every vehicle meeting another has to put one wheel into the mud which is anything from 1 to 2 ft. deep. This road is the only one to feed the British Army by, and is flat except where it climbs up the circular mounds on which are built Cassel and Bailleul. We met an unending stream of cavalry, infantry, ambulances and army service wagons going towards the front, the men looking well fed and clothed, well shod, cheerful but serious, though quite confident. The great numbers of horses being shod struck me, though it was natural enough.

It appeared to have struck the French authorities after 2 months' occupation of our front that a narrow road was a great drawback and they had turned some thousands of French and Belgian territorials to carry the *pavé* to the whole width of the roadway. I found Gen. Morland at his *poste de commandement* near the village of Kummel established in an *estaminet*, one room for himself and his staff, the other for the dispatch riders and telephones. This was about 4,000 yards from our trenches and just in front of his divisional artillery position which fired over our head during lunch, luckily the Germans were short of ammunition and only sent one or two shells our way. The attack which was to have been general on Monday, owing to the French being late as usual, and though we took a small wood of about 2 acres, it cost us 16 officers and 360 men killed and wounded and then could make no use of it as the Germans held a salient covering it. The road we came up by was liable to be shelled at any moment but a peasant woman was walking slowly up leading a little child of 7 or 8, to call in her cow in a neighbouring pasture, and ploughing had just been finished in the field behind the inn. In this field we stood after lunch watching the shells of either side bursting over the German and British trenches. The ground we were on sloped gently up from the Ypres valley and the position in front was like this

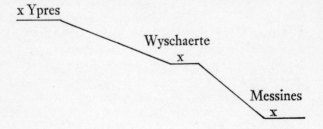

Ypres being out of sight over the hill, and the church towers of Wyschaerte and Messines just visible in the mist. There was little sickness, about 8 cases of typhoid, due to trenches taken over from the French. These frequently buried their dead in their trenches and on at least one position had made a parapet of dead bodies of their comrades covered with a little earth. The chief trouble was swollen feet and legs due to standing for day and night in the half-frozen mud, which gets over boots and under putties and which is the most prominent feature of the whole scene. The camps are more than ankle-deep with it, it is literally feet-deep in some of the roads. The trenches are half-full of it and men have actually to be hauled out of it with ropes. It is easy now to understand how men can be buried in it by the effect of a shell, and suffocated before they can be rescued. Morland said it was curious, considering the thinness of a telephone wire and its flat position lying on the ground, how often it was cut by shell fire. It appeared that some ladies of easy virtue had established themselves in Ypres, although it was being shelled, having brought out ambulances and got passes from the French medical authorities. Our staff cleared them out pretty quickly. . . . The Germans apparently for sanitary reasons tie their dead in bundles of four and send them to Antwerp to be cremated. Everyone spoke in high praise of their courage, and Morland said their minor tactical movements were very skilful since they constantly held posts which we should have abandoned, this he thought was partly due to their absolute disregard of losses incurred.

Sir J. French asked me to dine to meet Prince of Wales but I had to get back. I heard very good accounts of the Prince's intelligence, keenness and good humour. . . .

22 December

At our meeting today K. proposed to organise the 6 new armies of about 130,000 each under the command of Douglas Haig, Smith Dorien, Arch. Hunter, Ian Hamilton, Leslie Rundle and Bruce Hamilton in the order named.

K. told us he could get no news from Russia, but that he believed the Russian resistance was collapsing for want of ammunition, and he had heard the Russian troops had both in attack and defence to rely on the bayonet. We instructed Grey to telegraph to Russia for information of a reliable kind which was essential to our strategy in the war—and K. to arrange for a conference between Sir J. French and Gen. Joffre.

K. said his news about Russia was disastrous. Whereas our orders for ammunition placed already provided 20 rounds for *every* gun, and the French numbers were the same, the Russians only ordered 3½ officially, and unofficially it was only 2. Notwithstanding the withdrawal of 40 German divisions the Russians had decided to abandon Warsaw and retire to the line of the Bug. The Grand Duke was not allowed to know too much, and the Russian War Minister was corrupt and useless. My own belief is that K. himself is a most overrated man, very conceited, and though hard-working, much overweighted by the character of his labours. He is a pessimist and a bad *soldier*.

Apropos of the conference between Joffre and Sir J. French Ll.G. took occasion to repudiate very strongly any attempt to settle strategy in the Cabinet. We settled policy, but the C.s-in-C. arranged their work unhindered by politicians. W.S.C. sprang a scheme of wireless stations round the world, worked by the Navy and *essential* to it, on the Cabinet. He put its cost at about £840,000. As it gave me a pretext for getting rid of H. Samuel's wretched Marconi scheme, I offered no objection beyond warning the Cabinet the new proposal would cost £1½ millions.

I forgot to note that the day war was declared at midnight the P.O. cable ship at midnight cut all the German cables in the Channel. Today I learnt that the Germans had sent their cableship to Vigo to lie there and thence cut our Atlantic cables in the Atlantic. As however we had been so prompt she never heard of the declaration of war, and was interned by the Spaniards and a few days ago her Captain committed suicide from chagrin.

VIII

Intrigues Within?

January–May 1915

✳ By the end of 1914 it was clear that there was to be no swift end to the war. The war of movement of the early autumn had been replaced by the static struggle of machine-guns, wire and mud on the Western Front. One consequence of this was the search for an alternative strategy which led to the Gallipoli offensive. A second, more significant, result was the need for greater and greater quantities of munitions, especially high explosives. To ensure sufficient production of guns and shells necessitated more Government supervision and where possible, control. Growing complaints were to culminate in the 'Shells' crisis in May 1915. Overall, there was the increasing complexity and degree of state intervention required. Control of aliens, press censorship, recruitment of labour, the problem of drink—all exercised the Government. Yet to talk simply in terms of '*laissez-faire* versus control' is misleading. There was no hard and fast division of opinion on these lines within the Cabinet. Ministers urged intervention in some areas while loudly protesting against it in others. It is difficult to distinguish individuals as belonging firmly to one camp or another. What was happening was that different men reacted differently to the various problems confronting them. Yet slowly but surely the old *laissez-faire* and voluntarist Liberal concepts were undermined by the strains of war. In parliamentary terms, too, the Liberal Government's position was weakened. Even at the outbreak of war, after the by-elections since 1910, the Conservatives were the strongest party in the House of Commons. A Government majority depended not only on the support of Labour and Irish members, but on the fact that a rather higher proportion of Conservative members were away on active service than from the Liberal ranks. And there were also signs, though there is little indication of this in the diaries, that many Liberal backbenchers were either irritated by the Government's failure to adopt more businesslike methods, or alternatively, viewed with anxiety the abandonment of cherished Liberal principles and the erosion of individual freedom implicit in 'total' war.

12 January

Two things I may record. First the W.O. have arranged with Morgan Grenfell & Co. to buy in the U.S.A. all the copper in that market which does not seem to be on sale for home consumption. It will be kept and stored in the U.S. and only resold as friendly neutrals or we ourselves may require. This will stop the mouths of the Republican copper interests in that country who partly as traders, partly as politicians are hustling their Govt. on the point. Only the P.M., K., W.R. and I are supposed to be cognisant, but I doubt the secret being kept. Alone of all traders Morgan's, though only on this business, are allowed to use their private code.

Last night I dined with Lord Pirrie.[1] He let out that the Admiralty had given him an order to get hold of 10 or 12 tramp steamers of suitable sizes, and the moment any of our warships are sunk, or put out of action, to convert one of the tramps into a facsimile of the lost ship. He has already turned out an *Audacious* and by turning on the *whole* of his staff can copy any man-of-war in 2 or 3 weeks sufficiently well to startle the Admiral to whom it is sent with the likeness.

K. pronounced the 28th Division which he saw this morning, to be the very best he had dispatched to the front. Grey brought up the question of the *Dacia*, and *nem.con.* the Cabinet agreed we should refuse to recognise her transfer from German to American flag, let the growlings of their press be as loud as they liked.[2]

The taking up by the Admiralty of 1,400 ships for transports has, in conjunction with the detention of German and British shippings, caused very high freights and so raised prices. The P.M. raised the subject; W.R. promised to send us a memo and W.S.C. agreed to ascertain how many he could release. We decided to encourage the employment of women, but many trades are barred as said Ll.G., e.g. miners' and dockers' work. 'But they do such work in Zanzibar,' said K. at which we all laughed. Still it exactly and happily illustrates his knowledge of and attitude towards social questions.

Grey was asked to draw up a list of conditions on which we would admit food freely to Belgium. They were in a word that Germany would cease or cancel any requisitions of money or provisions on the country.

✳ At this stage a second 'Marconi' affair loomed over the horizon. In 1912 negotiations had begun for a contract between the Government and the

Marconi Company for the erection of six long-distance wireless stations for the Imperial Wireless Chain. The contract was ratified by the House of Commons in August 1913 and provided for possible cancellation of the second three wireless stations by the Government in certain circumstances. Hobhouse's involvement began at that time when he became Chairman of the Wireless Research Select Committee. After he became Postmaster-General, he went to Berlin in February 1914 with Sir Henry Norman, a wireless expert. The purpose of their visit was to examine the Telefunken Company's long-distance wireless installations, in terms of current wireless research rather than any commercial undertaking. During the summer work on the Marconi project was delayed and stopped entirely on the outbreak of war. In September Hobhouse produced a Cabinet memorandum describing the difficulties connected with the Marconi contract. On 14 September, after both Churchill and Kitchener had stated that they had no need for the project, the Cabinet agreed that the contract should be terminated. It was hoped to avoid the legal consequences which might follow this breach by providing an Admiralty contract as a consolation for the Marconi Company, but on 23 December it was revealed that verbal agreements between the Admiralty and the Company already precluded this course of action. Accordingly, on 30 December, Hobhouse gave the Marconi Company notice that the Post Office was cancelling the contract. On 11 January, after a flurry of correspondence, Godfrey Isaacs, the Marconi managing director, wrote to claim compensation for breach of contract. The Cabinet was to discuss the matter again on 21 January, but on the day before Hobhouse heard of serious allegations being made by Isaacs against him.

20 January

Murray[3] sent me over today a communication from a Naval Officer setting out a conversation he had with Godfrey Isaacs. G.I. was supposed to have been told by the Telefunken Co. of Berlin that H. Norman and I went to Paris in the summer of 1914 to hatch a plot against Marconi. Whether Isaacs has invented this story himself or whether someone has been getting at him I must find out. I imagine the latter, because he must know that dates would settle him at once if he had invented the story himself.

Heard today from Gen. Morland. Weather frightful and conditions worse even than when I was there, but spirit of men wonderful.

Their only alarm is lest we should give in. It's a pity they won't frankly tell us their needs, or induce K. to do so, and even a greater pity that they don't know what pains we take to meet their wants, that is as far as K. will tell us them. I am certain that there is some very serious difference of opinion between K. and French as to high explosive and shrapnel of which K. will say nothing; I can't, and subordinate commanders like Morland won't write to anyone in the Govt. because they think it is us who are starving them.

21 January

Cabinet today occupied with Marconi contract. H. Samuel who has got us into trouble by understating to H. of C. the cost of the Wireless Chain, went to P.M. (as the P.M. says or was sent for by P.M. as H.S. says) and the position of the contract came before a Committee of Cabinet of which McK., Simon, H.S. and I were members. We discovered that the Admiralty had *concluded* a bargain with Marconi, before W.S.C. told the Cabinet that he proposed to make and would consult me before he did make one and also before they told their own Civil Depts. As a consequence we are unable to use their contract in making terms with Marconi as to ours. The Committee agreed and Cabinet ratified, that we should write and withdraw our cancellation of contract so as to compel Company to go on with contract, or damages would be mitigated. Godfrey Isaacs is plainly an unscrupulous liar, for he told me in our private conversation that the Company would be only too glad to be quit of the whole work.

✳ The sequel to this discussion is fascinating. The story of Government expenditure on new advanced technology proving greater than expected is familiar to present-day readers. However, the admixture of more traditional notions of honourable commercial practice, an extraordinary appetite for, and delight in litigation, and the availability of some of the most remarkable legal luminaries of the age, made for a *cause célèbre*. The substance of Isaacs's charges was that in February 1914 Hobhouse and Norman had improperly invited the Telefunken Company to compete against the Marconi Company for the second part of the wireless chain contract. His information came from certain Telefunken directors whom he had met in Paris in June 1914. He claimed that when he confronted Hobhouse with these allegations, he had not denied them, indeed he had admitted the impropriety of a Minister taking such action, and asked Isaacs what he intended to do with this information. In an extraordinary choice of phrase, Isaacs claimed that Hobhouse had said 'You have your foot on my neck: do you intend to crush me, which would mean my leaving the Government, or are you disposed to help?' The implication that a Cabinet Minister should be in the power of a commercial contractor such as Godfrey Isaacs was of course outrageous, if it was true. Isaacs made these charges in a letter written to J. A. Pease in June 1916, and they were repeated when the Marconi Company brought its case for breach of contract against the Government in March 1918. On that occasion Marconi's counsel, Carson, made his opening statement and the Counsel representing the Government, who was of all people his former Ulster comrade F. E. Smith, the Attorney-General, immediately agreed to settle. Hobhouse had hoped to give evidence utterly refuting Isaacs's statements, but denied the opportunity, he instead made a statement in the House of Commons and published a letter in *The Times* saying that they were false. Isaacs thereupon sued him for libel. In the suit that followed, legal talents abounded. Hobhouse was represented by his former Cabinet colleague, John Simon, and Leslie Scott appeared for Isaacs. The case was tried before the inimitable Justice Darling who trenchantly summed up 'The issue here is very simple. One of these persons is committing the blackest perjury. The question is which of the two it is.' The jury found for Hobhouse, who was awarded damages and costs.

27 January

W.S.C. showed us today a remarkable photo of the German warship *Blücher* as she gave her last sideways roll over, and of the crew scrambling up the deck to the taffrail. The *Lion* and *Tiger* did all the fighting, as the other big ships were outclassed for pace, and the smaller and faster ships had to be held back for fear of obscuring the field of fire with their smoke. The secondary armament is clearly of no use nowadays—it's the big gun and its range which is going to decide a fight. The great pace at which the action was fought was most remarkable; Commodore Tyrwhitt said 29 to 30 knots.[4]

While W.S.C. was telling us *his* story, it was amusing to see K. pretending to look bored and uninterested, as if he had got something really worth relating. He had only 2 rather human stories, first that the mysterious headlights seen flashing over Sandringham during the recent raid were caused by the car of the rector returning home after dinner, and second, that the previous night some special constable having seen signalling from a church went post-haste to the nearest military station and got a company who in due course surrounded the church, but discovered it was held by soldiers, and prepared to give battle. Luckily at the very last minute the latter were found to be neighbouring Territorials sent there to practise signalling.

We then discussed the case of the *Wilhelmina*, laden with corn for Hamburg. Ll.G. and W.S.C. were for holding it up in any case, no matter what the U.S.A. might say. The P.M. and McK. for letting it through on the ground that the absence of an effective blockade made seizure contrary to international law; W. R. Lucas and myself were for telling the U.S.A. quite plainly that while we would pay a fair price for anything we stopped, we were not to be frightened or deterred from stopping anything or everything.[5]

3 February

Breakfasted with M. Nathan this morning. He is much perturbed at the state of Ireland. He says that Sinn Feinism though not large is dangerous, and that many of the minor Civil Service officials are imbued with it. Redmond whom I talked at length with yesterday told me that it was only a stage army of small significance, and that never had he had such good spirited or large meetings. J.R. grumbled at K.'s hostility, he permitted Ulster Volunteers to wear badges with the arms of Ulster, but not National Volunteers to wear the arms of Ireland: as to the National Volunteers, more had enlisted than of the Ulster Volunteers and K. was sending the former abroad half trained, and keeping the latter to be intact when the war was over, a policy K. is quite capable of conceiving and engineering. Nathan and Redmond were agreed as to the sullen state of Ulster, and N. had come over to ask Walter Long to move Carson towards peace. He found Long, for the first time, ready to counsel accommodation and agreed to sound Carson to make a speech approving of Redmond's recruiting attitude. The P.M. had agreed. Long said he expected Carson to be helpful. Nathan said the Irish detective service was better than he expected, and instanced their running to earth a stranger whose arrival in Ireland had been reported by him to the F.O. and by them to him in reply as an Admiralty agent. He told no one, but the R.I.C. one day told him the man's real name and occupation discovered apparently by the chambermaid of his hotel noting the initials of his shirts, a very poor tool of secret service.

8 February

I met tonight Capt. Younger of the Coldstream Guards who has been through the *whole* campaign, and is the only unwounded officer in the Regiment, through which has passed some 10,000 men. He said that the temper of the troops was such that as few prisoners as possible were being taken from or by the Prussians and Bavarians, the latter for plundering and cruelty being as bad as the former. Quite recently the Scots took 18 prisoners from the Prussian 112th Infantry whereupon the Irish Guards, who had been tricked by a white flag incident by this Regt. at the Aisne, attacked the Scots Guards, and tried to get at the prisoners who were however got away. The free use of whale oil had driven away frostbite, the men poured it into their boots and smeared their whole clothing with it. The use of iodine had been of invaluable service in preventing blood poisoning. One officer got a graze on the back of the hand, he said enough to get him a fortnight's leave at home. In 48 hours he was dead of blood poisoning due to the too highly manured earth having got into the wound, and no antiseptic being available. After the last attack on La Bassée, they had to go out of their trenches at night to push the dead Germans off the barbed wire where they hung so thick, like crows, that they obscured the field of fire. He said they would greatly prefer Gen. Haig[6] as C.-in-C. to Sir John French who never, not even at the battle of Ypres, came anywhere really near the firing line. The officer appointed to a machine gun was almost certain to be killed, and yet there always were volunteers for it. The prisoners they took had only 8 or 9 weeks' training, and officers were so scarce with the Germans that they were forbidden to leave the trenches for attack, the rank and file being led by N.C.O.s or driven forward with the officers behind—not from fear, but necessity to preserve their lives.

10 February

We had a long discussion as to methods of retaliating on Germany for her 'blockade'. W.S.C. was given the lines on which to make the Admiralty declaration but though I pressed it hard I couldn't get a decision as to whether cargoes purchased are to be paid for at the price of purchase plus freight, or at the price realisable at the port of consignment, although the first will discourage and the second violently encourage neutral trading with the enemy. . . .

16 February
Between the 3rd and 13th February we have lost 102 officers and 2,600 men killed and wounded, and neither side has anything substantial to show for it.

The plan for attacking Constantinople was discussed. On Friday at daybreak, the *Queen Elizabeth*, just completed, and a large squadron of old battleships armed with new guns are to lie off the town, well beyond the range of the forts' guns, and to batter to pieces at their leisure each fort in turn, until the way through to the Black Sea is clear. No risks are to be run, and the operation may take a fortnight or 3 weeks. Meanwhile the Greeks are to evacuate Lemnos, and we are to seize the island, station a division of troops there, and these subsequently are to occupy the Gallipoli peninsula. We are promised a military rising and ultimate revolution on the fall of the first fort. W.S.C. said policy was decided at War Council and he would take all responsibility. The raid at Zeebrugge was a considerable success, the most noticeable part being that the German airmen made no attempt to counter-attack.

We then discussed the reply to the American note about our use of neutral flags. We propose to detain all ships carrying cargo useful to Germany, or likely to arrive there directly or indirectly. Grey was of opinion that America would be very likely when she found her ships being held up to send them there under an escort of warships. We were unanimous that we must take that risk, though if that happened we should have to let them pass through. . . .

One driver in a battery at the front recently advertised in the *Daily Chronicle* that he was 'in the trenches and lonely': 3 days afterwards my officials sent on to him in one day 3,000 letters, 4 sacks of small parcels and 98 large parcels of an average weight of 10 lb.

18 February
. . . The news from Russia is very unsatisfactory, they report their losses at between 300,000 and 400,000 a month, a number which

seems incredible, even allowing for an eventual return of 60% to the colours. K. said the staff officers sent from Russia to confer with him were most casual and vague. They could only turn out about 45,000 to 55,000 rifles a month after six months of war, and instead of the millions of men they had previously spoken of now only be certain of *fully* equipping 900,000 by the end of May. They had borrowed field artillery and rifles from Japan. The latter they gave to their police and frontier forces taking the latter's rifles to their front-line troops. They would however send one good brigade to Serbia. We can get no details from the Russian H.Q. staff as to the recent fighting and they keep their attaché in the same ignorance. K. said he had recommended to them the half-million Vitali rifles he had proposed to buy for ourselves.

We think we have secured 300,000 Brazilian Mausers and 100,000 Argentine Mausers, for which the French promise us ample ammunition viz. 10 million rounds per month.

Harcourt brought up the case of S. Africa. The Union Govt. under pressure from us had sent home all our artillery at the Cape, and now find themselves requiring quick-fire and howitzers for the S.W. Africa campaign. We could only promise some 4.7 inch guns of which Churchill has a store, as he said, 'hidden away' with *plenty* of ammunition. . . .

W.S.C. said that they had news from Holland of 20 German submarines, starting from Kiel in the next 3 days, and that yesterday in their big net under the Forth Bridge, with meshes 12 ft. square, they thought they had caught one, but divers could find no trace. A very lugubrious day. We had two Cabinets 12 to 2 and 5 to 6.30.

24 February

Crewe made a very distinct moue at being asked today to put a F.O. paper in his pocket instead of receiving it through the usual channel of a circulation box: so much for being an ex-dandy.

We talked today about the results at Constantinople, the interruption of the bombardment will militate considerably against its early, and possibly against its eventual success.

Then W.S.C. gave us a characteristic outburst against the workmen on the Clyde and elsewhere as being mutinous and malingering and endangering thereby present and future naval operations. This morning Sir George Gibb[7] had been to see me about a war bonus for postal servants and told me that the employers had kept men's demands which were for 1d. an hour extra, waiting for 2 months before meeting them, and then had offered ¾d. instead of 1d. Beardmore and another firm being the sinners. The men had been working night and day shifts much in excess of normal hours for 7 months, they were tired physically, and on edge mentally and required very careful handling. K. supported W.S.C. by saying he couldn't get the large works to execute his orders in due course, or in his order of sequence. Ll.G. then proposed we should pass legislation to commandeer all works doing naval or military business for the Govt. or capable of doing it, that in respect of such works the Govt. should have power to compulsorily arbitrate in any wages dispute, and punish by fine or imprisonment any refusal of a man to work after arbitration, and also have power to keep all public houses shut until 11 a.m. I asked him what he proposed for men who simply threw up their work at the works, and went elsewhere for if he compelled them to return to their job he was proposing industrial conscription, and if he didn't employ compulsion he would possibly not keep dissatisfied men. To this he made no reply. W.R. pointed out that the men were not malingering, but worn out, and I added Sir Geo. Gibb's statement. Crewe supported Ll.G. while the P.M. observed the proposal was indistinguishable from socialism. K. then asked if he might assist at drafting a bill to which the P.M. replied with a grim smile that he should be very glad if he, K. would do so, and would make it as 'offensive' as possible.

2 March

Today K. and W.S.C. told us, with the air of importing a great secret, that their officers had decided to send to occupy Gallipoli 40,000 British and Colonial troops from Egypt, one French Division, one Naval Division from England, one Russian Brigade, and K. added as an afterthought Gen. Peyton's Division of Territorial Cavalry. So far as secrecy was concerned my brother-in-law John Fuller had heard this news from his friends at Brooks, where the servants were gossiping about it. Grey however added that Venizelos had telegraphed this morning to say that subject to consent of his King, who with his Court and high officers of Army was unfriendly to Allies, he would put at our disposal 3 Corps for purpose of reducing Gallipoli.

W.S.C. added to this that he proposed to bombard Smyrna and afterwards 'as there was a friendly and bribable Pasha' land a force to blow up forts and stores. Grey said he must warn us that Russia was very suspicious of Greece both in Asia Minor and at Constantinople. During first 10 days of blockade only 8 British ships sunk, and 5 British lives lost.

We then discussed reply to be made to the U.S.A. where Bryan is thinking not of England and perhaps not of America but of the political future of himself and his party. John Simon has proposed to bring in the Prize Court to adjudicate as to the disposal of enemy cargoes, but left to naval authorities the much more difficult and preceding question as to whether these were of enemy origin or destination. McK.'s quick mind saw the flaw and we postponed decision. We refused to entertain a policy of reprisals suggested by F.O. based on the condemnation by Prize Courts and transfer of enemy vessels detained not captured, at outset of War. We have already requisitioned and used them, and it would be very doubtful if a Prize Court would condemn them.

Runciman produced a Bill to commandeer the great armament works, but W.S.C. who early in the day had violently proposed that the Admiralty should take over the whole Mercantile Marine, now supported by K. denounced R.'s Bill as socialite and anarchic: the real fact being that he resented the idea of anyone touching the fringe of the Admiralty garment.

4 March
. . . After discussing till 1.45, we met again at 6 p.m. Grey began by saying that since the morning Imperiali had come to formally state on behalf of his Govt. that Italy was ready to intervene about the middle or end of April; that neither the temperament nor the finances of the people could permit a long war but they could hold out for a year in both directions. E.G. added that the matter was one of vital secrecy. I sent him a note to say that on Friday last I was told that 2 days previously the Italian military attaché had visited the W.O. with a request to be informed of the names of the officers commanding Corps and Divisions, and the composition and numbers of our forces at home and broad, justifying his request on the ground that Italy had decided to come in by the middle of April. I told E.G. that if the news leaked out, he must not therefore blame the Cabinet.

Grey also produced a further obstructive telegram from Russia saying that the Tzar 'would not tolerate Greek co-operation in the Dardanelles', and that Russia would send instead of a Brigade, an Army Corps. We all agreed that we could not accept this restriction on our acceptance of allies, and that Grey should reply that we had embarked on this enterprise of our own initiative (Churchill remarking that the French had declined to share in so risky an enterprise until we said that we should go on with it anyhow) that we derived no direct benefit from it, while Russia would be immediately benefited, and that the decision of the Balkans was hanging in the balance, and perhaps of ultimate victory, and while we recognised Russia's claims, we could not jeopardise our efforts for sentiment alone.

We then decided on E.G.'s reply to America, in the shape of an Order-in-Council, the second para in which is taken verbatim from the O.-in-C. of 1807 in reply to the Berlin decree of that date. It was proposed by Emmott that only certain ships should be stopped so that the Yankees might be let down lightly at first, but as few ships' cargoes are confined to one article alone, each ship would still have to be stopped and searched for contraband.

5 March

This afternoon Murray brought me a warrant of the Home Office requiring me to open all mail bags from Holland to America and to open any letters therein addressed to the Ritz Carlton Hotel at New York. As I was a Member of the Cabinet equally with McK. I could not therefore shelter myself under his authority, even if I had been willing to do so. I went down to see him and said that unless his reasons were overpoweringly strong, it would be impossible for me to allow this search to be made. He then said that they had long known the Ritz Carlton as the headquarters in America of the spy organisation: that on Tuesday last they had caught an American, who had only been 4 days in England, transmitting news of importance, but not of value, to the German centre in Holland by means of invisible ink, and that 3 others were taken at the same time, and it was most important to see what were the communications which passed between the 2 centres of organisation. I told him that I thought the justification enough for so serious a step as first destroying and afterwards reproducing the seals on the Dutch mail bags, besides opening the individual letters therein, but that he ought to realise the consequences of a discovery of our proceedings, which in the excited state of American opinion might well mean war with us. We agreed that neither the P.M. nor E.G. should be told, and we should be prepared to be the scapegoat.

9 March

Grey said that in accordance with an arrangement between Venizelos and himself, the former had sent a protest against our occupation of Lemnos. In order to make matters difficult for the Greeks and ourselves, the Greeks had just received from the Porte an announcement that they had agreed to cede Lemnos to Greece. It thus automatically becomes neutral territory, which we have seized. Ingenious but unavailing diplomacy. E.G. also said that France was putting it about, especially to Russia, that we were the obstacles to her realisation of the Constantinople proposal. If this be true it does not augur well for negotiations now or later. E.G. and the Cabinet then discussed the Dardanelles question. Ll.G. proposed that E.G. should go to Salonika with M. Delcassé to meet Sazonov. Grey said he had no personal objection to the Russian occupation of the western shore of the Dardanelles, with a strip east of the Enos-Midia line, and both shores of the Bosphorus, and K. said he had no military reason for opposing it. W.S.C. would have liked Tenedos and Imbros, but recognised first it would look like a threat to Russia, and secondly they could be reduced from the mainland. But he was bound to stipulate for Alexandretta and a hinterland. E.G. said this would clash with French aspirations of Syria and Palestine, Samuel then put in a plea for an English protectorate over this latter, which he said would be consonant with the wishes of the Jews generally. Montagu kept silent. I then said that we ought to remember that the Balkan states would hardly be pleased to find Russia on three sides of them, and our acceptance of Russia's proposals might have the effect of sending them over to the side of Germany. Grey said he would be bound to recollect this phase of the question, but he would prefer to have all the Balkan states in opposition rather to alienate Russia at this crisis.

Haldane pronounced very strongly against Grey going to Lemnos, he couldn't be spared and a conference as to the future couldn't settle the present. Crewe recommended a meeting on a British

battleship off the Dardanelles. Harcourt put in a caveat as to any
proposed distribution of the German Colonies. Emmott hoped
nothing would be done to wipe out the Germans as an Empire. It was
agreed to invite Sazonov to confer, as Grey said settlement at an
early date was essential.

16 March
... In the Dardanelles the minesweeping by night has been a failure,
and the ships are to be sent in to close range to engage and reduce
the forts.

Then we discussed the relation of the Govt. to the armament
firms. At our previous meeting W.S.C. had tried to get all negotiations between capital and labour centred in Ll.G.'s hands. McK.
had resisted this on the ground that W.R. (who was away unwell)
was already in touch with the employers, and should not be disturbed.

Today W.R. gave us a most lucid account of his interview with
Armstrong, Vickers, Coventry Co. etc. He had got them to agree to
accept financial supervision on condition that internal management
was untouched and that we should guarantee the previous dividend
plus 15% increase on the dividend itself; and certain depreciation in
excess of the ordinary as a set-off against continuous working. It was
accepted as an admirable arrangement and agreed that he and Ll.G.
should see the men the next day. Then we passed to Aniline Dyes.
£490,000 has been subscribed, and a further £88,000 conditionally.
We agreed to add £750,000, and this would enable us in 6 weeks
from the present to get from Switzerland a considerable amount of
dye stuff, and in 6 months we should be able to supply 30% of the
requirements of normal trade. It appears that Coats Spinning Co.,
are managed by a naturalised German, Lippi by name, and if we
let this chance slip they will monopolise the whole of the Swiss turn-
out, supply themselves cheap and the small dealers dear. Sir F.
Cawley[8] who violently opposed our scheme is deeply mixed up with
Coats. It has been ascertained that the Badische Soda Co., who
control the German dye industry, have a wholesale system of buying
the managers of cotton works in England by means of extravagant
commissions. The P.M. resisted the whole scheme, as bound to
result in 'protection' for the dye industry at the end of the war.
Montagu supported him. Emmott said it would be cheaper to sub-
scribe the capital now and scrap it after the war, than let Coats

monopolise the trade, or Lancashire go without dye. This voiced the general sentiment to which Lucas and I added that perhaps the Badische chemists would be no longer alive or in a condition to renew their activities after the war, and therefore one of the bogeys would disappear.

Ll.G. tried to foist on us a railway man from Canada as his universal provider of advice.

23 March

The Cabinet has lost or gained so much in personnel since last I tried note its members' characteristics that I will do so again. We sit round the table thus: Asquith, Harcourt, Beauchamp, Montagu, Emmott, Simon, Birrell, Pease, Samuel, Haldane, Grey (opposite the P.M.), George, Crewe, McKenna, Runciman, Hobhouse, Lucas, Wood, Churchill, Kitchener.

The P.M.'s abilities are as transcendent as ever: his qualities more noticeable. Temper, tact, courage, quite marvellous. Some of us think he is a little too considerate to the Opposition, but it is a wise fault.

Loulou Harcourt, subtle, secretive, adroit, and not very reliable or *au fond* courageous does not interfere often in discussion, but is fond of conversing with the P.M. in undertones; a hard worker, and a good office chief.

Beauchamp is a nonentity of pleasant manners, a good deal of courage, and a man of principle, but with no power of expression.

Montagu has a power of speech, clever, even brilliant; he will probably not desert his party, but always attach himself to its most conspicuous men, and is determined to achieve a career which he will probably do. He will probably swallow a good deal of boot blacking on the way. He has no courage, but some violence and bears malice and gossip.

Emmott is honest, slow, laborious, and has a whining mechanical voice which detracts from a good and sober judgement and hard work.

Simon, a most attractive personality; a ready wit, a persuasive advocate, I am told a very sound lawyer, a very hard-working colleague, and boundless ambition with whose aims he will let nothing interfere. He has his ear always on the ground, and though he will not advocate principles in which he does not believe, he will certainly push aside those in which he was trained, if they happen to stand in the way of political advancement. In private life a very lovable character.

Birrell, Pease, and Samuel do not seem to me to have changed. The last is very able, not liked or trusted by anyone, but much used, and his wits often drawn on.

Haldane has always repelled me. I hardly know him and mistrust him thoroughly. He does not now carry much weight in council, but the P.M. consults him very constantly, and accepts his advice.

Grey, we all like, admire, and respect, for his transparent sincerity and honesty as well as for his courage, skill and steadfastness. He is always open to argument (except on a point of principle when indeed he is apt to narrow his views from conviction to prejudice), most patient, courteous, and conciliatory with all, a nice sense of humour—a horror of self-advertisement, and a loathing of politics.

Ll.G. is in council as in every other relation wonderfully versatile, adroit and quick, with an unrivalled, indeed miraculous, power of picking other people's brains. He reads and educates himself continuously, but is contemptible as an administrator and his want of the knowledge of money values has cost us quite as much as his audacity and resource has gained. He is fickle, ungrateful, untruthful, but not I think envious, and quite appreciative of others' ability.

Crewe is liked and respected by everyone. He never intervenes without effect, or speaks at unnecessary length. His stammer drags out his utterances, and make them seem tedious, but if one has the patience to listen to it all there is nothing really superfluous. Not a strong man, or apparently a hard-working one, he knows his own mind and that is generally practical and progressive.

McKenna has one of the best and quickest intellects in the Cabinet, and has great influence with the P.M. He has a most retentive memory and much general knowledge, but he suffers from the subtlety of his mind, and verbal quibbles and precautions only irritate and do not convince his opponent. He is more unpopular in and out of the H. of C. than all the rest of the Govt.

Runciman carries considerable weight. He is lucid, concise and courageous, dislikes Ll.G. and K. very heartily, ambitious, and a little cocksure. A hard-working, very capable man of business, and a very honourable and straightforward colleague, as indeed is McKenna also.

12 Augustine Birrell, captioned 'The Passive Resister's Last Hope', by Spy in *Vanity Fair*. Hobhouse: 'Cynical, amusing, a bad administrator, but high principled and with plenty of courage'

13 Sydney Buxton, Hobhouse's predecessor as Postmaster-General, by Spy in *Vanity Fair*

Lucas, between whom and Runciman I sit, has not yet found his legs, is a good example of a Liberal peer, by conviction and training. Industrious after 11 a.m., courageous, rather advanced, hating the Germans and the Yankees.

Churchill as always, in a hurry to be conspicuous; he turns out *memorabilia* on international law, shipbuilding, blockade running, labour problems, and other *disjecta membra*, by the basketful. Nervous, fretful, voluble, intolerably bumptious and conceited, he squanders our time and his own in increasing orations. These are interspersed with tags of Latin and French which are a source of unfailing amusement and contempt for the P.M.

Kitchener who sits on the P.M.'s left has gained the unbounded confidence of the nation, the unquestionable dread of the British Officer, for qualities not really his own. He works hard, is outspoken, and hates red tape. But he does not really know W.O. requirements or difficulties, and is not at all a master of detail. I hear from many that he is very changeable and hasty, and in council conceals his ignorance of events and requirements by a fatuous smile of complacency which tries his colleagues sorely. Withal he is a snob. He is quite remarkably astute and untruthful, in all matters big and small. But he has faculty of getting work out of others, and is, I hear, loyal to his friends.

Cabinet today was taken up with the claims of Italy which stand to be satisfied, if she undertakes to come into the war. Germany we believe has offered Italy the Trentino, and Austria has agreed to surrender it, almost openly reserving the right to retake it at the earliest convenient opportunity. But the Italian Govt., which with the exceptions of Sonnino[9] and the Colonial Minister would like to accept this arrangement, has to reckon with public opinion, and accordingly Italy proposes for herself, as the reward for declaring war on *Austria*, the Trentino and the Northern Bay of the Adriatic down to Fiume. This latter to go to Croatia as now, after the war probably to Serbia.

Dalmatia is to fall to Italy, Albania would become a Moslem state with its capital at Durazzo, Greece to get Epirus. Italy gets Vallona. From Ragusa to the Drin, and thence to Voiussa excepting Durazzo would go to Serbia and Montenegro.

The P.M. said that as we were dealing with the most cynical and treacherous Govt. in Europe it behoved us to be most careful. Italy did not propose to declare war on Germany or Turkey. We agreed, on my suggestion, that it should be 'on Austria and her Allies' and that we should bind to prosecute the war with all her forces. Otherwise she was quite capable of merely occupying the Austrian provinces by arrangement, without engaging her own or the German forces. Churchill declared on behalf of the Admiralty that they did not mind the Adriatic becoming an Italian Lake and offered no objection to their retention of Rhodes. K. urged the acceptance of Italy's demands as likely to decide the Balkan States, who would judge that if Italy had come to the conclusion that we were going to win, it was high time for them to come down on the same side. What moral defence Italy has for declaring was on States with which she was and is actually in alliance it is not our business to determine. W.S.C. gave us an unsatisfactory statement about the Dardanelles; pretending that it was not unfortunate that three old battleships should be sunk, as they supplied crews for his newer ships. It also appeared that the *Queen Elizabeth* had something wrong with her port turbine engine which reduced her speed to 18 knots. The outer forts seem to have suffered some considerable damage, the inner ones little or none. The American Ambassador in Turkey reports that his visit to them showed little unrepairable damage. Runciman reported that it was possible we should have to face the prohibition of the export of coal.

26 March

W.S.C. today in saying that U29 had been sunk by a battleship in the North Sea ten days ago hinted darkly at the destruction of many German submarines, a hint which I believe to be without any foundation.[10] Grey said the Rumanian Minister had arrived hot foot from Bucharest to say that Rumania would at the beginning of May join the allies, without making any conditions, except that we should supply her with shell; the Minister in reply to Grey said he was not authorised to tell France or Russia what he had said, but had no objection to Grey repeating it. His Govt. were very anxious Italy should come in, but their own participation was not conditional upon Italy's.

W.S.C. raised the attitude of Germany to Holland as evinced by their capture of 2 Dutch ships, and the deliberate sinking of one other. K.'s view was that the Germans had a million unoccupied men who could be profitably employed in overrunning Holland and seizing the mouths of the Scheldt and Rhine.

I think it more likely that their mentality is such that they still believe they have only to rattle the sabre and all will obey. Holland has been obliging to England, sink a Dutch ship or two, and she will cease to be obliging to England and become instead subservient to Germany. Nothing but crushing disaster will cure this mad arrogance. We had a long discussion on a proposal of mine to give a war wages bonus to postal servants whose weekly pay was below 30/- and 60/- of a sum of 3/- and 2/- respectively. I admitted the certain extension of the grant to other civil servants, and the probability of it to others working for Govt. but asked how could we refuse to a postman on 23/- what we had given to a railway man on 24/-. Ll.G. and Montagu proposed to reject the request. Crewe supported it, but pointed out the danger of extension, so did Haldane. So far as facts are ascertainable the 'price' increase is 5/- not 3/- but they, the workmen, must share the burden of war with richer classes. Eventually the P.M. suggested referring to Sir G. Askwith's[11] Committee for advice on the question of prices.

Samuel and Pease then brought up registration and with it the postponement of the general election. Ll.G. was for postponement. Harcourt against, on the ground that we could not afford to cut into the Parliament Act so early in its life. Ll.G., after Crewe had mentioned 'Coalition' as the possible price of Opposition agreement, declared such a course improbable. Whereat McK., W.R., and I winked knowing what he and W.S.C. and we believe K. had been up to, and the reason why Balfour had been admitted to the Labour Conferences against our general wish.[12] The P.M. remarked he could not believe the Opposition wished to have any responsibility for the conduct of the war.

Meanwhile K. has objected to every proposal of Ll.G.'s for a superman,[13] and McK.'s H.O. inspectors have collected the facts, and tabulated them; with the result that Ll.G. declared that McK. should do the work and not he.

7 April

Today we had a little breeze between K. and W.S.C. as the latter declared the W.O. were recruiting his Admiralty workmen; later on the encounter was renewed as K. was very unwilling to reveal the numbers of men recruited. He put it eventually at 2,100,000. He said he sent over weekly about 12,000 men of whom 4,000 were to replace casualties and 4,000 were only fit for lines of communications, and 4,000 to increase the size of the Army. Ian Hamilton[14] was being given 80,000 British troops and 120 guns for the Dardanelles venture on which he and his men leave Alexandria today; he has been allowed to choose his own officers and units from the Egyptian garrison. He evidently looks with some distrust upon this enterprise which K. describes as a most serious and difficult task. It is as well to recall that when it was first mentioned to the Cabinet McK. asked on whose authority it was undertaken. W.S.C. replied 'after consultation with the C.I.D.' and on McK. observing that the Cabinet had no responsibility for it, Churchill declared that he was willing to take the whole responsibility himself. It is evident that the Navy has hitherto failed completely so far in its task, and though it has been reinforced by 4 battleships and a squadron of destroyers, and aeroplanes it is clearly a dangerous and very doubtful venture. The Naval forces are to be protected from mines by a net stretched from land to land in front of them. W.S.C. reported that the Grimsby trawlers, who are mine sweeping, did not object to the risk of being blown up by mines, but declined entirely to face shellfire, and have had to be withdrawn.

The P.M. who has taken Grey's place temporarily, reported that Russia was now regarding Italian claims with more toleration, and would be content to preserve the Serbian commercial rights on the whole of the Dalmatian coast, reserved for them, leaving the islands to Italy; while we were talking a telegram came in from Sazonov saying that he was prepared to do this but if Italy insisted on anything more, he might now have to give way, but he would take it out of her elsewhere. Asquith added that Imperiali told him that Italy greatly distrusted France, misdoubted Russia, and that their real wish in coming in was to repay their debt to England; to prove this he added that there was a clause in the Triple Alliance agreement that no matter what occurred Italy was not to be called on to fight against the British. Moreover they could have got almost as good terms from Germany and Austria.

On this latter point Spender said to me that Sharpe the American Ambassador in Paris had told him they had made most careful inquiries in Vienna and that the Austrians were prepared, if necessity required, to yield Transylvania to Rumania and Gallicia to Russia or Poland, but never would they yield a foot of ground to Italy. He added that Von Bulow had warned Italy that Germany had concentrated special formations at Stuttgart which were to attack Italy through Switzerland who had agreed to such a course being taken.

The P.M. has sent for the Rumanian Envoy Miska, and asked him if they were still minded to come in unconditionally. He said that hardly could be said, for they would want compensation and must wait for Italy, but they meant to come in.

Then we discussed 'drink'—Ll.G. said that he did not desire or believe in total prohibition, certainly not of beer, though possibly of spirits; that the brewers were not unfriendly—and in reply to W.S.C.—that hurry was the worst thing he had to fear: he was consulting the Opposition of whom B. Law was friendly certainly.

13 April
. . . We had much desultory chat about the Dardanelles, which hangs in the wind. Ian Hamilton apparently unwilling to carry out the enterprise and afraid to represent it as impossible as K. has ordered him to put it through. The Greeks have apparently made up their minds to come in 'against the Turks', and this should help us—but our W.O. are not happy as to the possibility of success.

Italy is still shillyshallying, but Rodd writes privately to Grey, as being beneath the dignity of a dispatch that the Italian cook of the Austrian Embassy has had notice of discharge!

16 April
Yesterday we had a very stormy meeting.[15] K., the moment we met, said he had something very serious to say. Yesterday at a meeting of the War Munitions Committee the Chancellor of the Exchequer and Montagu had informed the Committee that the number of troops in France was 500,000, and this in spite of the entreaty he had made the figures he supplied to the Cabinet should not be divulged; he felt a great responsibility to the Army for having furnished these figures, since the knowledge of them by the enemy might have serious results, and as they had been divulged by his fault he could only resign his position as Secretary of State and immediately withdraw from the Cabinet. Ll.G. replied that at the first meeting of the

Committee Von Donop,[16] the Master-General of the Ordnance, had produced figures to the Committee which showed that we had 2 armies in France, and not 4, and that by July supply to these of all munitions would have overtaken demand. He thereon gave the Committee as a basis to work on the number of 509,000 which K. gave the Cabinet two days before. It would be a mere farce for them to be working on figures which were inaccurate, and neither he nor any other of its members would stay there 5 minutes if they were not to be trusted with the real numbers and requirements. W.S.C. then chimed in to support Ll.G. and said that these figures were probably known approximately to a good many—I interrupted to say they were known to a writer in *The Times* the previous day—and to the Paris correspondent of the *Tribuna*—and that no great responsibility for their being mentioned to a confidential Committee could therefore exist, that everyone had had successes and failures, and if things went amiss sometimes no great harm was done. Grey remarked that K. had some cause of complaint as he had particularly asked these figures should be kept secret. Ll.G. answered very hotly that it was childish to withhold such facts from a body which was set up at K.'s request, of which he was Chairman, against his own wish, and only because of K.'s insistence and the P.M.—he was quite ready to resign that or any other position, but he could only continue as long as he was in full possession of all facts and figures. Crewe and Harcourt tried to mediate and then K. broke in saying it was plain he had lost the confidence of his colleagues and must cease to co-operate with them, picked up his spectacles, pushed back his chair, and took 3 slow, very slow steps to the door. McK., W.R., Lucas, Harcourt, Crewe and some at the far end of the table called out 'no, no'—Grey and P.M. said nothing. Ll.G., W.S.C. and I also said nothing, they because they were angry, I because I was certain the whole thing was pure farce. Either K. wished to try his strength with the public against the Govt. or his case being a bad one, that he wished hereafter to be able to refuse to give information. He tried 'resignation' 3 times with Cromer, and when on the third time it was accepted by telegram and a remark that a cabin on the first homeward ship reserved, it was not again referred to, or proferred. If now accepted it would have made a great fuss, and he would have had to explain that he had resigned because he had withheld from one of his most important military colleagues important information or had authorised that colleague to supply the Chancellor of the Exchequer and a Committee set up in response to a national request with false information, by either of which courses he endangered the state and because his colleagues thought such conduct unwise and corrected it, he retired from Office. That K. has got some underhand game on is almost certain, but that he play it with such bad cards is not likely.

Grey told us Sazonov had raised new difficulties as to Italian participation, over the position of Albania. The Cabinet refused to grant a 'war bonus' to postal servants, on the ground that all classes must share in the war burden, and if increase was made to postal wages on the score of the rise in prices, it would have to be given to all other Govt. employees, and to all men whose employers had no increased profits to pay them out of. I argued that they had put themselves out of court by giving the railwaymen a bonus and that L.C.C. and many other local authorities had followed suit, and that I was certain they would be driven to pay with a bad grace what they now refused to give.

21 April

Runciman gave me a detailed account of the various intrigues of the past three months. It began with W.S.C., Lord Northcliffe, Balfour and Garvin.[17] The idea was to get rid of the P.M., Grey, and the rest of the Cabinet, and to substitute Balfour for Grey, and to keep Kitchener and Ll.G. who was an essential element of success. The conspirators went to K. who asked what was to happen to 'the old man' with whom he was working closely. The only answer he got was a shrug of the shoulders. Then W.S.C. put it to him as to which side he inclined, and he replied he would stay where he was. Then Northcliffe and his brother Rothermere differed as to Grey, and R. had power enough to stop *The Times* attack on Grey, but E.G. told W.R. that no one had added so much to the burden of his work, or disputed the decisions of the F.O. and Cabinet so violently or obstructively, as W.S.C.

Then W.S.C. turned to Sir John French as a substitute for K. and spent his weekends at the front colloguing to this end. The scene then shifted to Ll.G.'s Munitions Committee. The plan to which Balfour was apparently privy was to pass the word round that K. had supplied false information to the Committee and deceived the

War Office as to their requirements and necessities, and so to hunt
K. out of the W.O. and replace him with French. About ten days
before this happened K. had written to W.R. and got him to a tête-à-
tête dinner, and told him of what he had heard about French's
goings on—and that he very nearly recalled French, leaving Douglas
Haig out in his place, and thanked Walter for giving him a hint 3
months ago as to possible intrigues. We discussed the P.M. who is
aware of all these movements through his jackal Montagu, who
howls in sympathy with any camp. H.H.A. has not the courage or
perhaps the energy to tackle W.S.C. who amuses him—and whom
he thinks will not really be dangerous in his time. Montagu some
2 or 3 years ago repeated to Mrs. Asquith a chance sentence of R.
McK. that the P.M. seemed to be jealous of Grey to anyone who did
not know them both, and a scene took place between all the parties,
with the result that McK. shut his house to M. for six months. He
also repeated Mrs. Runciman's phrase describing the P.M. as
'brains in aspic' which had divided the two ever since. Grey's eyes
have been very bad, specks on the retina, he employs with great
reluctance a Secretary, to read and write for him at the F.O.

＊ Rumour such as this was ripe during March and April 1915. McKenna
and Runciman especially nurtured acutely over-developed suspicions
of their two brilliant colleagues, Lloyd George and Churchill. The plot
described by Runciman on this occasion is highly unlikely—what is
more significant is the way in which such suspicions and fears became
magnified under the stress of war and the nagging criticism of the press.
Asquith himself took the stories less than seriously. Lloyd George made
vehement—and probably truthful—denials of any intention of ousting
the Prime Minister.[18]

22 April
K. speaking of the treatment of English wounded and prisoners said
that things were reported to him from the front far more barbarous
than anything he had known in the Sudan, and he hoped that after
the war no German would be allowed to trade, much less to reside in
this country and that from the Kaiser—who was principally responsible for these atrocities—downwards, the authors and instigators
should be held personally responsible.
. . . We discussed drink. McK., W.R. and I were for total pro-

hibition of spirits which we believe the country were quite prepared for with reasonable compensation to the spirit manufacturers and vendors. Ll.G. was very uncertain as to his proposals. He would have liked as usual to do something startling, and to buy up the whole of the liquor trade which he said the brewers were ready to accept; it would be impossible to pay them for war disturbance, reduce the consumption of drink and hand them back a damaged and declining trade. Birrell declared Ireland would not stand prohibition of all spirits, though ready to accept prohibition areas. The north were sober people and would welcome it, and declare that they were sacrificed to and ruled by the drunken south, if there was no prohibition, but he could not recommend it for the whole country. W.S.C. argued strongly for canteens and regulations, and prohibition areas. I said that smuggling would go on extensively in such cases, and couldn't be stopped. The P.M. advocated increased taxation, canteens for food and drink under disinterested management. To this Ll.G. agreed, coupling it with the purchase of breweries and licensed houses in the areas. Harcourt objected strongly to the principle of purchase.

24 April
We observed today our silver wedding. Nina is very well generally, and I don't feel any older than I did 10 years ago.

27 April
W.S.C. again today attacked E.G. for his views about the use of fire balloons which the former desired to let loose in June on the German harvests and the latter thought illegitimate. K. asked us to consider whether he should give orders for the preparation of poisonous gases, as he wished Cabinet assent 'before he fell to the level of the degraded Germans'. We agreed he should use anything he could get invented. Grey told us that the Italian Ambassador had at 3.30 today signed the Declaration of September, and the alliance was now quadrupled. The P.M. thanked Grey on our behalf, and we 'hear heared' with hearty appreciation. E.G. was clearly very pleased and relieved. W.S.C. then vehemently went for Grey over the necessity of bringing in Bulgaria by discarding Greece and taking from her Karaka. The Queen of Greece had become openly a German agent and we have had to dismiss the Greek military attaché here. Grey

handled him very well, and without giving the Greeks away, said he would do what he could with Bulgaria.

28 April

On Wednesday I got a very important decision from the Cabinet. Ll.G. and Montagu had opposed the grant of war bonus to postal servants, which I had advocated because a similar grant had been made to railway servants, and it was impossible to discriminate. Thereupon the postal employees had appealed for arbitration. I said I thought it was impossible to resist the claim, as we had insisted on it for private employees but that if the Cabinet wished to resist, it must be clearly understood that there would be no drawing back at the last moment under parliamentary pressure. Thereon the P.M. said we could not refuse arbitration under the circumstances, but we must support before the arbitrator the Govt. view that a bonus was not right. All the trouble comes from Ll.G. having no financial (or other) principles or training and from the P.M. having no energy to spare for co-ordinating Departmental decisions. . . .

10 May

I went to France, via Boulogne, and to St. Omer, thence to Poperinge, staying with Sir R. Maxwell the Q.M.G. I found that since my previous visit in December we had lost rather than gained ground, but while Sir John French had given up his absurd habit of telling his men that one successful attack and they were through the German line, and the whole campaign would finish, yet in general everybody at H.Q. was confident. Gen. Haldane, Commanding 3rd Division whom I saw for an hour, was equally so, but complained of the bad quality of the shells lately supplied. He was against retaliation by means of gas. Gen. Morland of the 5th Division who had suffered more from gas than any other unit, was strongly for its employment; he said the men had suffered horribly. While I was talking to him near the village of Poperinge in came the news of the loss of practically the whole of a battalion of K.O.Y.L.I. The staff of this Division was plainly overwrought by a series of fights for Hill 60, which had lasted nearly 3 weeks without cessation. I learn that this day, Friday May 7th, had been intended for a great advance by the French, supported next day by the British, but the French being as usual late, the attack was postponed. The whole route followed from Boulogne to St. Omer, and thence to Paris was beautifully tilled and cultivated, not a field left fallow, and all done by boys and women—here and there a few men, but very few. The roads had much improved, both in width and texture. The inn at St. Omer was clean and comfortable, and plenty of food as very reasonable prices was everywhere obtainable.

In Paris I stayed at the Ritz Hotel which was very empty but I lunched and dined with Princesse de Faucigny Lucinge, 18 rue de la ville l'Eveque. Parisians, everyone told me, were greatly chastened and sobered, as well they might be with the Germans for 9 months only 30 miles away. The shops were open but empty, no taxis and not many horse vehicles. I met the Infante Eulalie, Mr. and Mrs. Bliss of the American Embassy, the Marquise de Semouilles and Sir F. Bertie. The latter was plainly of opinion that our yielding the Bosphorous to Russia was hopelessly wrong.[19] I got back to England on the 9th for Monday's Cabinet on the 10th.

We have apparently lost 16,000 men at Gallipoli from the Army, besides those from the Navy, and the whole operation has been brought to a standstill. W.S.C. cannot be got to give us any information, and takes refuge in generalities. Nothing could be more unsatisfactory. K. is sending out 2 Divisions, and the French are sending out another general to replace D'Armade. Enver Bey is supposed to be commanding the Turks. E.G. and W.S.C. had another difference about Italy, and the latter who needs men even more than ships for *his* Gallipoli enterprise, puts every obstacle in the way of Greece coming in.

We had some talk about aliens, some being for interning *all*, but W.R. and W.S.C. were for observing the scrap of paper which naturalised aliens have acquired. K. remarked that no injurious action had been traced to any alien at large, while P.M. declared that nothing would induce him to repudiate any grant of the full privileges of citizenship to all naturalised persons. . . .

IX

After the Fall

May–October 1915

✳ Despite the strains to which the Government was exposed, Asquith was
confident enough to declare on 12 May that Coalition was 'not in con-
templation'. Yet within a week events had led to a dramatic reconstruction. On 14 May Colonel Repington's dispatch published in *The Times*
claimed that allied progress on the Western Front was fatally impaired
by the shortage of shells. The charge was part of a Northcliffe vendetta
against Kitchener, but was eagerly taken up by the more belligerent
Conservative (and even some Liberal) backbenchers as a general attack
on the Government's munitions policy. Then on 15 May the growing
tension between Churchill and the First Lord of the Admiralty, Admiral
'Jackie' Fisher, over the Dardanelles culminated in the latter's dramatic
resignation. This double crisis hit Asquith on the weekend of 15–16
May. Traditionally historians have argued that one or other, or the
combination, of these problems 'caused' the downfall of the Liberal
Government, which was so fearful of a Conservative attack in the House
of Commons over these issues that Asquith chose Coalition rather than
face defeat. Now in fact, as suggested earlier, the relative numbers of
Liberals and Conservatives on active service rendered this possibility
less likely. A recent commentator has argued persuasively that these
events were the occasion not the cause of Asquith's decision.[1] The
decisive factor was not the House of Commons—after seven years as
Premier in the most turbulent circumstances, Asquith was armoured
against criticism there—but the fear of a wartime election in which the
Liberals would probably be annihilated. Under the 1911 Parliament
Act an election was due by January 1916 at the very latest. Whereas the
Conservatives were united in their patriotic determination, the Liberals
were hopelessly divided in their attitudes to the war. Some still believed
that British involvement was wrong, others disliked increasing state
intervention, many were ardent anti-compulsionists, most disliked the
harsh treatment of aliens necessitated by the war. It was an election not
a debate that Asquith feared; it was an election, not a coalition, that the

Conservatives desired. Hence Asquith's dramatically swift decision which dumbfounded his colleagues and dismayed his party. Its suddenness could only be justified by the need to prevent the Liberal Party from following a suicidal determination to fight out a wartime election. This motive, of course, could hardly be stated. That many Liberals could not come to terms with the new situation is clear from Hobhouse's diary. The shock of these events is implicit in every reference.

17 May

On Monday after questions I went into McKenna's room at H. of C. and found him and Geo. Lambert[2] in earnest conversation. I went out, but McK. followed me to my room and said that on Thursday (or Friday) night Lord Fisher[3] came to him bringing 2 notes, one for W.S.C. and one for the P.M. saying that he could not continue at the Admiralty if W.S.C. remained as First Lord. McK. had done all he could to persuade him to alter his mind, but failed, and the notes were dispatched. On Sunday he had seen both the P.M. and Ll.G. The latter did not see the seriousness of Fisher's resignation, but was convinced later that W.S.C. could not stay. While we were talking Bonham Carter[4] came in, his face as grey as possible, with a circulation box, which I opened. Inside was about half a quarto sheet of manuscript from the P.M. intimating that in order to prevent an acrimonious and damaging discussion on the supply of munitions he had decided to request the resignation of his colleagues so that the Govt. might be reconstituted on a broader basis. Some perfunctory words were added that it gave him the deepest pain to part, even temporarily from devoted and loyal colleagues. This precious document was as unexpected by McK. as by myself. The P.M. had taken the matter very seriously, the Admiralty were undoubtedly seriously embarrassed by the drain at the Dardanelles upon men and ships, and W.S.C. had been ordering fleets and ships about without consultation, much less concurrence of Ld. Fisher. The latter had unquestionably communicated with the Opposition and they, headed I have little doubt by Balfour who has had a room at the Admiralty, and can supply any lacunae of detailed mistakes and differences, have threatened the P.M. with an attack on W.S.C. in the Commons and on K. in the Lords upon the alleged shortage of shells.

Nor must it be forgotten that Ll.G. who is now playing to the middle-class gallery, has ever since his conferences, public and private in 1909 [sic] been on intimate and friendly terms with A.J.B. The one wants to revenge himself on the Tories who ousted him, the other is in a hurry to seize the chief place, just as Chamberlain was in a hurry to supplant Mr. G. With these reflections in mind, I went, after dining at Sir J. E. Ferguson's,[5] to see McK. and Runciman at the former's house. There I found the Jekylls, Ian Macpherson,[6] and Jack Tennant the latter of whom seemed to have but little knowledge of the details of his own department, and was absolutely in the dark as to the political crisis. It seems that after leaving me McK. had picked up W.R. and they had gone together to the F.O. to see Grey. The latter had heard absolutely nothing of these doings, was deeply hurt at the concealment practised, and at once wrote to Asquith, bidding him for the sake of Italian intervention to keep all secrecy until after Thursday. Just then Haldane came in and was asked if he had heard the news, 'No, where from, the Dardanelles?' 'No, from Downing St,' and on being told nearly fell over his chair. As a result of Grey's note we received while we were speaking a second 'circulation', enjoining us to keep these events to ourselves and to continue the administration of our offices. We gathered that the request for resignation was decided on just before question time today, and written without consulting anyone except probably Ll.G. The P.M. had not been to see the King.

19 May
Yesterday it was impossible to get any news. Today Runciman and Mr. Thomas, Labour M.P. for Derby[7] lunched with me at the P.O. Up till 10 a.m. this morning E. Grey had had *no* communication with the P.M. and was in entire ignorance of the course of events. Edwin Montagu was acting as go-between and henchman to the P.M. and the Tories. Mr. Thomas was bitterly opposed to coalition and said the bulk of the Labour men were equally so. Henderson[8] had been asked to join the new Govt. and personally had agreed, but the party was to meet this afternoon and decide on confirmation of H.'s acceptance or the reverse. (They did eventually confirm it by a small majority.) Ll.G. had approached him, as a Welshman and a Labour man, some time ago to share in his schemes, but knowing Ll.G.'s reputation he avoided his overtures. Lately he had marked the goings and comings of Ll.G. and A.J.B. to E. Montagu's house in Queen Anne's Gate, and had scented mischief. He had lately been

with the Army in the trenches, and had encountered sharp criticism of K.'s administration and seen much backbiting on the part of officers. He thought from his own experience that the W.O. had been very slack. Instanced an offer of the W.O. Railway Management Committee to do all railway repairs in *one* workshop, and use all other shops and plant for making shell which offer was first hung up and then rejected; and again an order given to the Midland Railway for stretchers at 19/6, on which subsequently owing to a rise in prices the M.R. asked for an increase of 1/- a pair. This was refused, and an order for stretchers at 35/- per pair placed with another firm. He predicted a stern refusal by organised labour of anything like conscription.

After he left us at H. of C. to which we had driven R. said that E.G. with whom he had breakfasted was chiefly concerned with the proceedings of the Russian Army. According to a letter, of which I had otherwise heard, the Empress Marie had written to Queen Alexandra that their troops were largely armed only with bayonets tied on sticks; from this subject, W.R. could hardly get him away. He hated the coalition, was very sore at being kept in ignorance of Asquith's proceedings, and very disinclined to go on. (It seems that half an hour after W.R. left him a letter came from the P.M. asking E.G. to come to Downing St., and the statement made in the H. of C. was the result.) I forgot to note that yesterday I dined with Alick Murray and that Lord Rothermere (Harmsworth),[9] was present and said he was certain that Ll.G. had told Sir H. Dalziel[10] who had passed it to the press, so as to stop any possible back-sliding by the P.M. Few of the party credited the news!

After the P.M.'s statement the Liberal party adjourned upstairs to hold under the presidency of Sir T. Whittaker[11] an indignation meeting. Many hard things were said, and so high was feeling flowing that O. Partington[12] whose judgement is not always sound got alarmed, and ran for the P.M. With great difficulty he induced him to attend the gathering, but in an address of great tact and cunning, for there was as much of the one as of the other, he completely placated the angry assembly. Simon, and it is interesting to record this, told O.P. that it would be well to let the meeting blow up steam, and show the P.M. he could not count on the blind adherence of the party. I reached the same view to O.P. before J.S. and Gulland.[13] It is a pity that they were [?not] allowed to explode and thereby give the P.M. the backing he must have if he is not to capitulate to the Tory demands in full.

20 May

Lord Crewe went to No. 10 yesterday and there found with the P.M., Ll.G. and W.S.C., the latter of whom was offered the Colonies though the author direct and indirect of the commotion! Crewe in talk with W.R. spoke in terms of great indignation with W.S.C. as the cause of the 2 great difficulties of the Liberal party, viz. the present imbroglio and secondly the Ulster plot. Of this latter Crewe said he had discussed the matter with the P.M. and the plan had been to engineer a revolt in the Army, which a loyal Navy under Churchill were to suppress. It is impossible to conceive such wickedness, and that the P.M. should have any confidence in or any dealings with such a colleague will be a blot on his name. I can only rejoice that I knew nothing of this, and that when I warned the P.M. of the state of feeling in the Army, I was in no position to know of W.S.C.'s manoeuvres.

Loulou Harcourt is to retire at his own request. Haldane because the Tories insist on this—and the P.M. who could keep Grey in the dark, can quite easily desert his closest personal friend; Samuel involuntarily also. Redmond has been offered the Post Office: and refused it. McK. is fighting for the retention of Lord Fisher as First Sea Lord; but both Balfour wishes to get rid of him, and the P.M. who regards him as the match which set the heath on fire. It seems that the P.M. resisted the first threat to debate the Dardanelles and war munitions, and yielded to a second. The failure of the *Daily Mail* and *The Times* attack on K. will, too late, have shown him the advantage of a little courage.

23 May

There has been a recast of the new parts owing to the receipt by the P.M. of the resignation of Sir John Bradbury, Permanent Secretary of the Treasury. When asked for his reasons as he is a young man, and only 2 years at his post, he replied that he would give them if required, but they were the same as those which had produced the retirement of his two immediate predecessors, and if Ll.G. returned to the Exchequer he must resign though willing to take any other post however humble. Accordingly McK. goes to Exchequer where he will do admirably, and they are to invent a new post for Ll.G.

14 Lloyd George in 1912. Hobhouse: 'An unrivalled, indeed miraculous, power of picking other people's brains'

15 Charles Hobhouse in later life

The disintegration of the Liberal Party is complete. We shall not return to power for some years, and only then because Labour is as broken as ourselves. Ll.G. and his Tory friends will soon get rid of Asquith, and the one or two genuine Liberals left of whom Grey and Crewe and W.R. are the most conscientious.

25 May

Yesterday I heard from W.R. that he had no intimation from the P.M. as to his office, and knew neither whether he was to go or stay until he read in the paper the list of the Cabinet.

Tonight I received a brief letter from P.M. regretting the severance of ties, and thanking for services rendered and hoping for a speedy reuniting. All of which is the purest bunkum. Jack Pease who is also 'out' was personally assured by Asquith that he at any rate 'would be all right'.

The newcomers will have to justify their appointments, and our party who care or dare to criticise must confine their remarks to the Tories who have supplanted Liberals.

27 May

This morning I heard from Samuel that he deeply regretted supplanting a colleague, and only did it at the insistence of the P.M. Unfortunately Jack Pease met him yesterday, and asked him how he *could* take the place of a friend and colleague, to which he had replied 'Oh well one must look after oneself.'

17 June

During the last 3 weeks I have learnt some fresh facts. Today I had a long talk with McK. He says the P.M. has been most miserable about his share in the upset, and this Mrs. Asquith confirmed by saying to me that for 3 days after his decision to ask for our resignations, he was constantly in tears. According to R. McK., Ll.G. and B. Law were the people who actually persuaded the P.M. and W.S.C. had no knowledge of what was on foot as to the alterations in the constitution of the Govt. and is much disgusted at the turn things have taken. McK. added that there was hopeless financial disorder at the Exchequer, so great indeed that we could not have carried on for another three months, if no change had taken place at the Treasury. He said that at first Ll.G. had determined to continue there, and wanted Law to do 'munitions'. Law had refused, and said he would go to Exchequer. After much wrangling Crewe had proposed McK. for that post, and to Ll.G.'s surprise B. Law had jumped at this arrangement. He thought that Ll.G. and Law were playing for conscription or a general election.

I made a short speech in H. of C. last Wednesday against conscription which had considerable effect, and not only saved the Govt. from a disastrous division on the Munitions Bill, but I am told had largely decided the Cabinet to stay further action thereon. The Conscriptionists will probably proceed by way of compulsory registration, and there will be difficulty in resisting that. One result of *The Times* and *Daily Mail* proceedings has been that their circulation has decreased; H. Chaplin says he knows 60%. O. Partington who provides them with their raw paper tells me that they ordered from him quantities a month ago greatly in excess of their usual supply. Two or 3 days ago they said they would not now require these special supplies, and reduced their ordinary requirements.

The Labour M.P.s tell me that while not more than 6 or 7 of them would fight industrial conscription, *all* would go to any lengths to resist military conscription.

22 June

It seems that Fisher's first note to the P.M. only alluded to W.S.C.'s continuance at the Admiralty, but later he made his own retention of the First Sea Lordship dependent on Churchill's exclusion from the Cabinet. Thereupon W.S.C. called Balfour to his aid, and the latter then said he could not go to the Admiralty if Fisher was kept on the Board of the Admiralty. During the recent Zeppelin raid John Fuller, who is in charge of special constable area, visited his police headquarters. On the floor were 7 unexploded bombs laid out in a row, and labelled with police labels as 'unclaimed property'.

I have talked to several of the King's Messengers to the Fleet. They are generally agreed that there is a great deal of drinking going on amongst the wardroom officers. It would not be unnatural if it was so, for a ten-month blockade must be frightfully monotonous. The result however may be disastrous. Yesterday the *Roxburgh* of the 'County' Class was torpedoed in the North Sea, and only just crawled back to port while the submarine got away uninjured, and 2 destroyers were lost last week. How much of these losses may be due to bad lookouts can't be estimated but it is reasonable to connect drink, neglect and loss together. Mr. Aider, a Norwegian merchant of standing, came to see me yesterday after visiting Germany and Austria. He said they had plenty of food and metals, but money was very short and credit bad. There was some doubt as to victory, but none as to defeat being possible.

Lord Cowdray had been giving the F.O. much trouble by trying to bring the U.S.A. into Mexico. If they got seriously involved they might want munitions there, which they are now selling to us.

W.R. gave me a description of the Tories in Cabinet. Carson very adroit and resourceful; B. Law ineffective and puny, and openly flouted by Curzon; Lansdowne most useful; Chamberlain insignificant and unsuggestive; Long, very quarrelsome; the P.M. on the defensive, very apprehensive, and at last alive to the consequence of his slothfulness and timidity. Ll.G. hand in hand with B. Law and ignored by A.J.B. the latter immersed at the Admiralty. Ll.G. and the P.M. hostile to and watchful of each other, the latter very insistent on the grounds for anything said by the former. I met T. P. O'Connor[14] on Sunday. He said that Dalziel, Freddy Guest, Sir J. French's A.D.C., he and Marlowe, Editor of the *Daily Mail* dined together the night before *The Times* 'attack' on K.—Guest brought over memos, and letters from French which he read aloud, and which convinced T.P. as to K.'s laches and thereon he and Marlowe concocted the attack.

After the Cabinet resignation he went to see Asquith and told him the Irish feared H.R. was gravely jeopardised, and their only hope was in himself. A. replied that while he remained, and he had every hope of remaining and intention, they need have no fear. T.P.O'C. spoke openly of their dislike of Ll.G. who would sell them or anyone else on the slightest provocation if only the price was high enough.

Donald of the *Chronicle* told W.R. that he was *present* at Walton Heath when Ll.G. practically dictated the *British Weekly* article on conscription—Ll.G. talked and Robertson Nicholl took notes and phrases, and reproduced the harangue almost verbatim.

17 July

Jack Pease is staying here. It seems that in Dec. last, the P.M. told him he would be wanted in April (1915)—he was to replace Birrell as Chief Secretary in Ireland. A.B. to go to D. of Lancaster. Again when the trouble came lately the P.M. assured him that *he* would be undisturbed at the Board of Education, now he has been turned out for a man who has no knowledge of education for others or himself. Again when some years ago Jack was offered a very good industrial appointment the P.M. begged him not to accept it, as 'he relied so much on his (J.P.'s) judgement'! French, Gen. Wilson and Sir W. Robertson have last week been at the Cabinet meetings. The quarrelling between K. and French has been very sharp; it appears undoubted that F. asked for high explosive and K. began by sending 8% and lately 15%. Behind this lies however the fact which ought to be known to French that the French artillery in the course of firing their 'curtains' of h.e. shell have burst 800 guns and killed 3,200 men: and this is Von Donop's defence against attacks by Ll.G. etc.

25 July

W.R. and his wife came to stay. He was with K. recently who showed him a printed dossier of Von Donop's orders for munitions etc. Von D. started with 27 large contractors; these developed into 279, and these again with sub-contractors into 3,000. It seems as if he has promptly ordered everything the Munitions Committee authorised him to place.

We have been sending out 8,000 to 10,000 men daily for 3 weeks past, and have taken over the line north of Dixmunde up to the Belgian right except 2 miles which the French hold. It is an article of faith in the French Army, having obtained landing places at Calais and Boulogne, we intend to keep them after the war, and for this reason Joffre refused to leave hold of some portion of north France, though his ostensible reason for clinging to it is that the Belgian troops are sure to break some day, and in that case the French officers who speak their language will be better able to rally them than English ones who can't converse! ...

... Ll.G. prompted Dalziel's attack on W.O. administration the other night, and made the feeblest of defences, and the printer of Hansard whether by accident or of malice and wit, printed Dalziel's speech under the name of Ll.G. W.R. said Ll.G.'s handling of the press during their journey to Cardiff etc. and his address to the would-be strikers was quite marvellously adroit and successful. He was always protesting against the 'odious' photographers, and then smoothing his hair and adjusting his collar and stopping at a convenient corner to allow them to catch him. His latest phase is to accuse Girouard of treachery to Von Donop, and he will eventually offer him up as the victim when the Ministry of Munitions breaks down.

✳ Out of office, Hobhouse found he had time on his hands. He made a visit to his old friend Nathan in Ireland, and then went to France, where he busied himself about munitions problems.

1 September

I came to Dublin staying with M. Nathan at the Under Secretary's Lodge in Phoenix Park, *en route* to Belfast to investigate a new method of retting flax by bacterial treatment. M.N. gave me two examples of Irish methods. A complaint had reached him from Belmullet that a theatrical company had been for 2 months in possession of the Town Hall and refused to depart, and what were the police to do? Then 2 German officers had escaped from a detention camp, and procured priest's clothes and managed to elude detection for some days. Finally they came to some town, walked boldly into the hotel, and ordered bacon and eggs. Unluckily it was a Friday which they probably didn't know, and no priest could have such a breakfast, and so discovery resulted.

M.N. tells me he refuses to let Ld. Wimborne, the Lord-Lieutenant see any papers or take part in administration. I think he is clearly wrong; no good comes from treating intelligent men as puppets. It is also clear that he gives Birrell as little information as he can, which luckily is all A.B. requires. When the Irish changes were recently being made, A.B. remarked of the Irish Law Officers, Gordon[15] the Attorney-General and O'Connor[16] the Solicitor-General, that it was a very good combination to have one a lawyer and the other a gentleman. . . .

M.N. has been successful here so far, the worst they can say of him, and Losey is that he entertains the 'widow Green' to lunch at Jammet's Restaurant, but won't lunch with friends at the Kildare Street Club. He told me that Lucas was offered the Ld.-Lieutenancy at the changes, but declined it. Wimborne seems to be doing well. The favourite story against Lady Aberdeen is that shortly before they left she ran over a little dog of some lady, but stopped, apologised profusely, and promised to send one of her own dogs of which

she breeds many. So she did, but accompanied it with a bill for £5
due for the new dog, to herself.[17]

19 September

I went to France on Sept. 9. My oldest friend, and relation, John
Fuller, was buried at Neston on the 8th. He had talents, wealth,
much charm of manner, and a most affectionate and lovable nature,
but he threw away all these advantages through indulgence in
alcohol. I shall miss him very much.

I travelled over with Birrell and Mr. Bailey of the Irish Land
Commission.

. . . Birrell thought the Cabinet would break up as Ll.G. and
W.S.C. would not stay if they could not get conscription. A.J.B.
held aloof from his Tory colleagues, was absorbed in his work, and
strongly against conscription. B. Law was useless in Council;
Carson surly, captious, critical; Curzon helpful, and not too talkative. The P.M. was at present adamantine against conscription. K.
wanted it only when he gave the signal, and only as a last resort. I
dined on my arrival with the Princesse de Lucinge at 18 rue de la
ville L'Eveque, as indeed I did each night: great economy exercised,
a few servants, motor seldom used, work every day in the Duchesse
de Rohan's Hospital from 8 a.m. till 7.30 p.m. with only 2 hours off.

I lunched next day Sept. 10 at Embassy with Lord Bertie; I
met Baron Gunzberg, who is never far away from Ld. B., he is a
Russian Jew who was allowed to serve in the Imperial Hussars of
the Guard, ran through much of his money, left the service, remade
his fortune, a good man of business, but honest straightforward and
agreeable. I learnt that by a *very* recent arrangement the conduct of
both English and French armies was entrusted in future to Joffre
and the French staff. Sir John French remaining as a figurehead, and
making promotions etc. while the 3 Army commanders ran the
actual local campaign. I also learnt partly from LeRoy Lewis the Military attaché here, partly from Gunzberg, and partly from a French
Col. of Artillery who is their chief expert on shells the following
story. When M. Millerand became Ministre de la Guerre, he
wanted like most new brooms to make and leave his mark. He ordered
that shells should be drilled and bored, an operation easier and
quicker than 'forging', the former method. Three results followed:
each shell required 13 measures of steel instead of 8; thousands

could be delivered instead of hundreds; and the base of the shells proved so weak that 1,000 French guns were burst. Eventually Creusot Schneider and Montbard, the big shell factories refused to go on making drilled shells, the facts became notorious, a secret Senatorial Committee made inquiry and condemned the new methods. A Ministerial crisis ensued, Millerand justified himself before a hostile Chamber by saying 'the public demanded numbers and I had to provide them' and only escaped by Viriani's amazing eloquence. When the Munitions Dept. began work, Gunzberg wrote to Sir Lionel Philipps,[18] his partner or friend in England, and also to Moir[19] of the Munitions Dept. warning them of the difficulties experienced by the French Govt., and of the danger to life and material caused by the use of 'drilled' shells. In a letter to Moir he pointed out that he would lay down a factory in England, or he would receive English experts in his works at Montbard to show them how to make the forged shells, and he added that if he did the former and only received the lowest payment the British Govt. gave to anyone for shells he would recoup himself in 2½ months at the outside for the whole of his outlay. To these representations Moir sent an answer, which he showed me, evidently desiring to do as G. suggested, but unable to move. LeRoy Lewis told me that he had satisfied himself that the statements of Gunzberg were true, that he had read and sent to the W.O. the report of the Senatorial Committee and that he had written to both Mr. West and Mr. Moir warning that if disaster followed on their adherence to discredited methods he would make public his and their share in the proceedings. He added that he had heard that some British guns had lately burst, a fact confirmed to me by Norton Griffiths whom I met on the boat going homeward, and who is in charge of the Mining Dept. at G.H.Q. and who said one big gun and two 4.7 inch guns had recently burst. It is perhaps interesting to add that Ivor Philipps,[20] Ll.G.'s Munitions Parl. Sec. was sent over to confer with the French on this very accident, but as he told me himself, he knew nothing of metals or shells, and couldn't speak or understand French.

It seems that forged shells are made from metal, stirred when red hot with a square hammer-shaped revolving spoon, which expels the air bubbles etc and the metal is pressed by hydraulic presses over the shaped centre or core.

Gunzberg also said that Creusot told him that they had a contract for 25,000 tons of steel with an English hard steel firm. These people delivered 5,000 tons, of which 87% Creusot rejected and cancelled the contract, but gave them an order for soft steel. A little later these people came to Creusot, asked to be released from this contract, and offered to pay for release because said they, the British Govt. has offered them a large contract at £19 per ton of the same quality as Creusot had contracted for £11. . . .

. . . Sir John French seems a stupid obstructive man. He is disliked by the French authorities for this cause, and showed both these qualities to Ivor Philipps, who whatever his abilities is a most pleasant and willing officer. P. who came out to talk about munitions, passing through St. Omer reported himself to French, who glanced at him, didn't speak, and turned away. Later in the day P. again met F. at Amiens by accident, saluted him, and again met with the same treatment.

14 October

I have this afternoon seen the P.M. on the subject of shells and ammunition for the third time. The first time was on Sept. 27, then on Oct. 6 and now today; on the first two occasions after lunching at No. 10. today at H. of C. On Sept. 27, Cowans, the Q.M.G.,[21] said they had just heard that the *Aquitania* which had taken 6,000 men out to the Dardanelles had been missed by a torpedo, off Gibraltar by 12 ft. The *Olympic* with a similar number of men had reached Gibraltar from Liverpool in 47 hours. On Oct. 6 Orpen[22] the painter was present, he and the P.M. were laughing over a ludicrous story of Sargent[23] painting Lady Sassoon, and producing as he does when he dislikes his sitter, a caricature. The lady dissolved in tears, before Sargent, who insisted that he painted what he saw, and if she wanted something different she could get any Tom, Dick or Harry to do a likeness. He could alter nothing—and she had better bundle out of the room. The P.M. tried to intervene, and at last Sargent picked up his brush and said, 'You declare your hands aren't a greenish yellow—how do you like this?' and picked out a tube of vermilion and painted them a raw beef tinge—'Is that English enough for you?'

I told the P.M. on Sept. 27 the gist of the story Gunzberg related to me, and he agreed to send to Ll.G. the copy of the letter G. wrote to Moir, of the Munitions Dept. offering to set up a factory, and warning him of the excessive prices and profits. On Oct. 6, I asked how things were going, said I had heard from L. Lewis that an inquiry had been started in France, that it was very likely that those interested in prices would try to switch off on to the subject of fuses, from methods of manufacture, and begged him to try to get a real investigation. He promised, and asked me to get further information.

On Oct. 7, I crossed to France, and saw my two informants for Ll.G. They gave me information which showed that the French saved nearly 3/- on each rough shell, and nearly 11/- on each h.e. fuse besides weight and steel; that the Montbard Co. could put up here machinery and in 3 months turn out 6,000 shells a day, and save money sufficient to repay the whole capital outlay. It seems the French fired in 8 days 2,908,000 75 mm. shells of which 485,000 went in one day, and 220,000 large calibre out of a *total* supply of 7 millions before the offensive began. As a result of this great expenditure the action had to be broken off, until fresh supplies had accumulated—the French at once ordered a fresh factory at Montbard.

The P.M. was very attentive, thanked me unusually warmly for the information and sent the memo I left with him at once to Ll.G. Also this afternoon I saw W.R. He gave an interesting picture of Cabinet discord; Lansdowne, Curzon, Law, A. Chamberlain were for leaving the Cabinet if conscription were not proposed. Law chiefly because the Gallipoli peninsula was not abandoned and Chamberlain because of his position as a reversionary leader. Curzon qualified his desire to resign by a declaration that in that event his criticism would be confined to any subject of actual disagreement. Balfour and Long would remain in whatever happened, to carry on the Govt. A.J.B. being against and Long for compulsory service. With them would go Churchill who was pining to get abroad to the Dardanelles, and Ll.G. who saw no opening to a leadership, and was much afraid that he had muddled the Ministry of Munitions, for which he would be called to account, and thought he had better get out of harness while there was yet time to throw the blame on someone else. The P.M. was still a convinced voluntaryist, but equally determined on keeping the Govt. together, and was trying to find a hypothetical formula of a Bill falling due 3 months hence! McKenna who was the P.M.'s only confidant was determined to resign as was W.R. and these two thought Loulou would also go, if conscription was carried in Cabinet. K. had been won over, and had told the Cabinet he wanted 35,000 men a week, whereas his departmental people had only asked for 30,000. Simon characteristically could only express his determination to stand by the P.M. Henderson had a violent altercation with Ll.G. and told him and the Cabinet squarely that Labour would resist conscription by every means, in and out of Parliament.

I went down for two weekends to Nuneham to shoot partridges, who were not shot last year and had really got too numerous. Our guns, varying from day to day, were J. Pease, Tennant, the Speaker, Fritz Ponsonby, D. of Marlborough, E. Grey and Ed. Montagu— we got 1,828 in 4 days. I then went to Blenheim and 425 in one day with 4 other guns. E. Grey's position is that he loathes conscription only a little less than he does the Coalition—but that he fears the effect of a breakup upon the *Entente*. His own withdrawal, the special hatred of Germany for him considered, would have a damaging result. Russia in particular would find it hard to get over. But for that consideration, he would resign tomorrow, as he told me himself, and set off on a walking tour from Land's End to John o'Groats, a 6 weeks' job which would be long enough to enable him to forget the war. One eye has a third of the vision, the other eye a half, obscured—and he is indescribably weary of it all.

✳ This is the last diary entry Hobhouse made. At the end of September he was warned by his doctor, backed up by other medical opinion, that he had only a month to live. He was suffering from an internal growth which in their opinion was inoperable. However, he went ahead and had an operation. As he later noted 'when however they got me on the operating table they discovered their growth was a huge stoppage. I escaped therefore with a shock, and an illness due only to the gradual poisoning of the system by the stoppage.' But it is more appropriate to end with the letter which he wrote to Asquith, thinking himself *in extremis*, on 16 October 1915.[24]

> 47 Rutland Gate,
> S.W.
> 16.10.15

My dear Prime Minister
This is in all probability the last time I shall address you, since

tomorrow or Monday I am to be operated on for bad internal trouble. I should like to thank you for the promotions in political life you have given me, and for the personal kindness you have shown. I am sorry I am not still in harness, and though I was sore at exclusion, I know the many difficulties. I have wished to live to see England victorious, and with such ability as I had I have worked to make her conquer. I most earnestly ask that our country should be saved from the horrors of failure, and that you may guide us into safety.

   Very sincerely yours,
   C. Hobhouse

Epilogue

The diagnosis proved false, however, and he was able to return to rather subdued political activity. Like many Liberals, by this time he viewed the Lloyd George Coalition Government with distaste. He was also well aware that his future political prospects were slight. By 1918 he was even proposing to resign his seat at Bristol if some suitable sinecure, such as a Directorship of the Suez Canal Company, could be found! As it happened it proved unnecessary. Caught in the snare of Lloyd George's 'Coupon' election in 1918, Hobhouse went down in defeat with the rest of the old Asquithian Liberal Party. Facing a Coalition Liberal and a Labour candidate he finished bottom of the poll in East Bristol. His was the indignity of being the first ex-Cabinet Minister ever to lose a deposit in a British election, the system of deposits having been introduced by the 1918 Representation of the People Act to discourage 'freak' candidates. The fact that he was in good company—Asquith, McKenna, Runciman, Simon, Samuel and McKinnon Wood were among the former Ministers defeated—hardly dispelled the gloom of the end of his parliamentary career.

Although he made one more attempt to win election, curiously enough in the very constituency, North Buckinghamshire, where he had begun his political life, he suffered a heavy defeat by the Conservative and Labour candidates there in 1922. He never re-entered Parliament. As the fortunes of the Liberal Party waned further so his political activity became more and more honorific. He was President of the Western Counties Liberal Federation from 1924 until 1935 and he became President of the National Liberal Federation from 1928 to 1930. He had succeeded his father as the 4th Baronet in 1916. Increasingly his main interest lay in running his estate. Nina Hobhouse died in 1927. Four years later he married Aimee Gladys Brendon. He died at Monkton Farleigh on 26 June 1941.

Notes

I IN AND OUT OF THE HOUSE *pp.* 19–48

1 G. W. E. Russell (1853–1919): Liberal M.P. 1880–5, 1892–5; Indian Under-Secretary 1892–4.

2 The speech was a defence of Rosebery's Ugandan policy which implied a British occupation if the British East Africa Company withdrew from the area. It contradicted Gladstone's own policy of evacuation.

3 Charles Saville Roundell (1827–1906): barrister; Liberal M.P. 1880–5, 1892–5.

4 Robert Lowe (1811–92): Liberal M.P. opposed to parliamentary reform 1866–7, led 'Cave of Adullam' who joined with Conservatives to defeat 1866 Reform Bill.

5 Second wife of Sir Michael Edward Hicks Beach (1837–1916) (1st Earl St. Aldwyn): Conservative M.P. 1864–85, 1885–1906; Chief Secretary for Ireland 1874–8 and 1886–7; Chancellor of the Exchequer 1885–6 and 1895–1902. She was the sister-in-law of Mrs. Fuller, Nina Hobhouse's mother, whose home was Neston Park.

6 J. W. Mellor (1835–1911): Liberal M.P. 1880–6, 1892–1904; Deputy Speaker 1893–5.

7 Liberal M.P. 1892–5, 1896–1923.

8 Yorkshire country seat of Lord Ripon.

9 Sir Arthur Hobhouse (1819–1904): created 1st Lord Hobhouse 1885; Bencher of Lincoln's Inn; Member of the Judicial Committee of the Privy Council; married Mary, sister of Lord Farrer of Abinger (1819–99).

10 Sir Edward Fry: Lord Justice of Appeal 1883–92.

11 Sir Charles Parry Hobhouse (1825–1916): the diarist's father.

12 George Joachim Goschen (1831–1907): Unionist Chancellor of the Exchequer 1887–92; First Lord of the Admiralty 1895–1900; 1st Viscount 1900.

13 Henry Hartley Fowler (1830–1911): Liberal M.P. 1880–5, 1885–1908; President of Local Government Board 1892–4; Indian Secretary 1894–5; Chancellor of the Duchy of Lancaster 1905–8; 1st Viscount Wolverhampton 1908.

14 The mustard manufacturers, J. Colman & Sons of Norwich.

15 Joseph Arch (1826–1919): Liberal M.P. 1885–6, 1892–5; founder of Agricultural Labourers' Union 1872.

16 Liberal Chief Whip 1895–9.

17 The Sheffield Attercliffe Liberal Association had refused to nominate a prominent local Labour trade unionist and had chosen a local Liberal employer as candidate in this predominantly working-class constituency. In the three-cornered contest that followed the Liberal retained the seat, but the Independent Labour candidate polled over a thousand votes to demonstrate the ability of Labour to stand as an independent political force against the prejudices of middle-class Liberal caucuses.

18 The Yorkshire estate of Lord Farrer of Abinger.

19 William Brooks, eldest son of 1st Baron Crawshaw, uncle of Nina Hobhouse. His wife was the youngest daughter of Sir Michael Hicks Beach.

20 Henry Hobhouse (1854–1937): barrister; Liberal M.P. 1885–1906.

21 James Bryce (1838–1922): historian and jurist; Liberal M.P. 1880–1907; Chancellor of the Duchy of Lancaster 1892–4; President of the Board of Trade 1894–5; Chief Secretary for Ireland 1905–7; British Ambassador to the United States 1907–13; 1st Viscount 1914.

22 The arbitration of the Anglo-French fishery dispute over the French right to dry fish on the 'French' coasts of Newfoundland, settled by 1904 colonial agreement.

23 Son of 5th Earl Spencer, First Lord of the Admiralty 1892–5; was himself Liberal M.P. 1880–1905; succeeded as 6th Earl 1910.

24 Sir Francis Lockwood (1847–97): cartoonist and *Punch* contributor; Liberal M.P. 1885–97; Solicitor-General 1894–5.

25 Arthur Wellesley Peel (1829–1912): Liberal M.P. 1865–95; Speaker of the House of Commons 1884–95; 1st Viscount 1895.

26 Arnold Morley (1849–1916): Liberal M.P. 1880–95; Chief Whip 1886–92; Postmaster-General 1892–5; no relation to John Morley.

27 The Unionist Party candidate, Sir Matthew White Ridley (1842–1904), had held junior office and was to be Home Secretary 1895–1900. Created 1st Viscount in 1900.

28 Prince Alfred, Duke of Edinburgh (1844–1900), second son of Queen Victoria, had been granted an annuity of £10,000 in 1873. Parliament had the right to revoke this grant if he succeeded to any foreign principality. In 1893 he succeeded to the Dukedom of Saxe-Coburg and Gotha. Twice in the next two years the House of Commons voted to end the annuity, the debate on both occasions revealing violent pro- and anti-monarchist factions.

29 Paul Kruger (1825–1904): President of the Transvaal.

30 Sir Edward Strachey (1858–1936): Liberal M.P. for South Somerset 1892–1911; created 1st Baron Strachie 1911.

31 Liberal M.P. for Reading 1892–5, 1898–1904; director of Huntley & Palmer, biscuit manufacturers.

32 Margot Asquith, his second wife, had been dangerously ill during her first confinement in May 1895 and lost the child. She suffered from persistent ill health for many years after, although she had two children in 1897 and 1902.

33 Benjamin Jowett (1817–93): Master of Balliol College, Oxford.

34 Springkell, near Ecclefechan, Dumfriesshire, home of Sir John Robert Heron-Maxwell (1836–1910).

35 Llysdinam Hall, Breconshire, home of Charles Dillwyn-Venables-Llewelyn, cousin of Nina Hobhouse.

36 Henry Fawcett (d. 1884): Liberal M.P. 1865–84; Postmaster-General 1880–4; Professor of Political Economy, Cambridge University 1863–84.

37 Salisbury City constituency had only about 3,000 electors. The by-election result was: A. H. E. Allhusen (Con.) 1,425; J. M. F. Fuller (Lib.) 1,278.

38 Colonial correspondent of *The Times.*

39 Mr. and Mrs. George Pargiter Fuller, Nina Hobhouse's parents; her brother Robert; and Mrs. E. H. Clutterbuck of Hardenhuish Park, Chippenham.

40 Ulysses S. Grant (1822–85): President of U.S.A. 1872–6; his father was a tanner.

41 Country house near Neath, Glamorgan. Harcourt, defeated at Derby on 13 July 1895, was able to stand successfully at West Monmouthshire on 23 July. Not until 1918 did general election polling take place all on one day.

42 Eshton Hall, Gargrave, Yorkshire, home of Sir Mathew Wilson (1827–1909).

43 Hobhouse's recollection was not quite accurate. Edward Fitzgerald's first edition of *The Rubáiyát of Omar Khayyám* has
     That every hyacinth the garden wears,
     Dropt in her lap from some once lovely head.

44 Herbert Spencer (1820–1903): philosopher and author.

45 Thomas Henry Huxley (1825–95): Professor of Biology, Royal College of Science 1854–85; President of the Royal Society 1885–6.

46 Private Secretary to War Secretaries 1882–93 (Campbell-Bannerman 1892–5).

II INDIAN JOURNEY *pp.* 49–70

1 George Wyndham (1863–1913): Conservative M.P. 1889–1913; Private Secretary to Arthur Balfour 1887–92; Under-Secretary for War 1898–1900; Chief Secretary for Ireland 1900–5.

2 John Bailey (1864–1931): barrister, author and literary scholar; Assistant Private Secretary to George Wyndham.

3 Lord Stanley of Alderley (1827–1903) in fact married, in 1862, Fabia, daughter of Señor Dom Santiago Federico San Roman, of Seville.

4 Joseph Chamberlain married for the third time in 1888, Mary Endicott, daughter of the United States Secretary for War. Jesse Collings (1831–1920) was Chamberlain's longstanding political ally, first as a Radical and later a Liberal Unionist M.P.

5 Sir Maurice William Ernest de Bunsen (1852–1932): envoy extraordinary to Portugal 1905; later Ambassador to Spain and Austro-Hungary.

6 Liberal M.P. 1892–1908; Attorney-General 1905–8.

7 1st Baron Burghclere (1846–1921): Liberal M.P. 1885–95; President of Board of Agriculture 1892–5.

8 The Royal Commission on the Care and Control of the Feeble Minded, which reported in 1908 (Cd. 4202, 4215).

9 Buxton was M.P. for Poplar, where the local Board of Poor Law Guardians was in open conflict with the Local Government Board. At the end of 1905 the L.G.B. was preparing to hold an inquiry into the administration of Poor Relief in this particular area of high unemployment.

10 Financial Secretary at the War Office was T. R. Buchanan (1846–1911); Under-Secretary at the Local Government Board was T. J. Macnamara (1861–1931).

11 Claude Hay (1862–1920): Conservative M.P. 1900–10.

12 William Boyd Carpenter (1841–1918), Bishop of Ripon 1884–1911; James Edward Cowell Welldon (1854–1937), Canon of Westminster Abbey from 1901; Frederick Brotherton Meyer (1847–1929), President of National Federation of Free Churches 1904; James Guiness Rogers (1822–1911), Chairman of Congregational Union of England and Wales 1874.

13 Sir Charles Tennant died on 4 June 1906, aged 83. He left an estate of £3 millions, which was to be divided between his sons. His will specifically stated that he had already provided for his widow and daughters by their respective marriage settlements. Asquith, whose means were not extensive, may well have lamented the absence of any further bequest to his wife, Margot, Sir Charles's daughter.

14 Alfred Lyttleton (1857–1913): married Margot Tennant's sister, Octavia Laura (d. 1886); Unionist Colonial Secretary 1903–5.

15 George Whiteley (1855–1925): Conservative M.P. 1893–1900; Liberal M.P. 1900–8; Liberal Chief Whip 1905–8; 1st Baron Marchamley 1908.

16 Russian Foreign Minister.

17 Lady Dorchester (1830–1914) and Lady Roden (1833–1916) were Charlotte and Sophia Hobhouse, the second and third daughters of John Cam Hobhouse, 1st Baron Broughton (1786–1869).

18 Sir Godfrey Baring (1871–1957): Liberal M.P. for Isle of Wight 1906–10.

19 Douglas Kinnaird (1788–1830): Byron's banker and literary agent after he went abroad in 1816.

20 4th Earl Minto (1845–1914): Governor-General of Canada 1898-1904; Viceroy of India 1905-10.

21 Edward Norman Baker (1857–1913): Member of the Council of India from 1905.

22 William Lee Warner (1846–1916): Under-Secretary, Government of India from 1887.

23 1st Baron Shuttleworth (1844–1939): Liberal M.P. 1869–80, 1885–1902; Chancellor of the Duchy of Lancaster 1886.

24 Thomas, 3rd Baron Denman (1874–1954).

25 T. Ashton (1855–1933): Liberal M.P. 1885–6, 1895–1911; 1st Baron 1911.

26 Lt.-Col. Edward Tufnell (1848–1909): Conservative M.P. 1900–6.

27 6th Earl of Radnor (1868–1930): Conservative M.P. for South Wiltshire 1892–1900.

28 Frederick Robert Moor (1853–1927): Premier of Natal 1906–10.

29 Sir Wilfred Laurier (1841–1919): first French Premier of Canada, 1896–1911.

30 George James Wardle (1865–1947): Labour M.P. 1906–20.

31 John Ward (1866–1934): Labour M.P. 1906–29.

32 Runciman Papers; University Library, Newcastle-upon-Tyne; WR 17.

33 Members of Council of India.

34 Report of the Royal Commission on Decentralisation in India, Cd. 4360.

35 Sir George Sydenham Clarke (1848–1933): Governor of Victoria 1901–4; Secretary, Committee of Imperial Defence 1904; Governor of Bombay 1907–13; created 1st Baron Sydenham of Combe 1913.

36 Sir Arthur Lawley (1860–1932): Administrator, Matabeleland 1898–1901; Governor of Western Australia 1901–2; Lieut.-Governor of Transvaal 1902–5; Governor of Madras 1905–11; succeeded brother as 6th Baron Wenlock 1921.

37 Sir Charles Edmund Fox (1854–1918): married Ethel Mary Hobhouse, Charles Hobhouse's eldest sister in 1876; Chief Judge, Chief Court, Lower Burma 1906–17.

38 Sir Herbert Thirkell White (1855–1931): Chief Judge, Chief Court, Lower Burma 1902–5; Lieut.-Governor of Burma 1905–10.

39 Sir Andrew Fraser (1848–1919): Lieut.-Governor of Bengal 1903–8.

40 Sir Lancelot Hare (1851–1922): Lieut.-Governor of East Bengal and Assam 1906–11.

41 On 23 December 1907 there was an attempt to murder C. B. Allen, the British magistrate of Dacca, as he was waiting for a train at Goalundo railway station. He was shot and seriously wounded by three Bengali youths. Contemporaries believed that such terrorism was the natural consequence of the revolutionary agitation of the Extremist Party.

42 British resident at Katmandu.

43 Members of the Council of India.

44 The Maharao of Kotah succeeded in 1889; ruler of half a million Hindus, he had an income of £186,000 per year.

45 The Maharaja (Holkar) of Indore succeeded to his throne in 1903. He ruled over nearly one million Hindus in an area extending to almost half of the Central Indian Native States. His annual income was about £475,000.

46 Bal Gangadhir Tilak (1856–1920): leader of the Extremist Party in Congress; imprisoned in 1897 for inciting violence and sedition, he believed that revolution was the only way to gain complete freedom from foreign (British) rule; sentenced to six years' imprisonment for sedition in 1908.

47 Gopal Krishna Goghale (1866–1915): leader of Moderate Party in Congress; believer in constitutional reform to avert terrorism; his evidence to the Commission was of great importance, advocating the creation of the village *panchayats* which the Commission were to recommend as the basis of local self-government.

48 To counter the Russian 'menace', in 1905 Kitchener had proposed a major reorganisation of British military forces in India and the construction of strategic railways to control the passes on the North West Frontier. There was considerable Liberal opposition to the massive expenditure involved. Morley was always wary of the annexationist implications of such a policy. Hobhouse's comments suggest a more pragmatic approach, rather concerned about military efficiency than Liberal principle.

49 Quetta suffered a catastrophic earthquake in 1935 which affected an area 130 miles long by 20 miles across, killed 10,000 and made 20,000 homeless.

III LLOYD GEORGE THE IRRESPONSIBLE *pp.* 71–104

1 The source for this statement is probably Morley himself. He rather half-heartedly suggested himself as Chancellor to Asquith, but Asquith never seriously considered such a proposal. He may have thought of acting as Chancellor himself at one stage but once the Premier abandoned that plan he was left with Lloyd George as the obvious choice. Cf. J. Morley, *Recollections* (1917), vol. 2, p. 251; R. Jenkins, *Asquith* (1964), p. 183.

2 Sir Dighton Probyn (1833–1924): Keeper of the Privy Purse and Extra Equerry to King Edward VII.

3 Edward and Alexandra. Edward VII (1841–1910) married in 1863 Princess Alexandra, eldest daughter of King Christian IX of Denmark.

4 Gully, Peel and Brand were the sons respectively of Viscount Selby, Speaker of the House of Commons 1895–1905; Viscount Peel, Speaker 1884–95; and Viscount Hampden, Speaker 1872–84.

5 On 7 November shots were fired at Sir Andrew Fraser, the Lieut.-Governor of Bengal, in the Y.M.C.A. in Calcutta. It was the second of several attempts on his life. A contemporary commented that the desire to kill Sir Andrew Fraser in India had become 'fashionable'!

6 Robert Donald (1861–1933): Editor of the *Daily Chronicle* from 1902 to 1918.

7 Opinion differed on the success of the substitution. Lady Minto, a hostile witness it should be said, claimed 'Mr. Hobhouse had not sufficient grasp and knowledge of the subject to enable him to preserve an unruffled air of confidence when difficult questions were suddenly asked upon matters of detail, some of which had not been completely solved by the Government of India, and Morley became uneasy and restive.' Countess of Minto, *India, Minto and Morley 1905–10* (1934), p. 300. Morley, however, commented with satisfaction on Hobhouse's performance. Morley, *Recollections* (1917), vol. 2, pp. 306–7.

8 Sir Jacob Sassoon (1844–1916) had only been created baronet in February 1909. He never gained a peerage, nor did Sir G. Donaldson (1845–1925) despite various public benefactions ever receive a baronetcy. Sir Steyning Edgerley (1857–1935) had been a member of the Decentralisation Commission.

9 Sir Ernest Cassel (1852–1921): banker.
Sir Henry Babington Smith (1863–1923): Secretary to the Post Office 1903–9.

10 See Edward David, 'The New Liberalism of C. F. G. Masterman 1873–1927' in *Essays in Anti-Labour History* (1974), edited by Kenneth D. Brown.

11 Herbert Lewis (1858–1933): Welsh Liberal M.P. 1892–1906, 1906–18, 1918–22; lifelong associate of Lloyd George; Junior Whip 1905–6; Parliamentary Secretary, Local Government Board 1909–15, Board of Education 1915–22.

12 R. C. Lehman, Liberal M.P. 1906–11, never gained office.

13 Charles Trevelyan (1870–1958): Parliamentary Secretary, Board of Education 1908–14, resigned on the outbreak of the First World War. He later held office in the Labour Governments of 1924 and 1929–31.

14 J. Sinclair (1860–1925), 1st Lord Pentland: Liberal M.P. 1892–5, 1897–1909; Secretary for Scotland 1905–12.

15 Viscount Harcourt's country seat in Oxfordshire.

16 Prince Arthur, Duke of Connaught (1850–1942): third son of Queen Victoria; married in 1879 Princess Louisa of Prussia; Princess Patricia was their third child.

17 Sir Robert Chalmers (1858–1938): Chairman, Board of Inland Revenue 1907–11; Permanent Secretary, Treasury 1911–13; Governor of Ceylon 1913–15; Joint Permanent Secretary, Treasury 1916–19; 1st Baron 1919.
Sir Laurence Guillemard (1862–1951): Deputy Chairman, Board of Inland Revenue 1902–8; Chairman, Board of Customs and Excise 1909–19.

18 In the Lords debate on the Parliament Bill on 10 August Rosebery had made a miserable speech explaining that he would vote for the Government but he was at pains to emphasise how reluctant he was to do so.

19 Sir E. P. Tennant (1859–1920): Liberal M.P. 1906–10; Asquith's brother-in-law.

20 Stuart Rendel, 1st Baron Rendel (1834–1913): Liberal M.P. 1880–94; managing partner, Armstrong's Engineering Company.

21 The position of the old Gladstonian, Morley, was curiously ambivalent. As one of the group advocating immediate action to alter the Lords' veto powers, he seems to have willed the end but not the means, regarding the threat to create peers with disfavour. 'Untouched' is ambiguous: the 'vetoists' saw the veto as the evil to be remedied, not the composition of the Lords.

22 Patrick O'Brien: Irish Nationalist M.P. 1886–92, 1895–1917.
William O'Brien: Independent Nationalist M.P. 1910–14, led opposition to the Budget, bringing pressure to bear on Redmond.

23 Private secretary to Lloyd George and Winston Churchill at Board of Trade 1906–8, and to Lloyd George as Chancellor of the Exchequer 1908–10.

24 Sir John Talbot Dillwyn-Llewelyn (1836–1927): Conservative M.P. 1895–1900; uncle of Nina Hobhouse.

25 Mrs. Alice Keppel (1869–1947): mistress of Edward VII.

26 Lord Farquhar (1844–1923): Master of the Household 1901–7; Lord Steward 1915, created Earl 1922.
Lord Beauchamp, 7th Earl (1872–1938): Lord Steward 1907–10; First Commissioner of Works 1910–14; Lord President of the Council 1910 and 1914–15.

27 Charles Hardinge (1858–1944): Permanent Under-Secretary, Foreign Office 1906–10 and 1916–20; Viceroy of India 1910–16; British Ambassador to Paris 1920–2; 1st Baron Hardinge of Penshurst 1910.

28 Edmund Gosse (1849–1928): author and essayist; Librarian of the House of Lords 1904–14.

29 6th Earl of Portsmouth (1856–1917): Parliamentary Secretary to the War Office 1905–8; was refused office by Asquith, who had once been his tutor and had little opinion of his ability.

30 Robert Donald, A. G. Gardiner and Clifford Sharp were the respective editors.

31 1st Earl of Cromer, formerly Sir Evelyn Baring (1841–1917): British Consul-General in Egypt 1883–1907; President of National League for Opposing Women's Suffrage.

32 The Conciliation Bill passed its Second Reading by 299 votes to 189. But the House immediately voted by 320–175 to refer it to a Committee of the whole House, thereby eliminating its chances of becoming law. What perturbed Hobhouse was the undoubted vote for the *principle* of women's suffrage.

33 Henry Peter, Baron Brougham and Vaux (1778–1868): Lord Chancellor 1830–4; reported killed after carriage accident on 21 October 1839; obituaries appeared on the following day; he was accused of deliberately reporting his death.

34 Mrs. Tennant had indeed formerly been H.M. Superintending Inspector of Factories, hence Hobhouse's description.

35 2nd Baron Nunburnholme (1875–1924): succeeded to the title in 1907; previously Liberal M.P. 1906–7.

36 Neil Primrose (1882–1917): son of Lord Rosebery; Liberal M.P. 1910–17; Under-Secretary for Foreign Affairs 1915; died of wounds received in action.

37 F. D. Acland (1874–1939) had been Liberal M.P. for Yorkshire, Richmond from 1906 until January 1910. In December he was elected M.P. for N.W. Cornwall. Strachey's seat, South Somerset, as Hobhouse feared, was lost to a Conservative in the by-election which followed Strachey's peerage in November 1911.

38 H. E. Kearley (1856–1934): Liberal M.P. 1892–1910; Parliamentary Secretary Board of Trade 1905–9; 1st Baron Devonport 1910.

39 Asquith was well aware of Lloyd George's negotiations and regarded them with some scepticism and no great alarm. There was little likelihood of collaboration between the bitterly antagonistic backbenches however much individual front-bench politicians might favour the idea of Coalition. Asquith's own position as Liberal leader was far stronger than Balfour's at the head of the Unionists. The latter's fear of being 'another Peel' and splitting his party effectively ended the discussions. But Hobhouse's alarm was shared by many Liberals.

40 This refers to the formal constitutional conference proposals and not to any Lloyd George Coalition talks. Lord Halsbury (1823–1921), a former Conservative Lord Chancellor, was to lead the 'last-ditch' fight against the Parliament Bill in the House of Lords.

41 The result in East Bristol was: C. E. Hobhouse (Lib.) 7,229; P. J. Hannon (Un.) 4,263. Hobhouse's comment on the closeness of the election result is a pardonable exaggeration. In fact nationally 80 more votes would have won 7 more seats for the Liberals. There were 15 seats lost by the Liberals by majorities of less than 100, but the Unionists lost 18 by the same narrow margin.

42 Edward Mylius had published in the *Liberator* a story that George V had secretly married in Malta in 1890, thereby implying that his marriage to Queen Mary was bigamous. Mylius was tried for criminal libel, found guilty, and sentenced to twelve months' imprisonment in February 1911.

43 Lord Cawdor, 3rd Earl (1847–1911): one of the four Unionist representatives at the constitutional conference, the others being Balfour, Austen Chamberlain and Lansdowne. Asquith, Birrell, Crewe and Lloyd George represented the Liberals.

44 Sir Henry MacMahon (b. 1862): Chief Commissioner of Baluchistan from 1905; officer in charge of the visit of the Amir of Afghanistan to India 1907.

45 W. St. John Brodrick (1856–1942): Conservative M.P. 1880–1906; War Secretary 1900–3; Indian Secretary 1903–5; 9th Viscount Midleton 1907; 1st Earl 1920; Hobhouse criticised his maladministration of the War Office in letters to *The Times* and articles in the *Contemporary Review*.

46 This was an over-sanguine view. George V had given the pledge with considerable reluctance and, disturbed by Conservative criticism of his position, he wished this to be made clear. He hoped to avoid having to create peers. The danger was that the 'ditchers' would misconstrue his natural reluctance as evidence that the Government was bluffing and so bring about the very contingency he wished to avoid.

47 Sir Arthur Thring (1860–1932): First Parliamentary Counsel 1903–17.

48 Sir Thomas Heath (1861–1940): Assistant Secretary, Treasury 1907–13; Joint Permanent Secretary 1913–19.

49 Sir Francis Hopwood (1860–1947): Permanent Secretary, Board of Trade 1901–7; Permanent Under-Secretary, Colonial Office 1907–11.

50 R. D. Holt (1868–1941): Liberal M.P. 1907–18.

51 Delcassé, the French Premier, had been forced to resign by German diplomatic pressure at the time of the first Moroccan crisis 1905–6.

IV CHANCELLOR OF THE DUCHY *pp.* 105–127

1 Count von Aehrenthal (1854–1912): Austro-Hungarian Foreign Minister.

2 Formerly the British military attaché in Persia, acted as Shuster's financial assistant.

3 Hobhouse omitted to mention the third committee of the Cabinet which was set up, on Welsh Church Disestablishment, at that meeting. The Home Rule Bill and the Welsh Church Bill were to take virtually all 1912 for their drafting and passage through Parliament.

4 General Sir William Nicholson (1845–1918): Chief of General Staff 1908–12.

5 There were actually two propositions which were approved unanimously: 1. That no communications should take place between the General Staff here and the Staffs of other countries which can, directly or indirectly, commit this country to military or naval intervention. 2. That such communications, if they relate to concerted action by land or sea, should not be entered into without the previous approval of the Cabinet. Cf. Asquith Papers, Bodleian Library, vol. 6, ff. 79–80.

6 J. A. Spender (1862–1942): Editor of the *Westminster Gazette* 1896–1922; friend and later biographer of Asquith.

7 Asquith's house in East Lothian, Scotland. There on 20 October McKenna warned Asquith that he would reveal the Anglo-French talks to his Cabinet colleagues.

8 Barclay and Buchanan were British Minister at Teheran and British Ambassador at St. Petersburg respectively.

9 John Dillon (1851–1927): Irish Nationalist M.P. 1880–3, 1885–1918.

10 Sir Fairfax Cartwright (1857–1928): British Ambassador to Austro-Hungary 1908–13.

11 Lord Acton (2nd Baron Acton) (1870–1924): British Chargé d'Affaires, Darmstadt 1911–14.

12 Sergius Sazonov (1866–1927): Russian Foreign Minister 1910–17.

13 The *Majlis* was the Persian elected assembly. Hobhouse's spelling is his own.

14 Sir William Edward Goschen (1847–1924): British Ambassador, Vienna 1905–8; British Ambassador, Berlin 1908–14.

15 Count Metternich (1853–1934): German Ambassador, London 1901–12.

16 Vernon Hartshorn (1872–1931): President, South Wales Miners' Federation.

17 Prince Louis of Battenberg (1854–1921); 2nd Sea Lord 1911–12; 1st Sea Lord 1912–14; took name of Mountbatten 1917 and created 1st Marquess of Milford Haven 1917. The idea of a Malta conference was originally mooted by Asquith, so it was not just a harebrained idea of Churchill's as Hobhouse rather implies. Talks between Asquith, Churchill and Kitchener did take place at Malta at the end of May, resulting in a draft agreement that France should

be asked to look after the Mediterranean while Britain protected the Channel. This draft was the basis of discussion in the C.I.D. and Cabinet over the next few months.

18 Hobhouse's secretary at that time, Mrs. E. G. Wilson, recalls 'Mr. Hobhouse told me with a chuckle that he "had made the King spend a lot of money"' on this occasion.

19 Hugh James O'Beirne (1866–1916): Councillor, St. Petersburg Embassy 1906–16.

20 Vice-Admiral Lewis Bayly (1857–1938): Commander 3rd Battle Squadron 1913–14; Commander 1st Battle Squadron 1914; Commander-in-Chief, Western Approaches 1915–19.

21 This confirmed the formula arrived at in the Committee of Imperial Defence meeting on 4 July. In effect Churchill had got his way as far as the primacy of the North Sea was concerned against those, such as McKenna, who had wanted to divide our naval forces between the North Sea and the Mediterranean.

22 'Lulu' Harcourt was a fervent opponent of women's suffrage. Hobhouse was to some extent the author of his own misfortune. One of the suffragettes arrested for the fire at Nuneham carried a note which stated 'I myself have taken part in every peaceful method of propaganda and petition . . . but I have been driven to realise that it has all been of no avail, so now I have accepted the challenge given by Mr. Hobhouse at Bristol, and I have done something drastic.' Quoted in Andrew Rosen, *Rise Up Women!* (1974), p. 169.

23 Governor-General 1911–16.

24 Robert Borden (1854–1937): Canadian Prime Minister 1911–20. In July he agreed that Canada should meet the cost of three dreadnoughts as a contribution to Imperial defence. Churchill's visit was intended to arouse Canadian enthusiasm for the proposal, but this was not shared by Laurier's Liberal Party, who opposed the Navy Bill in the Senate. Because of the party controversy Churchill did not visit Canada.

25 Runciman Papers, W.R. 67.

26 Paul Cambon (1843–1924): French Ambassador in London 1898–1920.

27 In a snap division on a financial amendment to the Home Rule Bill the Government had been defeated by 228 votes to 206. It was an embarrassment but no more, and Asquith refused to contemplate resignation. His statement to this effect provoked uproar in the House on 13 November and the sitting had to be adjourned. But a week later a resolution embodying the defeated resolution was carried easily by the Government.

28 Sir Courtenay Ilbert (1841–1924): Clerk of the House of Commons 1902–21.

29 Churchill originally proposed pay increases costing £35,000 for officers' pay

and £700,000 for ratings'. When he was told only £300,000 was available, he produced proposals costing just under £400,000, and was then disappointed that Lloyd George insisted on cutting this still further to £366,000. Hobhouse's account makes no allowance for Churchill's benevolent intentions, especially towards the ordinary seamen.

30 H. W. Massingham (1860–1924): Editor of the *Nation* 1907–23.

31 Geoffrey Howard (1877–1935): Liberal M.P. 1906–10; 1911–18; 1923–4; Parliamentary Private Secretary to Prime Minister 1910; Vice-Chamberlain of the Household 1911–15; Liberal Whip 1915–16.

32 Sir Eustace Edward Twisleton-Wykeham-Fiennes (1864–1943): 1st Baronet 1916; Governor and Commander-in-Chief, Seychelles Islands 1918–21, Leeward Isles 1921–9.

33 Sir James Craig (1871–1940): Unionist M.P. 1906–21; M.P. in Northern Ireland Parliament 1921; 1st Prime Minister of Northern Ireland 1921–40; cr. 1st Viscount Craigavon 1927.

34 Thomas Sinclair (1838–1914): Leader Ulster Liberal Party 1868; Liberal Unionist 1886; President, Ulster Liberal Unionist Association 1886–90; Member of Standing Committee, Ulster Unionist Council.

V A VERY DISTURBED ATMOSPHERE *pp.* 128–154

1 The Franchise and Registration Bill reduced the qualifying period of residence from twelve to six months.

2 A. E. W. Mason (1865–1948): Liberal M.P., Coventry 1906–10; author, *inter alia*, of *The Four Feathers*, *The Turnstile*, *At the Villa Rose*.

3 C. M. Warmington, Liberal M.P. for Monmouthshire West 1885–95.

4 Lady Edith Lovelace, wife of 3rd Earl, d. 1932.

5 Sir Derek Keppel (1863–1944): Equerry-in-Ordinary to Prince of Wales 1893–1910, to George V 1910–12; Master of the Household 1912–36.

6 Randall Davidson (1848–1930): Dean of Windsor and domestic chaplain to Queen Victoria 1883–91; Bishop of Rochester 1891–5, Winchester 1895–1903; Archbishop of Canterbury 1903–28.

7 Reginald Balliol Esher, 2nd Viscount (1852–1930): Conservative M.P. 1880–5; Deputy Governor and Constable, Windsor Castle 1901–28; Permanent member Committee of Imperial Defence 1905–18.

8 26 March and 3 April. 'Yesterday' was the Cabinet on 9 April. This diary entry is in fact misdated in the manuscript as 9 April.

9 The 26th Earl of Crawford had died in January 1913, leaving a vast amount of material relating to the French Revolution. Born in 1847, the Earl had been

a Trustee of the British Museum, and was a past President of the Royal Astronomical Society.

10 No baronetcy appears to have been forthcoming. Nor is there any record of a knight of this name, but there was a Wiltshire J.P. called Robert Caird, born in 1850, who lived in Devizes, who might just possibly have been the person concerned.

11 Albert Augustus David (1867–1950): Headmaster of Clifton College 1905–9; Headmaster of Rugby 1909–21; Bishop of St. Edmundsbury and Ipswich 1921–3; Bishop of Liverpool 1923–4.

12 Sir Stuart Montagu Samuel (1856–1926): Liberal M.P. for Tower Hamlets, Whitechapel 1900–16. See editor's commentary below, pp. 136–7.

13 The maiden voyage of the German liner *Imperator* was postponed during the spring of 1913, allegedly because of acts of sabotage by workmen.

14 During 1913 Weetman Pearson (1st Viscount Cowdray, 1856–1927), the former Liberal M.P. 1895–1910 and 'oil millionaire', approached the Government with the suggestion that it should invest £5 millions in his Mexican Eagle Oil Company, in return for which he would ensure oil supplies for the Navy. The suggestion was treated with understandable caution in the light of Marconi.

15 Raymond Poincaré (1860–1934): French Premier and Foreign Minister 1912–13; President of the French Republic 1913–20.

16 F. W. S. McLaren (1886–1917): Liberal M.P. 1910–17; Parliamentary Private Secretary to Harcourt as Colonial Secretary 1910–15.

17 John Henry Ponsonby (1848–1916), of Brympton, Yeovil, Somerset.

18 Charles Thomas Studd (1861–1931): Missionary in China, India, and the Congo; founder of the Heart of Africa Mission and the Worldwide Evangelisation Crusade.

19 George V was irritated by Harcourt in this interview. He objected to Harcourt's 'bludgeoning words' and thought him 'most unsatisfactory'. See Harold Nicolson, *King George V*, p. 231.

20 Brodick, near Lamlash, on the Isle of Arran.

21 On the face of it, this was a curious comment. In Linlithgow on 7 November, in a straight fight with the Conservatives, the Liberals were able to retain the seat despite a swing of 8% against them, whereas in Reading on the following day, in a three-cornered contest, Rufus Isaacs's old seat was lost to the Unionists on an adverse swing of 11%. The intervention of a Labour candidate made the difference, but Asquith may have had in mind also the personal following which Isaacs had had in Reading which his successor lacked. The great imponderable, of course, is what effect the 'Marconi' allegations had on the Liberal vote.

22 James Larkin (1876–1947): Labour agitator and trade union organiser, sentenced on 27 October to seven months' imprisonment for sedition. The Irish Attorney- General, J. F. Moriarty (1854–1915), had led the prosecution.

23 George Earle Buckle (1854–1935): Editor of *The Times* 1884–1912.

24 Geoffrey Robinson (1874–1944): assumed name of Dawson by Royal licence 1917; Private Secretary to Lord Milner in South Africa 1901–5; Editor, *Johannesburg Star* 1905–10; Editor of *The Times* 1912–19, 1923–41.

25 Sir G. Prescott (1875–1942): Military Secretary to Lord Wimborne when the latter was Lord-Lieutenant of Ireland 1916.

26 Lady Randolph Churchill (1854–1921): widow of Lord Randolph Churchill, mother of Winston. Lady Gwendoline Churchill (1885–1941) married Winston's younger brother John Spencer ('Jack') Churchill in 1908.

27 Winston Churchill to Lloyd George 12 July 1912. Randolph S. Churchill, *Winston S. Churchill* (1969), vol. II, Companion, part 3, pp. 1609–14. The letter was marked 'Confidential' and 'Not circulated'.

VI CHURCHILL AND CRISIS *pp.* 155–177

1 A Cabinet Committee had produced two schemes for a reformed Second Chamber. The first envisaged direct popular elections, which Hobhouse seems to have favoured. But it was the alternative scheme, whereby the members of the House of Commons divided into regional groups would elect members of the Upper House, which the full Cabinet had approved on 15 December.

2 Simon also wrote to Asquith to say that the loss of Churchill over the estimates would not split the party. He implied that his resignation on this issue would be preferable to a departure over Ulster. Asquith Papers, vol. 25, ff. 148–9.

3 Joseph Devlin (1872–1934): Irish Nationalist M.P. 1902–22, 1929–34.

4 Sir Herbert Jekyll (1846–1932): Private Secretary to Lord Lieutenants of Ireland 1885–6 and 1892–7; Assistant Secretary, Board of Trade 1901–11; something of a connoisseur, he was McKenna's father-in-law.

5 The letter as sent, addressed to 'My dear George' (the correct form of his surname which Lloyd George disliked greatly), has some very slight alterations viz. 'I served under you so long that I think I ought just to let you know that I find myself still unconvinced . . . I wish to express my dissent from and my distrust of them.' Lloyd George Papers, Beaverbrook Library, C/5/2/1.

6 The letter asked Asquith to consider the effect of British naval expansion on Germany; the prospect of counter-escalation by her to meet the British programme; the parliamentary danger of Liberal 'economists' being joined by

the Labour Party and opportunist Ulstermen in opposition; the effect on by-elections, at a time when Home Rule depended on maintaining the Government in power; and that the required heavy taxation could be seen as a breakdown of Free Trade. All the arguments came from the traditional Liberal locker—certainly not from pacifist 'Little Englanders'. Asquith Papers, vol. 25, ff. 170–7.

7 Prince Henry of Prussia (1862–1929) was the younger brother of William II (1859–1941), German Emperor 1888–1918.

8 General Sir Henry Wilson (1864–1922): Director of Military Operations, Army H.Q. 1910–14; Assistant Chief of Staff to Sir John French 1914; Corps Commander; Liaison Officer with the French; British Military Representative, Versailles, 1917; notorious political plotter, he became Chief of Imperial General Staff 1918–22; created baronet 1919; murdered by I.R.A. 1922.

9 Brigadier-General Hubert Gough (1870–1963): commanding officer, 3rd Cavalry Brigade; later Commander of 5th Army in European War.

10 Lieutenant-General Sir John Spencer Ewart (1861–1930): Adjutant-General to the Forces 1910–14; G.O.C. Scottish Command 1914–18.

11 Lt.-Col. Charles A'Court Repington (1858–1925): *The Times* military correspondent; was to play a significant role in the 1915 'Shells' crisis.

12 Garnet Joseph Wolseley (1833–1913): Commander of Forces in Ireland 1890–5; Commander-in-Chief of the Army 1895–1900; created 1st Viscount 1885.

13 Bonar Law Papers, Beaverbrook Library, 32/2/46, 32/2/54 and 32/2/62.

14 S. O. Buckmaster (1861–1934): Liberal M.P. 1906–10, 1911–15; Solicitor-General 1913–15; Director of the Press Bureau 1914–15; Lord Chancellor 1915–16.

15 On 24 April the Ulster Volunteers had landed over 20,000 rifles and 3 million rounds of ammunition at Larne, Bangor and Donaghadee. The authorities had been unable to intervene and the operation was carried out with extraordinary efficiency. The arms were distributed amongst the Volunteer forces which numbered close to 100,000 men.

16 General Sir Nevil Macready (1862–1946): Director of Personal Services 1910–14; Adjutant-General, British Army in France 1914–16; Adjutant-General to the Forces 1916–18; Commander, Metropolitan Police 1918–20; G.O.C. Forces in Ireland 1920–2.

17 In the House of Commons on 21 May, during a noisy Unionist demonstration, the Speaker had asked Bonar Law whether this was 'with his consent and approval'. Bonar Law's swift reply 'I would not presume to criticise whatever you consider your duty, Sir, but I know mine and that is not to answer any such question' was crushing. (H.C. Deb. 5th ser., LXII, 2213–4.)

18 Masterman had been promoted to the Cabinet as Hobhouse's successor as Chancellor of the Duchy but had lost his seat at the by-election then necessary for any minister on appointment. He went to fight Ipswich with justifiable misgivings and was indeed defeated. Attempts to find another constituency failed and he eventually had to resign from the government in February 1915.

19 W. S. Glyn-Jones (1869–1927): Liberal M.P. 1911–18.

20 Parliamentary Debates, House of Commons, 5th Series, LXIII, 477, 1117, 1529; 11, 17 and 22 June 1914.

21 On 7 July the House of Lords voted that the India Council Bill should be read 'this day six months' i.e. that it should be rejected.

22 William Maxwell Aitken (1879–1964): Conservative M.P. 1910–16; created Baronet 1916; 1st Baron Beaverbrook 1917; Chancellor of Duchy of Lancaster and Minister of Information 1918; founded Beaverbrook Newspapers.

23 Prince Lichnowsky (1860–1928): German Ambassador in London 1912–14.

24 W. V. Harrell, Assistant Commissioner of the Dublin Metropolitan Police. On 26 July the Irish Volunteers had emulated the Larne gun-running on a much smaller scale at Howth, near Dublin. Harrell called out the military and later in the day troops opened fire on a hostile crowd in Dublin, killing three and wounding thirty-eight. The dramatic contrast between this violence and the authorities' failure to intervene against the Ulster gun-running needed no emphasis.

VII War-lords under Strain *pp*. 178–214

1 The Anglo-Japanese Alliance of 1902 was renewed in 1905 and 1911. Each Power agreed to come to the aid of the other if any unprovoked attack threatened its territorial rights or special interests in East Asia or India. Hobhouse was perhaps construing this *casus foederis* over-strictly.

2 Walter H. Page (1855–1918): United States Ambassador to London.

3 Rear-Admiral Sir Arthur Limpus (1863–1931): naval adviser to the Turkish Fleet 1912–14. Enver Bey (Enver Pasha) (1881–1922): member of Young Turk triumvirate 1908; Minister of War 1914.

4 The *Sultan Osman* was one of two British-built battleships purchased by Turkey. They were due to sail to Turkey at the end of July but on Churchill's initiative they were seized for use by the Royal Navy. The *Sultan Osman* joined the Grand Fleet as H.M.S. *Agincourt* on 25 August. Meanwhile Enver had signed a secret treaty with Germany on 2 August, and the Germans made haste to send the *Goeben* to Constantinople, giving the Royal Navy the slip in the Mediterranean, as a gesture of solidarity. Turkey entered the war on the Central Powers' side on 29 October 1914, and surrendered exactly four years and one day later.

5 General Sir John G. Maxwell (1859–1929): Chief Staff Officer, 3rd Army Corps; Commander-in-Chief in Ireland 1916; C.-in-C. Northern Command 1916–18.

6 Sir Horace Rumbold (1869–1941): diplomat; Councillor of Embassy at Tokyo 1909–13, at Berlin 1914.

7 General Joseph Jacques Césaire Joffre (1852–1931): C.-in-C. French Army 1914.

8 Sir Francis Bertie (1844–1919): British Ambassador at Paris 1905–18; created 1st Viscount Bertie of Thame 1918.

9 There were mercantilist wars with Holland in 1652–4 and 1665–7. It seems rather more likely that Hobhouse was thinking of the earlier conflict, which was caused ostensibly by the English Navigation Act of 1651.

10 General Sir Ivor John Caradoc Herbert (1851–1933): Liberal M.P. 1906–17, created 1st Baron Treowen 1917.

11 Variously spelt Hooghly or Hugli, one of the river mouths of the Ganges flowing into the Bay of Bengal.

12 Lord Roberts of Kandahar (1832–1914): V.C. 1858; Commander, Kabul Field Force 1879–80; Field Marshal and C.-in-C. of Forces in South Africa 1899–1900; created 1st Earl Roberts 1901; advocate of compulsory national service.

13 See editor's comment below, p. 217; diary 20 January 1915.

14 J. H. Whitley (1866–1935): Liberal M.P. 1900–28; Deputy Speaker 1911–21.

15 William Crooks (1852–1921): Labour M.P., Woolwich 1903–10, 1910–21.

16 On 22 September the cruisers *Aboukir*, *Cressy* and *Hogue*, engaged on the Dogger Bank patrol, were torpedoed within minutes of one another with the loss of over 1,400 lives. Churchill was held responsible by a hostile press, but had in fact ordered the ending of such patrols before the disaster took place. Unfortunately his order was not acted upon in time.

17 The Germans began the destruction of Louvain on 26 August 1914.

18 The Shatt-al-Arab is the estuary into which both the Tigris and Euphrates Rivers flow before joining the Persian Gulf. The *Odin* was part of the small force protecting the Anglo-Persian oil refinery at Abadan. Once war between Britain and Turkey was declared the *Odin* took part in the capture of Basra, thereby securing control of head of the Gulf.

19 Albert I of Belgium (1875–1934): succeeded to the throne 1909; took command of his troops and fought with them throughout the war.

20 Albert Ballin (1857–1918): German ship-owner; owner of Hamburg-Amerika line. He had dined with Churchill on 24 July and they had discussed the pros-

pect of war. Ballin's visit to London at this juncture was intended to spy out what Britain's position would be in the event of a Franco-German war. There is no reference to such a letter from Churchill, as far as I am aware, in any other source.

21 There is some discrepancy here between Hobhouse's version of this singular event and that given in Roy Jenkins, *Asquith*, p. 345. Asquith's letter to the King, on 14 October, reporting that Cabinet meeting (CAB 41/35/52) does not record the names of those voting, merely the numbers. Nor does Asquith's copy of his letter (Asquith MSS, vol. 7, ff. 217–18). Jenkins gives no reference for his account.

22 Major-General Sir John Hanbury-Williams (1859–1946): Chief of British Military Mission with the Headquarters, Russian Army in the field 1914–17.

23 Field-Marshal Ferdinand Foch (1851–1929): General commanding 13th Division, 1911; Marshal of France 1918; Generalissimo of Allied Forces, France 1918.

24 Jan Christian Smuts (1870–1950): commanded Republican Forces, Cape Colony, in Boer War; commanded forces in British East Africa 1916–17; South African Minister of Defence 1910–20; Prime Minister 1919–24, 1939–48.

25 Ironically, in April 1913, Churchill had aroused hostility amongst some of his naval staff by circulating a memorandum entitled 'The Time Table of a Nightmare' which envisaged such a German invasion. Presumably he would have claimed in October 1914 that his efforts had eliminated the possibility which he had feared. See Randolph S. Churchill, *Winston S. Churchill*, vol. II, *Young Statesman 1901–1914*, pp. 613–27.

26 Brigadier-General Christian Frederick Beyers (1869–1914): Chairman of Peace Conference at Vereeniging; Commandant-General, Citizen Forces, Union of South Africa; drowned when trying to escape from Government forces during rebellion.

27 Christian de Wet (1854–1922): General and Commander-in-Chief of Free States Forces during South African War; Minister for Agriculture, Orange River Colony 1907–15; rebelled, defeated and captured; sentenced to six years' imprisonment and £2,000 fine.

28 There is no report of this squabble in Asquith's letter to the King.

29 Johannes Wilhelmus Wessels (1862–1936): advocate; later Judge of Appellate Division, Supreme Court of South Africa.

30 Vice-Admiral Sir S. C. J. Colville (1861–1939): commanding 1st Battle Squadron 1912–14.

31 General Sir William Robertson (1860–1933): Commandant, Staff College 1910–13; Director of Military Training, War Office 1913–14; Quartermaster-General, British Expeditionary Force 1914; Chief of General Staff, BEF 1915;

Chief of Imperial General Staff 1915–18; cr. 1st Baronet 1919; Field-Marshal 1920.

32 General Sir Thomas Lethbridge Napier Morland (1865–1925): Brigadier-General commanding 2nd Infantry Brigade, Aldershot 1910–13, 2nd London Divisional Territorial Force, 1914; old friend of Hobhouse in 60th Rifles.

VIII INTRIGUES WITHIN? *pp.* 215–241

1 William James Pirrie (1847–1924): Chairman of Harland & Wolff Shipbuilders, Belfast, created 1st Baron 1906, Viscount 1921.

2 The transfer of flag in wartime had been disallowed both by the British Declaration of London and the German Prize Manual which governed the policies of the chief belligerent powers at sea. The *Dacia* had been sold to a New York firm and given an American register in order to enable her to take a cargo of cotton from Texas to Germany, at a time when there was little available American shipping. In the event the *Dacia* was captured by the French and her cargo was seized.

3 Sir George Evelyn Murray (1880–1947): Secretary to the Post Office 1914–34.

4 In the Dogger Bank action on 24 January the German battle cruiser *Blücher* was sunk and the British battle cruiser *Lion* was disabled and had to be towed to harbour. It was a decisive British success, however, Commodore Tyrwhitt was captain of the light cruiser *Arethusa* which played a major part in the battle.

5 The *Wilhelmina* was seized at Falmouth and her cargo of wheat put into the Prize Court, the British claiming that a food cargo came within the definition of contraband under international law.

6 General Sir Douglas Haig (1861–1928): Chief of Staff, India 1909–11; Commander, 1st Army Corps 1914–15; followed Sir John French as Commander-in-Chief, British Expeditionary Force 1915; Field-Marshal 1917; created 1st Earl Haig 1919.

7 Sir George Gibb (1850–1925): Member of Government Arbitration Board 1915–18.

8 Sir Frederick Cawley (1850–1937): Liberal M.P. 1895–1918; Chancellor of the Duchy of Lancaster 1916–18; created 1st Baron Cawley 1918.

9 Sidney Sonnino (1847–1922): Italian Prime Minister 1906, 1909–10; Foreign Minister from November 1914, concluded Treaty of London 26 April 1915 and denounced Triple Alliance with Germany and Austro-Hungary on 4 May.

10 The U29 had been responsible for the sinking of the three 'Cressy' cruisers and the *Hawke* mentioned earlier. U29 was rammed and sunk by the battle-

ship *Dreadnought* when she made an attack on the Grand Fleet on 18 March. Hobhouse's suspicions about Churchill's optimism were justified. Although several submarines had been driven off or chased only two were in fact destroyed during the last two weeks of March.

11 Sir George Askwith (1861–1942): Controller-General, labour and statistical department, Board of Trade 1909–11; Chief Industrial Commissioner 1911–19; created 1st Baron 1919.

12 i.e. the Cabinet Munitions of War Committee.

13 Lloyd George had called for a businessman of 'push and go' to expedite the supply of munitions. The expression, first used in a debate on the Defence of the Realm Act in the House of Commons on 9 March, was taken up by the press. In the end the man, or superman, was to be Lloyd George himself, but the businessman adviser was to be George Macaulay Booth (b. 1877). See Duncan Crow, *A Man of Push and Go : The Life of George Macaulay Booth* (1965).

14 General Sir Ian Hamilton (1853–1947): Commander of Mediterranean Expeditionary Force 1915.

15 Asquith significantly makes no reference to this row in his letters to the King.

16 Major-General Sir Stanley von Donop (1860–1941): Master-General of Ordnance 1913–16.

17 J. L. Garvin (1868–1947): Editor of the *Observer* 1908–42; Editor of the *Pall Mall Gazette* 1912–15.

18 See Editor's Introduction.

19 According to Bertie's diary, he was less favourably impressed by Hobhouse's 'pro-Russian' arguments regarding Constantinople and the Straits. *Diary of Lord Bertie of Thame 1914–18*, edited by Lady Lennox (1924), vol. 1, pp. 162–3.

IX AFTER THE FALL *pp.* 242–257

1 Martin D. Pugh, in his excellent article, 'Asquith, Bonar Law and the First Coalition', *Historical Journal*, XVII, 4 (1974), pp. 813–36.

2 George Lambert (1866–1958): Liberal M.P. 1891–1924, 1929–31; Civil Lord of the Admiralty 1905–15; Chairman of the Liberal Party 1919–21; cr. 1st Viscount 1945.

3 John Arbuthnot Fisher (1841–1920): Controller of Navy, Lord of Admiralty 1892–7; C.-in-C. North American and West Indian Station 1897–9, Mediterranean Station 1899–1902; Second Sea Lord 1902–3; C.-in-C. Portsmouth 1903–4; First Lord of the Admiralty 1904–10 and 1914–15; Chairman of Royal Commission on Oil Fuel 1912; Chairman of Admiralty Inventions Board 1915–16; created Baron 1909.

4 Sir Maurice Bonham Carter (1880–1960): Private Secretary to Asquith 1910–16; married Asquith's daughter, Violet; Assistant Secretary, Ministry of Reconstruction 1917, Air Ministry 1918.

5 Sir Jabez Edward Johnson Ferguson (1849–1929): Liberal M.P. 1885–6, 1892–1900; owner of Springkell, Dumfriesshire, where the Hobhouses often stayed.

6 Ian Macpherson (1880–1937): Liberal M.P. 1911–31; Private Secretary to Under-Secretary of State for War (H. J. Tennant) 1914–16; Under-Secretary for War 1916–19; Chief Secretary for Ireland 1918–20; Minister of Pensions 1920–2; cr. 1st Baron Strathcarron 1936.

7 James Henry Thomas (1874–1949): Labour M.P. 1910–36; Minister in Labour Governments 1924 and 1929–31.

8 Arthur Henderson (1863–1935): Labour M.P. 1903–18, 1919–22, 1923, 1924–31, 1933–5; President of the Board of Education 1915–16; Paymaster-General and Labour Adviser to Government 1916; Member of War Cabinet; Home Secretary 1924; Foreign Secretary 1929–31.

9 Harold Sidney Harmsworth (1868–1940): younger brother of Lord Northcliffe; proprietor of the *Daily Mirror* and the *Sunday Pictorial*; created 1st Baron Rothermere, 1914; created Viscount 1919.

10 Sir James Henry Dalziel (1868–1935): Liberal M.P. 1892–1921; Editor and owner of *Reynolds's Weekly Newspaper* (later *Reynolds News*) and the *Pall Mall Gazette*; created 1st Baronet 1918, 1st Baron Dalziel of Kirkcaldy 1921; close associate of Lloyd George.

11 Sir Thomas Whittaker (1850–1919): Liberal M.P. 1892–1919; temperance advocate; Chairman, Select Committee on Parliamentary Procedure 1914.

12 Oswald Partington (1872–1935): Liberal M.P. 1900–1910, 1915–18; Junior Whip 1909–10, Whip 1915; succeeded to peerage as 2nd Baron Doverdale 1925.

13 John William Gulland (1864–1920): Liberal M.P. 1906–18; Junior Whip 1909–15; Joint Parliamentary Secretary to the Treasury 1915–17.

14 T. P. O'Connor (1848–1929): Irish Nationalist M.P. 1885–1929; Editor of the *Sun*, *Weekly Sun*, *T.P.'s Weekly*.

15 John Gordon (1849–1922): Liberal Unionist M.P. 1900–16; Attorney-General for Ireland 1915–16.

16 Charles Andrew O'Connor (1854–1928): Solicitor-General for Ireland 1914–16.

17 Lady Aberdeen, wife of the Lord-Lieutenant, was highly unpopular in Dublin for her interference in public affairs. It was felt that she should have remained 'ornamental rather than departmental' by many officials.

18 Sir Lionel Philipps (1855–1936): Member of South African Parliament; partner, firm of Wernher, Beit & Co.; former President, Chamber of Mines.

19 Sir Ernest William Moir (1862–1933): engineer; Member of Council of Ministry of Munitions; founded the Inventions Branch of the Ministry of Munitions; 1st baronet 1916.

20 Major-General Sir Ivor Philipps (1861–1940): Liberal M.P. 1906–22; Parliamentary Secretary (Military) to Minister of Munitions 1915; commanded 38th Welsh Division in France 1915–16.

21 General Sir John Cowans (1862–1921): Quartermaster-General of the Forces, War Office 1912–19.

22 Sir William Newenham Montague Orpen (1878–1931): British painter, born in Dublin, studied at Dublin Metropolitan School of Art and Slade School, London; Associate of Royal Academy 1910, Academician 1919; noted for vigorously characterised portraits; appointed an official war artist during First World War.

23 John Singer Sargent (1856–1925): American Painter and portraitist; made his name in Paris, moved to England in 1884; regarded as too *avant garde* for English taste; adjudged 'worst picture of the year' in Royal Academy 1886; later 'the greatest portraitist of the age'; official war artist.

24 Asquith Papers, vol. 15, ff. 32–3.

Index

People are entered in this index under the names and titles by which Hobhouse knew them; titles inherited or conferred after 1915 are not given. Hobhouse himself is referred to as C.H.